Cybermarketing Essentials for Success

Cybermarketing Essentials for Success

Craig Settles

Ziff-Davis Press
Emeryville, California

Development Editor	Leslie Heyden
Copy Editor	Jeannie Smith
Technical Reviewer	Chris Shipley
Project Coordinator	Barbara Dahl
Proofreaders	Madhu Prasher and Jeff Barash
Cover Design and Illustration	Regan Honda
Book Design	Lory Poulson
Word Processing	Howard Blechman
Page Layout	Russel Stolins
Indexer	Valerie Robbins

Ziff-Davis Press, ZD Press, and the Ziff-Davis Press logo are licensed to Macmillan Computer Publishing USA by Ziff-Davis Publishing Company, New York, New York.

Ziff-Davis Press imprint books are produced on a Macintosh computer system with the following applications:FrameMaker®,Microsoft®Word,QuarkXPress®,AdobeIllustrator®,AdobePhotoshop®, Adobe Streamline™, MacLink®Plus, Aldus®FreeHand™, Collage Plus™.

If you have comments or questions or would like to receive a free catalog, call or write:
Macmillan Computer Publishing USA
Ziff-Davis Press Line of Books
5903 Christie Avenue
Emeryville, CA 94608
800-688-0448

ISBN 1-56276-328-8

Manufactured in the United States of America
10 9 8 7 6 5 4 3 2

*Dedicated to the memory of my
grandmother, Annie Murphy Jordan,
whose frequent words of wisdom
included, "Every day, sing a little song,
say a little prayer, read a book—
it's like putting gas in your car."
I hope to live as long and be as wise.*

Acknowledgments

In a project like this where you interview a whole lot of people, it's tough to give everyone who deserves it credit without writing an extra couple of chapters. In order to save a few trees, I will offer acknowledgment throughout the online segment to those people whose day(s) I interrupted to collect tons of information, insight, and advice. Without these generous and knowledgeable souls, this book would not have been possible.

Introduction: Just the FAQs, Ma'am

Discussion groups on the Internet and online services post Frequently Asked Questions (FAQs) to introduce people to the group and the benefits of participating in the discussion. *Cybermarketing Essentials for Success* is a creative discussion about marketing online. Therefore, I wanted a creative way to introduce you to the book and the benefits of participating in this discussion. Hence, the FAQs.

When you're thinking about buying a book, you probably have some questions about the book or the author. You flip through the table of contents, the introduction, and even a few chapters to see if you want to buy the book or put it back on the shelf. Before you put me back on the shelf, let's look at the FAQs.

What is *Cybermarketing Essentials for Success* about?

This book shows you how to use cyberspace—the commercial online services, bulletin board systems (BBSs) and the Internet—to increase your marketing and business communication effectiveness. Regardless of the size of your company or the industry you're in, you will get valuable information about this exciting new business communication channel.

Why should I buy this book?

Cybermarketing Essentials for Success cuts through the hype, hope, and hysteria surrounding the Information Superhighway to give you a clear picture of the opportunities this communication channel offers.

This book helps you understand cyberspace, the people who hang out there, and why you can't market to them the same way you market to people via TV and magazines. People in cyberspace act and respond much differently than typical consumers. You must understand these differences in order to successfully market online.

This book gives you a framework to develop the appropriate cybermarketing strategy, and a step-by-step approach to produce creative tactics that dramatically increase market awareness for your products or services.

Who can benefit from reading *Cybermarketing Essentials for Success*?

Cybermarketing affects departments within a company beyond marketing. Likewise, it impacts the decisions and actions of other people besides those in the marketing department. The stories and recommendations presented in this book should be read and absorbed by a variety of executives, managers, and general staff:

- This is a great handbook for managers and staff in marketing, sales, service, and other departments that will shoulder direct responsibility for making cybermarketing work. People at advertising and PR agencies and marketing consulting firms are included in this group. You'll find real-life examples and a process for making cybermarketing decisions and developing specific activities. It will help spur your creativity and offer ways to present your message that get results. The online supplement will give you additional lessons, plus access to a valuable network of your marketing challenges.

- Entrepreneurs, presidents and CEOs who want to communicate more effectively with customers, prospects and their industries, take their companies into new markets, and increase their business growth will definitely benefit from this book.

- You will receive a good overview so you can see the whole picture of marketing in cyberspace. You will learn about the potential benefits and pitfalls of this exciting marketing channel that everyone's talking about. You will also get insights and advice from others who are already doing it so you can make wise decisions about going online.

- Business managers and consultants, as well as people who just want to find out what all the Info Highway hype is about, will find this a valuable book. If you are called upon to give your advice or general input about this brave new world called cyberspace, this book offers good food for thought.

What exactly will I learn about cybermarketing in this book?

You will first get a detailed breakdown of the different areas of cyberspace and an overview of how to use each of these areas in your marketing efforts. You will also get a fairly detailed profile of the people who hang out in cyberspace.

(I should caution you now, though, that you can never really understand cyberspace until you've been there. Unless you're already an active member of an online services, such as America Online or Microsoft Network, or you're an active Internet user, plan to go online before you do anything else.)

Cybermarketing Essentials for Success will show you:

1. How to market more effectively and for less money to your existing customers

2. How to provide faster, better, and less expensive customer service and support

3. How to generate prospects that can eventually become customers (though not necessarily through online sales)

4. How to increase the impact of conventional marketing such as advertising, direct mail, and press relations

The chapters on cybermarketing tactics will help you develop tactics that build brand awareness and loyalty so customers keep coming back. You will see how to create direct response promotions that increase the number of people who download your materials, and you'll learn how to implement market education activities that build your position as an industry leader.

This book will show you ways to demonstrate your products online, and in some cases, actually distribute them in cyberspace. I also outline tactics for enhancing your press relations efforts, conducting market research in ways never before possible, and building systems to better support your staff, resellers, and others with whom you do business.

You will also learn how your business operations beyond marketing and sales are affected by cybermarketing. When cybermarketing begins to play a serious role in how you do business, departments such as customer service, human resources, and finance are affected much differently than they would be with traditional marketing campaigns.

To help you understand these changes, companies with aggressive cybermarketing activities describe how they developed communication, document management, and work flow systems within and between departments. Though this may seem challenging, these are relatively painless modifications that reap significant benefits.

How is this book unique from other books about online marketing?

Other books may tell you how to market online, but this book shows you what works in cyberspace. Pick up an Internet Web browser or Microsoft Windows 95 to access the online supplement to *Cybermarketing Essentials for Success*. See exactly what companies are doing to market creatively in cyberspace and draw people to their areas.

There are links to the Internet sites of the companies I interviewed so you can see real-life implementations of the strategies and tactics I present in this book. A few of the companies developed special online documents that expand on some of my points. Others are offering special discounts on products just for people who read this book.

This book is also unique because it can be a two-way discussion. Through the online component, you can correspond with me by e-mail to offer suggestions for adding related online content or for the next edition of the printed book. There is also a special cybermarketing chat room available for you on the Microsoft Network to discuss cybermarketing issues with other readers.

Another thing you won't find in other books is an attempt by the authors to build communities around their books.

In *Cybermarketing Essentials for Success*, I address the value of building strong online communities of customers who support and contribute to the development and enhancement of particular products. Both customers and companies benefit in the long run.

I believe that building an online community of readers will help you and others derive significant long-term value from your investment in this book. That is the ultimate goal of the online book supplement and other online marketing information areas I will set up in the upcoming months.

Is this just another textbook on marketing theory?

Absolutely not. This book is based on careful research of companies who are successfully marketing in cyberspace. I interviewed people who are in the trenches daily, implementing proven tactics and continually creating new ones to address new situations. Some of these people have been marketing online for years.

You will read about online pioneers like Geoworks Software, CUC International, Hyatt Corporation, and JP Morgan, who are establishing cybermarketing standards for their respective industries. You will see how United Airlines and multilevel marketing giant Amway use cyberspace to enhance business operations, and how entrepreneurial firms like Software.Net and Roswell Computer Books are making their mark online.

There are also accounts of the cybermarketing efforts of my company (Successful Marketing Strategists) on behalf of clients who include AT&T Global Business Communications and leading software developers Symantec, Maxis (makers of Sim City), Day-Timer Technologies, and Software Publishing Corporation (makers of Harvard Graphics).

I discussed my ideas on strategies and tactics with the people I interviewed, and you can read their responses here. By and large, these cybermarketing veterans agreed that the approach I'm advocating here is the right one for companies who want to make the most of cyberspace.

No, *Cybermarketing Essentials for Success* definitely isn't about theory. It's about going out there and getting the job done right.

How else does this differ from traditional marketing books?

This book further differs from traditional marketing books in that I discuss business issues they usually do not address. Issues such as developing work flow systems between departments, integrating customer service and support directly with marketing efforts, and weaving through the politics of getting companywide buy-in to marketing activities.

I also omit discussions you might typically find in marketing theory books because cybermarketing is new and changing daily. Issues such as market segmentation and establishing market share are not main considerations in cyberspace. At least, not yet. I keep the tone here relaxed and relatively jargon-free. Cyberspace is a fun place to be. Marketing there should be fun too. Remember the maxim about all work and no play.

You will find very few hard-core, rigid rules in *Cybermarketing Essentials for Success*. Given the swiftly changing nature of the beast, I believe open-ended guidelines that give you a general marketing framework are more effective than strict rules. You can customize these guidelines to fit the particular needs of your company and product or service.

Why is cyberspace important?

The way the media describes it, you'd think cyberspace is a physical place similar to a giant shopping mall. Companies "build" displays and firewalls. People "meet" in chat rooms and forums. And you regularly hear about "break ins" and security breaches.

Forget all of that for a minute. This is what cyberspace really is.

Regardless of which site you "visit" in cyberspace, you will always find a computer with a data storage area, software that manages access to information in the storage area and (in some cases) allows people to talk to each other, and a telephone line that lets people access the site from their office or home computers.

Thousands of sites in cyberspace are linked by an international network of public and private phone lines, allowing users to move from one site to another on the same phone call so to speak.

What makes cyberspace a valuable marketing tool is the fact that these sites draw millions of people. Often called cyber surfers, they search for all sorts of information, exchange information with others, and engage in often lively conversations about every topic imaginable. Many of these people may be ideal prospective customers for you.

Cyberspace is also valuable because you can communicate to cyber surfers rather inexpensively. Though you can spend tens of thousands of dollars for an internal Internet setup, many companies go online for much less ($1,500–$3,000). The biggest investment often is the time required to develop the appropriate information for your cyber outpost.

Will I make a quick fortune on the Information Superhighway if I read your book?

Probably not. This is not a book for "get rich quick" schemers and scam artists. Instead, this is a discussion for smart people. People who want to grow their business by marketing more cost-effectively and building strong customer relationships. People who are smart enough to know that you have to work hard at it.

Cyberspace is a new communication medium that is unlike any other marketing vehicle. It requires that you take the time to learn how to use this medium properly. *Cybermarketing Essentials for Success* gets you moving in the right direction. If you're already marketing in cyberspace, this book will help you get more mileage from your current efforts.

But I read about people who generated lots of sales leads online. What about them?

It's true that some people will get lucky and offer the right product or service that, with little effort, lands them on "Life Styles of the Rich and Famous." But consider this: If you make a big splash selling green, two-pronged widgets, what do you do when 10,000 people come online selling green, two-pronged widgets? How do you differentiate yourself?

Your new $1,000 Internet Web home page can look better than Microsoft's home page. But practically everyone knows Microsoft and trusts them to be around for a few decades. They may not know you from Adam or Eve. How do you compete in this situation?

And what happens if online discussion groups get so cluttered with ads that users drop out of these groups altogether? Or what do you do if cybersurfers get electronic zappers that automatically delete unsolicited ads before they hit surfers' e-mailboxes?

Appropriate cybermarketing activities and hard work are the answers to these questions. This book will help you with the cybermarketing. You have to supply the hard work yourself.

Are there any technical terms I should know before I begin reading?

There are a few terms that I use frequently with which you should become familiar.

Content—Whatever information (software files, graphics, promotional materials, etc.) you post in your online areas for people to read and download.

Cybermarketing—Developing and implementing marketing activities that you use with the online services, BBSs, and the Internet.

Download—Make a copy of a file you find in cyberspace and store it in your computer.

E-mail (electronic mail)—Electronic messages you create and send to others using e-mail software, or software provided by the online services and companies that provide you with access to the Internet.

Flaming—The sending of nasty or derisive e-mail messages to a person or company because an action taken by that person or company offended the flamer.

Forum—An area set up on an online services for a company to store their content and interact with customers and prospects through e-mail or through real-time discussion.

Online area—Whatever site in cyberspace you use to store your information (online service forum, BBS, Web site). Chapters 3 and 4 explain the respective online areas in detail.

The Net—A commonly used name for the Internet.

What should I do next?

I think now is probably a good time to buy the book, head to your favorite reading spot, grab your favorite beverage on the way, and read about this new age in marketing communication.

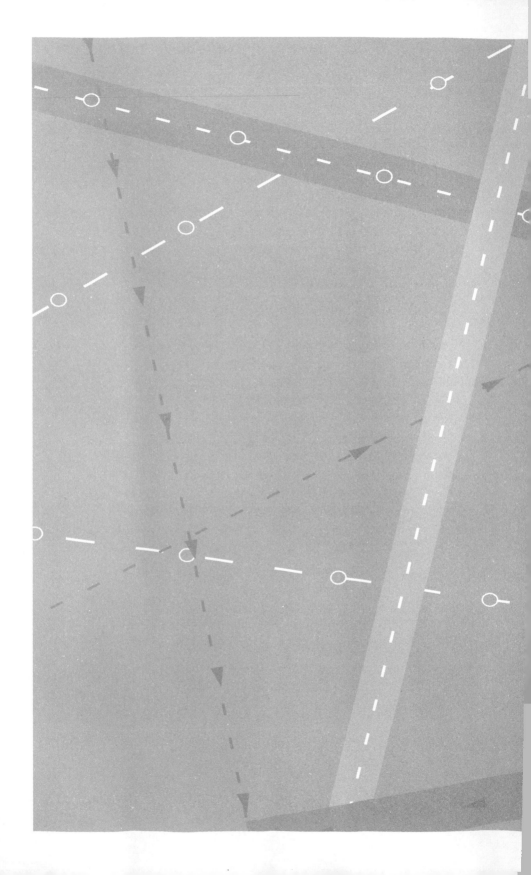

Chapter 1: The Dawning of the Age of Cyberspace

Once upon a time, so one theory goes, some White House gnome, who will probably remain forever nameless, slipped the words *Information Highway* into one of Vice President Al Gore's speeches. As with many things D.C.-bred and media-borne, these two words took on a life of their own, weaving themselves into the fabric of our daily lives.

The Information Highway: Taking Us to a Better Place (Maybe)

Everywhere you turn—TV, radio, movies, and the comic strips for crying out loud—you hear wondrous tales about the Info Highway that's going to take us to a better place.

From the midst of all this hoopla, the Internet (commonly called the Net) is arising as the clear and present embodiment of the Info Hypeway. With this evolution comes a marketer's dream of a lifetime: 30 million, mostly college educated, high-income consumers tethered together through a communication medium where you can advertise with minimal effort and cost.

What's wrong with this picture? First, anything that sounds this good, this easy, and this cheap usually isn't, including marketing through cyberspace. Second, even though cyberspace promises to deliver endless pots of gold, there's not a good map for finding that gold. By the way, I define *cyberspace* as not only the Net, but also bulletin board systems (BBSs) and online services.

Few people really understand cyberspace and the cybersurfers who hang out there. That's a problem. A big problem. My company, Successful Marketing Strategists, began tackling this issue in 1994.

Cyberspace: Observations and Conclusions

We provide traditional marketing services, such as the development of strategy, marketing materials, and press relations campaigns, to high-tech companies. Our staff knew there was marketing potential in cyberspace, but because this medium was so new, we needed to do lots of research to understand how to help companies capitalize on this potential.

We received a directive from our client, AT&T Global Business Communication Systems, to explore the opportunities for and obstacles to cybermarketing for one of their software products. I will give details about some of the work we did for them later in the book, but the efforts we made on their behalf helped us to really understand cyberspace.

After visiting each of the main online services' offices, meeting with people who knew the ins and outs of cyberspace, and spending more than a few hours surfing the Net, it became apparent that a lot of people were missing the mark. They were using print and television advertising models in a medium that definitely was in need of a new form of marketing communication.

Stories abounded about companies whose promotions were about as exciting as stale bread. When people weren't telling us about boring, lifeless ads, we were reading about Net surfers rising up in arms over intrusive ads that were spoiling the pristine cyberlandscape. It seemed some new rules were needed, so I wrote a few.

Actually, I wasn't cocky enough to call them rules. That would be the same as volunteering to wear the first sheriff's badge in Dodge City circa 1870. Everybody would be gunning for me, and I just got to town.

Instead, I referred to them (and still do) as guidelines for helping companies develop effective strategies and tactics for marketing in cyberspace. You can read my in-depth presentation on strategy in Chapter 6, and my discussion of tactics in Chapters 8–15. However, in 1994, these guidelines started as two pages of cybermarketing theory. I needed theory validation, so I went on a press tour.

A press tour is a series of in-person meetings with editors at publications who are interested in what you have to say. Most people I met on my tour agreed that online marketing was in a sad state, and my theory seemed to make sense. Many of them encouraged me to write a book. One editor, Dennis Eskow, made the right introductions, and here you have the book.

After dozens of lengthy interviews with cybermarketing veterans, hours upon hours spent exploring cyberspace, and jobs with a few major cybermarketing clients, I can now say with conviction that our aim was true. Cyberspace is a New Age communication medium that requires more than Olde World marketing. It requires new thinking, new strategies, and a new approach.

Cyberspace even requires a new kind of marketing book to really help you understand what's going on. That's why there is an online supplement to *Cybermarketing*. Until you actually go online and see the things I'm talking about here, you will not fully appreciate and understand the strategy and tactics presented in this book.

New Age Communication Meets Olde World Marketing

The Internet, BBSs, and commercial online services such as Compu-Serve and America Online (AOL)—cyberspace—represent New Age communication technology.

Cyberspace lets us have instant access to information anywhere on the planet, pull documents the size of telephone books through tiny telephone lines in minutes, and grab late-breaking news faster than Murphy Brown. People can zip past mountains of information to find just the one piece of data they need, then leave cyberspace without seeing one iota of additional material.

In cyberspace, the power of the individual is tremendous. A solitary person working at her desk can bring a world-wide industry powerhouse to its knees at the altar of humility. We saw a good example of this recently with Intel.

Intel, the largest PC chip maker in the world, went through PR hell because of a Pentium chip flaw. Tons of bad press and millions of dollars in replacement costs started with one person posting a message on the Net after discovering the problem. This story will be covered in more detail in Chapter 13.

Cyberspace lets you engage in two-way communication with individuals in ways never before possible. A company's online interactive system can let thousands of customers select information tailored to their specific needs, send their feedback instantly to the company, and in response, they receive additional information delivered automatically to their e-mail boxes.

Unfortunately, many people who are used to conventional marketing have not adapted well to communicating in cyberspace. They typically run campaigns which bombard consumers with one-way sales messages that reflect the limitations of print, TV, and radio media. I refer to this as Olde World marketing.

When you only have 30 seconds to deliver your message on TV or radio, or you can only afford to run a ¼-page magazine ad, a lot of valuable information is sacrificed. Even though brochures can present longer messages, they still have practical limitations of space and costs. What's more, none of these marketing tools offers prospects an opportunity to interact with your company.

Compounding these problems is the fact that many companies build barriers to customer communication rather than fostering feedback.

Distributors and retailers have virtually become a dam blocking direct company-customer interaction. Customer support and telemarketing are often outsourced, putting yet more distance between customers and businesses.

Conventional marketing's inability to give customers enough information, or a way to interact directly with companies, limits the kind of communication that can help companies develop better products and build stronger customer loyalty. These limitations simply aren't present in cyberspace, which is why you need a new marketing approach with this medium.

What Happens When Olde Meets New?

What happens when Olde World marketing meets New Age communication? Here are two pretty good examples.

Do We Get Fries with That Ad?   The folks at McDonald's, certainly no slouches in the marketing world, decided that Ronald McDonald should stake a claim in cyberspace via a forum on America Online. Among the many pieces of information they posted there (such as the nutritional value of Big Macs) was an actual 30-second TV commercial—about as Olde World as you can get.

Why would anyone who pays $5 or $6 an hour to be online retrieve an ad that takes four hours to download, especially since they can see the same ad on TV for free? That's $24, plus users couldn't do anything else with their PC while they were downloading. What's more, relatively few people even have full-motion video and sound capabilities built into their PCs to actually view this ad.

Needless to say, the critics had some choice words. One editor observed that the McDonald's online area was as exciting as day-old french fries. More importantly, online users (who are the primary target audience) were not amused or moved to action by such Olde World marketing tactics. They zipped right past this nonsense without even giving it a glance.

By the way, don't bother trying to find this particular piece of work. It seems that the McDonald's crew has quietly packed up its tent and returned to the cyberdrawing board. But stay tuned. Later in this chapter, I'll give my humble opinion of how McDonald's could have made this online venture a whopping success.

Sometimes these Olde World marketing methods lead to something far worse than being ignored—they lead to being flamed.

The Mother of All Flame Wars   Let me put flaming into perspective for you. For your business to be flamed in cyberspace is similar to having your mailroom filled with a gazillion pieces of hate mail, *and* having every billboard, TV station, and radio station nationwide broadcast what a "blankety-blank" you are.

People who are truly ticked off don't stop at sending nasty e-mail and posting derisive messages all over cyberspace. They get others in on the process to create a snowball effect that can be devastating. Under the right circumstances, it's similar to spontaneous combustion.

A particularly infamous story about advertisers who incurred the flaming wrath of Net users is about two lawyers who promoted one of their services online. They used a software program to repeatedly duplicate and post an ad to some 6,000 Internet discussion groups (newsgroups) with no attempt to target their audience. This is called *spamming* in Net circles.

Since newsgroups' discussions are delivered to people's e-mail boxes, users had to sort through and delete the spam to get to the information they subscribed to. This spamming was so bad, users were hit with these ads everywhere they turned. Users would clear out this junk e-mail from one newsgroup, just to have it appear again when they accessed another group.

Without going into the specifics (you can read the full details in "Canning Spam," *Internet World*, October 1994 at http://www.meckler web.com/mags/iw/v5n7/law.htm) let's just say that the backlash was quite intense.

So many e-mail flame messages hit the lawyers' Internet provider that the provider had to close its business for several days. Word of mouth throughout the Net was so ugly, other providers wanted nothing to do with these folks. If you want to see an Internet conversation instantly turn ugly, just open up with, "Hey, you know those lawyers on the Net?"

Of course, these are two somewhat extreme examples of marketing gone awry. Many attempts at marketing online don't draw controversy because they're so boring that no one ever stops by to see them.

Unless you enjoy creating great marketing pieces that no one sees, or you thrive on negative publicity, what do you do to make cybermarketing work?

As I mentioned earlier, there is a need for new thinking, new strategies, and a new approach.

Marketing with a New Attitude

Cybermarketing requires that you put everything you know about marketing on the shelf for a minute. Step back, look at cyberspace as a new marketing beast, and open your mind to a new way of thinking about marketing.

Cyberspace offers a unique way to communicate. The way you design and deliver information about your company, products, or services has to change to adapt to this new medium.

There are aspects of traditional marketing that can be applied to cyberspace, such as press relations, promotions, and research. But you need to put this knowledge off to the side so it doesn't cloud your understanding of where cybermarketing's potential lies and how to fulfill it.

Promotional materials online are different than most traditional marketing materials. Many online areas, such as BBSs and some of the online services, are technically incapable of presenting graphics, so you have to rely on the power of the written word. Also, online materials need to facilitate interactive, two-way communication between you and your customers.

Direct mail pieces as you know them, with envelopes, letterhead, and stamps, don't exist in the online world of bits and bytes. In cyberspace, you type one copy of a letter, pull up your e-mail database, and hit the Send command. Within hours, thousands of people receive your piece.

Answering a customer service question for a thousand people with a single phone call is probably a foreign concept to you. But when you post an answer to one person's support question in your online area, a thousand or more people can access that same answer when they visit that area. What's more, it usually takes less time to answer someone by e-mail than by phone.

You also have to change the way you view the marketing roles within your organization. Cybermarketing soon will reshape the lines of responsibility that separate marketing from customer support, product development, and other departments.

The computer jockeys who maintain your online areas will need to understand the company's marketing objectives and tactics. Marketing people will have to get past any technophobia to learn the difference between forums and newsgroups and become conversant with HTML (hypertext markup language), which is a format for information posted on World Wide Web servers.

Looking at the Big Picture

To help as you learn this new way of marketing, this book will give you the Big-Picture view of cyberspace. Even the way people refer to the Internet shows why it's important that you always look at the Big Picture.

The Internet is often equated with the Info Highway or cyberspace. But in reality, this highway also includes the online services and BBSs. People who ignore the latter are missing valuable marketing opportunities.

Running a cybermarketing campaign with just the Net is like running a press campaign that focuses only on *The Wall St. Journal*. *The Journal*, like the Net, has a huge audience and a great deal of influence. But your press campaign would also include trade publications and local newspapers. The online services and BBSs are the equivalent of the trade and local presses. They have audiences who may not be on the Net, but people you nevertheless want to reach.

Cyberspace is dynamic and continually evolving, which is another reason you have to check the Big Picture regularly. This is one reason for the online supplement to the book. By the time this book hits the streets, cyberspace will have changed. Only by having information online can I hope to keep you current with these changes.

Distinctions between commercial online services, BBSs, and the Net are blurring as the services and BBSs throw open gateways to the Net. Who knows what cyberspace will look like tomorrow as creative souls come up with better ways to link PCs with the rest of the world.

What happens to your marketing when cyberspace weaves its way into more standard media such as TV and radio? Work is already underway to provide cable TV feeds through online services.

The technologies that influence cyberspace, or are influenced by cyberspace, are changing daily. These too are part of the Big Picture.

Communication technologies will determine whether or not the typical person in your target market is able to receive your cybermarketing message. For example, until modems offer higher data transmission speeds for lower costs, a large chunk of the market will not be able to access some parts of cyberspace, such as the World Wide Web, where you may plan to post information.

Electronic transaction software companies and financial institutions are collaborating to develop new technologies that will affect your ability to process orders in cyberspace. Software giants, retailers, and even telephone giants like AT&T are forming partnerships and acquiring companies to try to influence how companies do business online.

With all of these changes swirling around cyberspace, how can you afford not to keep an eye on the Big Picture?

Chapter 2 gives you a fairly in-depth profile of cybersurfers, the people who hang out in cyberspace. Although you will find as many categories for surfers as there are people on the planet, there are some characteristic traits that can help you get a good handle on who these people are and how you should approach them.

Chapters 3 through 5 will help tremendously with your Big-Picture view of cyberspace. Here, you will read about the character and characteristics of BBSs, commercial online services, and the Internet. By studying each area by itself, you will see the distinct marketing role each plays, and better understand how to integrate the three into your cybermarketing efforts.

To keep up with the frequent changes that affect cyberspace, I suggest you regularly access the book's online supplement. Here, you will be able to keep a finger on the pulse of the online community and be able to make some sense out of everything that's going on there.

The Golden Rule of Cybermarketing

While you're contemplating the breadth, depth, and changing nature of cyberspace, remember that this is a new medium. Aside from acts of blatant commercialism, rudeness, violation of the rules of Netiquette, or just plain stupidity (all of which can get you flamed), there are few things you should not or cannot try.

For now, you have just as much opportunity to write new cybermarketing rules as anyone else. Once you have taken time to understand the complexities of cyberspace, and the fundamental issues of strategy and tactics covered in this book, let your creative mind run free. Try anything once! Experiment with a vengeance.

"What do you mean, no blatant commercialism? What is marketing if not blatant commercialism?" some may ask. "Isn't that what we're here for?" Well, yes and no. This is where new thinking and creativity really come into the picture.

The people online are not the same people who sit brain dead in front of their TVs. Surfers go online to find something or someone that they specifically want, and then they get out. If they see your material, it will likely be by accident. But if you try to actively seek out these people with your online marketing materials, you risk offending them.

Therefore, when you think cybermarketing, do not think "sell, sell, sell!" Think of yourself first and foremost as an information provider. This is the one rule that I highly recommend you follow in cybermarketing.

Provide information to people most likely to benefit from it and be sure your information offers the significant value which cybersurfers expect.

Follow this one rule and you will keep people coming back for more information and eventually they will become your customers.

This is probably the biggest challenge of cybermarketing—changing the way you think of your marketing objective. For now, selling products online is a very elusive goal. However, the value of cyberspace as a communications vehicle is unsurpassed. I will later show you how being an information provider can dramatically decrease the cost, and increase the efficiency, of doing business.

What If They Had Understood the Big Picture

Let's apply the "information rule" to the online marketing adventures of McDonald's and the lawyers I discussed earlier.

McDonald's Serves It Up Right   How could McDonald's have changed its cybermarketing approach if they had focused on being an information provider? To be fair, if you looked past the 30-second ad they posted, McDonald's did have information online as well. It just wasn't very compelling. Reading about the nutritional content of a Big Mac holds little value for most people.

But what if McDonald's had posted nutritional information about food in general? Granted, they market fast food for people who are in a hurry and don't want to cook, or who want a break from the brown bag lunch. But many people also fix regular meals for themselves and their families. Many people are concerned about eating healthy food at least once in a while.

The ability to do a quick search for the nutritional content of ingredients for a meal a person plans to fix would have been popular. An interactive database of information that surfers could access to create a selection of meals based on specific nutritional or caloric requirements (with a McDonald's menu item occasionally slipped in) would also have been popular.

What about kids, the mainstay of the McDonald's empire?

I know someone online whose six-year-old daughter also comes online and talks to some of Mommy's friends. Actually, quite a few people I meet online have young children. These are parents who would love to hang out with their kids at fun places. Regular visits by Ronald McDonald could have been a major boon for both McDonald's and AOL.

What's the financial benefit to McDonald's of these various ideas? Branding. That traditional marketing tactic of creating loyal customers for your brand.

By creating information that people regularly access because they derive some benefit from it, or creating a fun area for kids to visit, Mc-Donald's could have increased brand loyalty as the sponsor of these areas. If you regularly stop off at McDonald's while traveling the Info Highway, who are you likely to visit when driving on the regular highway.

Legal Beagles on a Leash   As much as it pains me to do this, and at the risk of being flamed for the effort, I feel that I should also show how our lawyer friends possibly could have achieved their purpose without creating such an uproar. I've often felt it's unfair to criticize without offering an alternative, so I guess I should practice what I believe.

The two attorneys, based in Arizona, offered online a service that helped immigrants enter the lottery for a U.S. green card. Their in-your-face approach sent a lot of people into a seething rage. However, what about people in the U.S. and abroad who really wanted to know about the lottery?

If the Dynamic Duo of the Desert had set up an Internet site as an immigration information center, posted valuable content, then linked their site to every possible *and appropriate* directory on the Net, their traffic could have been intense. Add to that posting in newsgroups that would have been appropriate for this information, and traffic could have been tremendous.

What kind of information? Well, obviously information about their service. Also, a guide to surviving the government procedures on immigration (which are bad even by regular standards of bureaucratic madness), and information about existing and pending legislation affecting immigration. They could have included a list of safeguards for hiring immigrants as nannies for individuals with aspirations to political office, and they would have had quite a popular site.

(Of course, it's questionable how safe the site would be from flame throwers once word got out that the $100 legal service could be performed by immigrants themselves with the aid of a 32-cent stamp. But that can be flame fodder for someone else's book.)

Chapters 2 and 9 cover in more detail this issue of providing information as a way to build brand loyalty.

Before moving forward, let's take a look at a couple of cybermarketing pioneers, CUC International and Geoworks.

They had the vision to capitalize on cyberspace before most of the world even knew there was a cyberspace. These two companies saw cyberspace as a new forum for communication that could expand their marketing opportunities. That vision served them both well. Besides taking you on a brief trip down Memory Lane, there is a valuable point I want to make here.

The Way Back Machine

During the early days of television, when life was only black and white, the Rocky & Bullwinkle cartoon show was quite popular. One segment of the show involved Sherman and Mr. Peabody (a boy and his scientist dog), who took trips in a contraption called the Way Back Machine to visit historical events "way back" in time.

The graphics and animation were a bit crude by today's standards (okay, maybe very crude), but the episodes were entertaining ways to pick up a few history lessons. Let me take you on a trip in my own little version of the Way Back Machine to pick up two cybermarketing history lessons that make an important point about why you need to be online.

CUC Makes the Right Moves

"Where are we going today, Mr. Peabody?"
"Let's go way back, Sherman, to 1982."
In 1982, CUC International sold annual memberships to buying clubs where people could shop for the best prices on goods and services.

CUC used a fairly simple business model. They empowered consumers by giving them objective, brand-neutral information on a vast array of products, let them make educated decisions about which products to buy, cut out the middleman to reduce costs and speed up delivery, and followed up sales with great customer service.

Hmmm. Sounds like a business that was primed for cyberspace. CUC offered lots of valuable, objective information, there was two-way communication between buyers and sellers even though CUC itself carried no inventory, customers could make their own decisions, and they received good service.

CompuServe, the granddaddy of online services, definitely felt CUC was ready for prime time online. They approached CUC and asked if the company wanted to bring its bustling business online. CompuServe didn't have to ask twice. "We jumped at the opportunity," recalls

CUC International's Product Manager of Interactive Marketing, Lew Bednarczuk.

CUC knew that service was their main marketing weapon, and they immediately saw cyberspace as an excellent service delivery vehicle. CUC enthusiastically embraced cybermarketing in spite of its uncertainty and often unquantifiable market results. They capitalized on the dynamic nature of cyberspace to experiment incessantly with new offers, ideas, and prices, up-selling, cross-selling, and probably even down-selling.

Continues Bednarczuk, "Since going online with CompuServe, we've participated in all kinds of tests for every new interactive technology that's been developed. We're on every major online service, and we're getting ready to make our presence felt on the Internet."

CUC in 1995 is a $1 billion company, with much of its revenues coming from cyberspace. Its four wholesale clubs collectively have 30 million members. Shoppers Advantage is a source of some 250,000 hard-good products. Premier Dining offers members 2-for-1 meal deals at over 10,000 restaurants nationwide. Traveler's Advantage is a service which finds the lowest available fares to anywhere customers want to go. AutoVantage is for people who are buying or selling a car, or for people who are looking for auto service and parts at the best prices.

As they prepare to set up on the Internet, CUC has no doubt that this is the way to go. "As long as we continue to add value to our customers, we will do well on the Net and on our other online areas," concludes Bednarczuk. "We will strive to be unique, to test every new marketing idea every way possible, and we won't give up in our quest to offer customers even greater service."

Geoworks: A Company Ahead of Its Time

"Where are we going now, Mr. Peabody?"
"Sherman, my boy, we're going to the year 1986 to catch up with another cybermarketing pioneer."

Way back in 1986, the Commodore 64 was still a popular computer for the home and some small businesses. A tiny company called Berkeley Softworks (now known as Geoworks) developed GEOS for Commodore, the first operating system for the Commodore computer. At the time there was an online service called Q-Link that eventually would become America Online.

Berkeley Softworks saw Q-Link as an ideal way for a small company to provide customer service and support.

"This turned out to be a smart move on our part because we couldn't afford to field a large bank of telephones," states Lee Llevano, Geoworks VP of Strategic Partnerships. "We posted answers to customers' questions on Q-Link where many users could easily find them. Another smart thing we did was to cultivate a loyal group of supporters who would hang out online and help other users, taking even more of the customer support strain off of us internally."

Besides providing customer support, the company created a nifty little in-house service as a sideline effort to get new customers. This service enabled users to upload to Q-Link important documents, such as proposals and sales presentations, that users had created with their Commodores using Berkeley Softworks's software.

These electronic documents were delivered online to a printing service that also used Q-Link. The service would print the final documents to hard copy using a laser printer and send them back to users by mail or overnight delivery.

A person with a $300 Commodore could produce stellar documents on a $4,000 laser printer that they otherwise couldn't afford to buy (this was before every copy center started offering laser printing services). The service, which made money, eventually became obsolete; however, it typifies the forward-thinking and creativity that finds new ways to increase exposure in cyberspace beyond distributing information and providing customer support.

As the years progressed, Geoworks began distributing software fixes, upgrades, and trial versions of new software online. Q-Link became AOL, which focused heavily on recruiting Macintosh users as subscribers to the service. Geoworks created a graphical DOS interface for AOL, which AOL in turn provided to PC users who signed up for AOL.

Geoworks later developed Ensemble, a graphical PC operating system packaged with some basic PC software applications and the AOL interface. By including AOL, Geoworks in essence sold customers online service and support in a box (I had wondered where Microsoft got the idea to include an online service with their new Windows 95 operating system).

Users would load their software and find an AOL icon along with the icons for the software applications. With a simple mouse click, users could go online as easily as they could open a word processing document, and navigate to Geoworks's customer support area.

Tying AOL directly into Ensemble not only made support easier, but once customers became regular online visitors, Geoworks had a captive audience to which it could regularly market upgrades and complementary products.

Geoworks today has shifted from marketing desktop computer software to providing operating systems to the manufacturers of handheld computing devices. Although this new market doesn't directly include end users, Geoworks still maintains its online presence to guarantee service and support to customers of its previous products.

Lesson from the Way Back Machine

Each time Sherman and Mr. Peabody returned from an adventure in the Way Back Machine, they would offer some lesson or other, usually through a truly awful pun.

I'll spare you the pun, but there is something very valuable to learn from these two stories. The heart of the lesson here is opportunity—see it, understand it, seize it now!

Many pioneering companies, without prompting from the media, looked into the abyss that is cyberspace and saw opportunity there. They probably couldn't quantify its full potential, but they understood enough to know that something good could come from this opportunity.

These pioneers took a chance, seized the opportunity by the horns, jumped on its back, and charged forward. Their rides have been good ones, though frequently bumpy. You'll read about a lot of them in the upcoming chapters.

However, many people today are still unsure of what opportunities really lie out there in cyberspace for their particular organization. Others see the opportunities, but they are not sure how, or even if, their companies should seize them.

These next chapters help you determine what opportunities the online world holds, and how to leverage these opportunities to your benefit. But if you still aren't convinced that you should take the plunge, consider this.

During the course of writing this book, I spoke with many people who have taken the cybermarketing plunge in a big way. Some are online veterans, and others have been online for only a few months. I asked them what opportunities await the companies that are sitting on the edge, staring into the abyss, wondering if they should jump in?

- Bill McKiernan, President, Software.Net (Internet software distribution company): *"I am convinced that this is the wave of the future. There are untold opportunities for companies to leverage their traditional marketing activities for greater market impact."*

- Gary Gluck, Business Development Consultant, Open Market: *"The opportunities here are vast. Think about cyberspace as another dimension that facilitates communication. We're at a point in its development that's similar to the time when telephones were first introduced.*

  "Now, just as then, you have a new medium that allows you to communicate with people from a distance the same as if you were standing right next to them. You can see how the telephone changed the way people do business. With cyberspace, though, there are so many opportunities you're almost unlimited in what you can do."

- Mark Stobs, Online Team Leader, Claris (PC software company): *"Leverage is a word we use a lot to describe the value of online marketing and support. We can post information online and it is seen by thousands of people who visit our forum or Web site, many times eliminating the need to call technical support or our sales number. That's leverage. And thanks to the hypertext nature of the World Wide Web, we can publish that information once and create links to it from other servers where Claris customers and potential customers visit, targeting market segments as specifically as we want."*

- Steve Case, President, America Online: *"There is enormous potential in this market because it truly is the birth of a new medium, just as radio and television were new mediums that fundamentally changed marketing practices and principles."*

- John Seamster, Director of Electronic Publishing, Borland International: *"Cyberspace is a great opportunity, given the real-time communication aspect of the technology. It gives you global access to customers in a medium that can deliver information in ways that traditional marketing with printed materials and other one-way communication materials can't."*

- John Duhring, Vice President Business Information Services, WAIS (provider of software and services to businesses on the Internet): *"Marketing online is a good way to get closer to customers. Literature distribution is immediate, and you shorten the loop between customer interest and order fulfillment."*

- Wayne Heitman, Principal Technical Consutant, Lotus Development: *"Given the way that people use cyberspace, it's the only way to go if you want to market more effectively in the 21st century. The cost is negligible when compared with traditional ads. I've felt that way for the last 15 years."*

- Russ Jones, Program Office Director for the Internet Business Group, Digital Equipment Corporation: *"I think online marketing is happening all around us. Some companies are doing it in ways that their customers don't even realize it's going on. If cyber-marketing is done well, customers will appreciate it.*

  "The key is to not tease them by offering them one thing, then leading them down a different path. You have to help people find the kind of information they want by being very direct about what your materials contain and delivering the type of information that you promise."

- Gary Hunt, Supervisor, Amway Business Network, Amway: *"Now is the right time to get going online. Everyone from the President of the U.S. to the average person on the street is talking about the Information Highway. This is a reality today. If you're waiting for some futuristic type of thing with more interactivity, your competitors are passing you by. People are expecting to see companies they know online now."*

- Hans Gomez, Senior Systems Analyst, Adobe Systems: *"We're just starting to explore. Some of the technologies used to manage marketing and business operations online are not standardized yet, so it's important for us to be here to see what other people are doing. Companies like Intel are trying to create showcases that we can learn from and improve upon in our online areas."*

Now that we've had a little pep talk from the field, let's take a look at cyberspace to get a better feel for this brave new world.

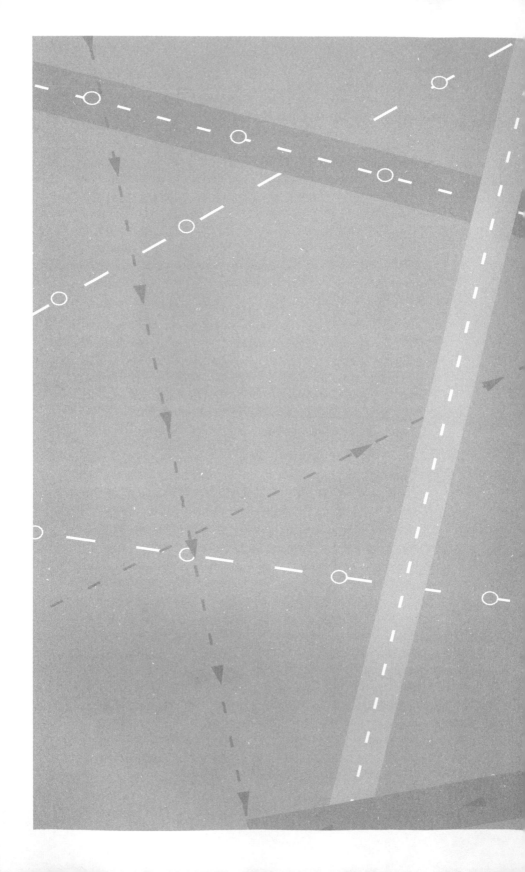

Chapter 2: Cyberspace and Those Who Dwell Within

Once upon a time there were six blind men out walking in the wilderness who happened to come upon an elephant. Since this was their first encounter with such a beast, they each went up and felt a part of the animal to try to understand what it was. Each man then tried to describe to the others what he had "seen."

"An elephant is a big wall," explained the man who had felt the elephant's side. "An elephant is similar to a snake," said the man who grabbed the elephant's trunk. "An elephant is like a rope in a compost heap," said the man who snagged the elephant's tail. And so on.

Like these vision-impaired wanderers of old, there are people today who run around claiming the Information Highway to be such-and-such, based on their limited view of the entire beast.

Online services, cybersex, the Net, flaming, home pages, interactive marketing, the World Wide Web, electronic chat, spamming—these are just some of the fragmented pictures that people have of cyberspace. But to use this New Age communication channel effectively, you need a clear and complete picture of this medium.

Let's take a close look at the environment in which you will be cybermarketing.

This Is Cyberspace

Even though people talk about it as if it were a place, you should treat cyberspace as a communication medium that is distinctly different than print, television, and radio media.

I will spend most of this chapter discussing the people who use cyberspace, since a thorough understanding of your audience is key to your cybermarketing success. I will start with a brief overview of the three areas of cyberspace. This will give you a good handle on the technology that makes cyberspace work.

BBSs

Let's start with your average personal computer (PC, Macintosh, and so on), add a sizable hard-disk drive, a modem, a phone line, and software that lets several people dial into your computer simultaneously to access files, add files, talk to each other, and so on. The software provides a menu structure and other features to help users navigate through the hard drive files with relative ease.

This computer workstation *et al.* is the heart of a bulletin board system (BBS), which in turn is the core concept of commercial online services and the Internet.

There are some 50,000 BBSs in the world of varying size memberships, with BBSs starting up and dying off daily. People become members by logging onto a BBS, providing information about themselves as prompted by the BBS, and sometimes paying a monthly or annual fee.

A BBS is typically run by one or two people called sysops (system operators) who develop, collect, and store the information that users access. Sysops also manage their BBSs and provide service to their members, who tend to be people with interests similar to those of the sysops.

A lot of sysops maintain BBSs in their spare time, but for other sysops their BBSs are their lives. A few sysops even try to make a buck or two with their BBSs.

Many BBSs are information sources for people of a particular profession, ethnic group, or religion and for people with just about every conceivable interest, hobby, and orientation. Some BBSs are places for users with these respective interests to talk to each other. Other BBSs are used by companies to communicate with their customers and to provide service and support.

Online Access is a monthly publication that covers cyberspace and frequently runs sizable lists of BBSs with descriptions and access numbers. *Boardwatch* is a monthly publication that focuses more on BBSs. A subscription to either or both can be a handy reference source to help you keep up with what's happening in this area of cyberspace.

Everyone who has a PC, a modem, and the phone number for a BBS can call into it from anywhere in the world and be a part of that particular cybercommunity. The number of people who can access a BBS at any one time depends on how many telephone lines BBS owners have coming into their systems.

Some BBS software now come with Internet *gateways* (devices that enable data to flow between these two online areas), so Net users can access BBSs without logging off the Net then logging on through a modem to the BBS. BBS members conversely can have easy access to the Internet. However, if it costs you a long distance toll call to access the BBS, the cost for accessing the Internet this way could be more than if you go directly through an Internet provider.

Online Services

Commercial online services take the BBS concept to a higher level. Instead of having one computer workstation with a modem, the services have several minicomputers and mainframe computers with humongous disk storage units and a serious bank of incoming phone lines.

Unlike BBSs, the services have carriers such as Sprint to provide users nationwide with local phone numbers, which then route users' calls to the services. Users benefit because they're not incurring the toll charges they would if they were calling BBSs outside of their local areas. However, users pay the services for the time they spend online. These charges can get to be quite hefty for people who surf until their eyeballs fall out.

Whereas a BBS usually has information on a limited number of topics and attracts a relatively homogenous audience, each online service has many diverse information and communication areas to attract vast, heterogeneous hordes of people. These areas are often called *forums*, and the text, video, and audio files stored there are commonly referred to as *content*.

The online services are managed overall by paid employees, although many of the forums are managed by the staffs of outside organizations that provide the content for these forums. Some users go online to visit only a few of these specific areas within a service, the way they would visit a single BBS, and then sign off. Others regularly explore the whole service.

The online services give users a broader choice of things to do, such as attend "live" interview sessions with celebrities, take college courses, buy products, or access news directly from wire services. Of these activities, it appears that e-mail and real-time discussions with other users in "chat rooms" are the most popular features.

Chat rooms are particularly useful for companies that have forums. These rooms, simply described, are an area in a forum which up to two dozen users can access at one time. Anytime one of these people types comments on his or her computer, everyone else in the room can read what has been typed. Companies can use chat rooms to conduct meetings between executives and customers even though the customers may be located all over the country.

The Internet

The Internet started in the 1970s as a U.S. Department of Defense effort to create a communications network that could survive a nuclear attack. They set up computers in various parts of the country and linked them all by special telephone cables. Today, each computer is configured similarly to BBSs and online services in terms of the basic component parts and is typically called an Internet site.

The Net has expanded to include thousands of sites all over the world that are linked by a combination of private, local, regional, national, and international phone lines. People at the different sites communicate with each other through e-mail and electronic discussion groups called listservs and newsgroups

E-mail is the biggest draw of the Net, especially now that it has become vogue for people to have Internet addresses on their business cards. Of the 30 million people who access the Net, most use it primarily to send e-mail.

However, newsgroups closely rival e-mail in their popularity with Net surfers. Newsgroups are electronic message boards where people post and respond to e-mail to keep up a running dialog around a particular topic, profession, or shared interest.

Newsgroups started as a way to help people from different universities easily collaborate and share data with others working on the same research projects. Now, there's a newsgroup for practically every interest and hobby you can imagine. Listservs are similar to newsgroups, and I will define them in greater detail in Chapter 5.

For storing marketing and other information for people to access, there are three types of Internet sites: ftp servers, gopher servers, and World Wide Web servers. I will also describe these in more detail in Chapter 5. But briefly, a server is a computer that is dedicated to distributing software files which contain documents, graphics, or other materials. Each type of server has a different way to store, display, and distribute this material.

Internet sites overall fall into two categories:

- In the first category, business, government, and nonprofit organizations have Net sites solely for their own use. These sites store employees' e-mail addresses and information that the organizations create to distribute internally or to people outside of the organizations. In-house staffs usually design and manage these servers.

- The second category of Net sites are commercial operations run by companies called Internet providers. Providers rent Internet access and computer storage space to individuals and organizations who want a presence on the Net without the expense of setting up and maintaining their own servers.

The Net as a whole is similar to online services in that it collects a widely divergent audience. However, unlike online services, there is no group or staff who controls the Internet and what is communicated to and from Net sites. The Net also has a chat feature called Internet Relay Chat (IRC) that is similar to an online service's chat areas.

Not having someone or some group to manage the Net can be a bit of a problem since there's no one to resolve problems that arise between, or because of, people who use the Net. Copyright disputes, false advertising claims, and so forth get worked out as best they can. Yet life somehow manages to go on in this self-regulated environment.

You should now have a general picture of what cyberspace is from a technical perspective. Let's look at the element of cyberspace that is most important to you from a marketing perspective—the cybersurfers who hang out there. Understanding these people is fundamental to getting the most value from this book.

Cyberspace Is Defined by the People Who Use It

There are as many different types of cybersurfers as there are types of people who walk the planet. This is why I cannot emphasize enough that you need to treat people in cyberspace as individuals who want their individual needs met.

At the same time, there are some common characteristics that many surfers share. These people are information junkies, they're intelligent, and they have a strong sense of community. These characteristics are so strong among cybersurfers that I will go as far as to say that you should etch them in your brain to use as guideposts to keep your cybermarketing on track.

Cybersurfers Are Information Hungry

Cybersurfers are information junkies, regardless of which part of cyberspace they navigate. They want lots of specific information. They want to meet people who have information to share.

Many of the people who go online are enticed by the lure of information. Information at their fingertips, instant and up-to-date. Information about their favorite hobby, politician, religion, or the migratory habits of the Hollingdale five-legged Rubber Neck Beetle.

Even though there is a lot written about the resistance of cybersurfers to ads, people do come online to get information about products they want to buy. But you have to keep in mind that users pay by the minute to surf. These folks have little interest in spending time and money on fluff material that is offered elsewhere for free.

People online want product specs and detailed cost-benefits analyses. They want to know exactly how and where your widgets are built, and what they do. If you are a service provider, prospects want proof that your service is credible.

WAIS is a Menlo Park, California firm that sells software that lets users easily search for and retrieve information from a company's Internet site. WAIS also helps companies design their Internet sites. John Duhring, VP of Business Information Services, believes there are three types of users in a given online area, be it a BBS, online service, or the Net.

Duhring observes, "There are new users who are not familiar with who you are and what you offer. Your online marketing provides them with ways to discover the value of what you have to offer through lots of promotional and background materials they can read and download.

"There are people who know about your company and the value that you offer, but they want shortcuts to get to the right stuff so they can quickly be on their way.

"The rest are regular visitors that you cultivate over time. These people really appreciate personalized information. The right kind of marketing will keep them coming back to see what your company has new to offer."

And what does all this mean to you? It means that if you want to reach these information hungry people in cyberspace, you have to play the role of information provider.

Feeding the Hungry

To win the hearts and minds of the information-hungry masses, you must become well known as the leading provider of information that people in your target audience want or need, even if it does not directly relate to your product. When people stop by to pick up this information, they will also see material about your company and products.

To put this in retail marketing terms, information is your loss leader. It's something valuable that costs you time to produce, but you offer it for free to get people to come in and buy the more valuable item—your product or services. When selling becomes more prevalent in cyberspace, you may want to charge for some of this information, but keep the price relatively small.

Do not, however, confuse "loss leader" with "bait and switch." If you bait the cyberworld with something that looks like valuable information, but switch it with sales fluff, you may as well put on your asbestos shorts because you're going to get flamed in a big way.

Some people look at me when I say this and ask, "How can I be an information provider?"

This is a good question, particularly for companies that have one product, such as office management software, an easy-to-understand service such as plumbing, or a product like pizza that is strictly advertising- and promotion-driven. Many people think that once they explain what their companies do, there's nothing else to say. However, that's not necessarily true.

Let's take the example of the office management software company. Managers in the company's target market would appreciate help organizing themselves, their people, and their companies' operating procedures. A well-written four-page monthly newsletter with helpful tips in these areas that is placed online would be a godsend for many of these managers.

The software company's cybermarketing efforts and the resulting word of mouth publicity would draw people to pick up the newsletter regularly. The newsletter could subtly build goodwill as the company's name becomes associated with helping people become better managers. What's more, users coming into the online area would likely pick up other materials that describe the software.

How about the plumber? As winter descends, the cold weather in many places can play havoc with pipes. A tip sheet with helpful hints to reduce the chances of pipes freezing and bursting that is posted on a local or regional BBS could get quite a few downloads.

This information distribution would increase the market awareness of the plumber in a favorable way. If the plumber included an e-mail address at the end of this document, a sizable number of people could write with questions that start a dialog with the plumber that could result in a steady stream of customers.

And now, a word from our local pizzeria: If these folks know their market, they know that some of their best prospects are people who frequently watch sports events. Working with the local newspaper in a joint promotional effort, the pizzeria could post in an online area schedules, stats, and an endless sea of trivia that sports fans find so captivating.

This is valuable information (to sports junkies) and it changes frequently, which would keep online traffic coming back. As people continuously visit this area, they would develop brand loyalty to the pizza parlor (the ultimate objective) that would lead them to call for a pizza when these users sit down to watch a game.

So you see, if you exercise your creativity, you can find a way to be a popular information provider. If you have a service company, you have a distinct advantage in this quest. Information is the keystone of many service businesses—providing it, finding it, analyzing it. So finding appropriate materials is fairly easy. But practically any company can rise to the challenge with a little effort.

When you evaluate ways to become a valued information provider, never overlook the opportunity to become an online spokesperson for your industry. Even if you're a one-person operation, when you're online, size doesn't matter. If you have industry insider information that people want, flaunt it. Give people a good reason to stop by your area to browse. Feed the hungry.

Cybersurfers Are Intelligent

Another characteristic of your typical cybersurfer is that they are fairly intelligent. For one thing, people online have figured out how to operate their computers and are capable of wandering through the cyberspace maze. Considering the difficulty many people have programming their VCRs, navigating cyberspace is not an accomplishment to take lightly.

Many cybersurfers want their minds challenged. Most of them are college graduates, hold jobs where they frequently engage their brains, and are technically proficient (especially those folks who are CompuServe and Internet veterans).

Of course, having intelligence and acting intelligently are not necessarily synonymous. Hang out in some of the online services' chat areas, and you will find a few people who are 50 cards short of a full deck. Unfortunately, these are the kind of people you frequently read about because they make good news copy. But consider them the exceptions.

Being intelligent folks, online users prefer to interact with your content, and sometimes with you, rather than have data passively fed to them. They want to probe, dig deep for answers, and do so at their own pace. When they do interact with you, users want more than just a canned sales pitch. If they don't find this level of interactivity and two-way communication in your area, they will quickly move on, never to return.

Traditional direct mail offers a good example of the value of interactive marketing. Studies have proven that if you mail response cards with a sticker that recipients move from one area to another, you will get more replies than if you use response cards without this sticker.

So, how do you win over these cybersurfers who are in search of intellectual stimulation? Adhere to the maxim "You can never have too much content, too many links, or respond too quickly."

Speak to Their Minds

Chapters 9 through 15 go into much detail about the type of content to post in your online areas. What I will say here is that you should think ahead, plan your areas well, and above all, deliver valuable information.

Keep in mind that you not only have to create an initial presentation of information, you also have to change portions of your content regularly. If people visit your area a second or third time and they don't see anything new, they will stop coming back. Some companies change elements of their online area weekly or even daily.

Another reason you need to plan ahead is that you are likely to have new information, new products, or new ideas that you'll want to add to your area. If you add this material randomly without any planning, your content will likely become disjointed and confusing. Surfers are intelligent, but your information layout and flow has to make sense, or they'll quickly lose interest.

When users get to your welcome screen, they need to immediately see what information is available and be able to navigate easily from general information to more specific information. When they find what they want, users should be able to take some action to get it—click a button to download items, send e-mail, complete a form, and so on.

You should check out Informix's Web site. This software company's layout looks nice without using large graphic elements that take forever to show up on your screen. Though it's simple compared to some Web sites, Informix's logical layout is easy for users to understand and navigate. What's more, they use the same graphics throughout the area, which further aids navigation.

Your content has to be complete and provide all of the information people want. The elements of your content (brochure, product announcement, and so on) do not have to be long. Often short one- or two-page documents are best. The elements have to be useful to those who access your material, either to inform, educate, entertain, or direct people to other sources of information.

Pass the Links, Please

Once you've prepared your content and designed your online area's layout, you need to determine how to link all of your content together and to other online areas. How well you link elements of your content will influence people's perception of the value of your area. Also, if you link to content other than your own, you can offer more information without having to actually develop it. Because you are linked to another site with information that is (or should be) clearly marked as belonging to another author or the owner of the online area where it is located, you do not have to worry about copyright issues.

Creating the right links for your content can get tricky, and you may have to experiment with this. Remember, surfers are individuals who want to be treated as such. Not everyone visiting your area will want to access the same elements or access them in the same order.

You therefore need to link content so it offers people the greatest amount of flexibility, and still maintains some semblance of logic. There are several ways to go about linking content.

You can literally link content by hyperlinking. This is done using special software to create pointers that electronically transport a person from a word or picture in an element to material located elsewhere within your content or somewhere else in cyberspace.

For example, someone reading your product brochure can click her mouse on the highlighted words *PC Week* and immediately travel to a *PC Week* article about that product.

Some places in cyberspace, such as the Web, the AT&T Interchange online service, and the Microsoft Network online service, offer the ability to create virtually endless links from your content to publication articles, databases, video clips, and anything else that's there. Your online area can literally become the gateway to the universe as long as it's linked properly.

Santa Cruz Operation (SCO), developer of a popular UNIX computer operating system, uses this approach. They hyperlink their Web server content to information from dozens of companies whose software supports SCO's operating system. Thus the company has expanded the amount of SCO-related content that customers can access.

In addition to hyperlinks, you can figuratively link content by writing directions that guide surfers from your area to other online areas with related additional information. When we wrote a cybermarketing plan for software developer Maxis, we listed areas of AOL and CompuServe with content that complemented Maxis's, and to which Maxis could create these figurative links.

Another way to create highly interactive content is to incorporate a software database of information that users can access. Software vendor Broderbund has a BBS with two interactive databases (one for novice users, one for advanced users) that customers dial into using their modems when they have problems. The database prompts users through a series of questions to guide them to solutions for their problems.

This database approach is great because it gives surfers complete control over accessing the information they need. The more control you give people, the more they will access your area. Besides customer support information, you also can put your sales catalogs in a database that helps users select products, calculate prices, and then order the products.

Quick response to users' online requests is another major factor in creating a positive interactive experience for users. The fastest way to kill your online traffic is to have word get around that you don't respond quickly to e-mail. By virtue of the fact that you're online, users expect you to have the resources in place for rapid turnaround of information.

Whatever procedures you put in place should enable you to respond to users within 24 to 48 hours, even if it's just to say that you're still trying to find answers to their questions.

The online services and BBSs offer opportunities to interact with your customers in real time via chat rooms and cyberauditoriums (similar to chat rooms, but they hold many more people). However, most of your online interaction with people will be via e-mail, either to process orders, provide customer support, or just answer general questions.

To guarantee quick response, you may need software that automatically delivers content to people, acknowledges requests for information, or notifies customers of shipping and delivery dates. You may also need to assign someone to personally send e-mail answers to inquiries or to call customers to solve problems.

The Adobe software company developed their own automation software to funnel user e-mail to the right departments, track its progress through the company, and ensure fast response. You may not be at the stage where automation makes sense; nevertheless the time may come when that will change.

Building Communities in Cyberspace— The Foundation to Good Cybermarketing

A culture exists online which is as distinct as that of another country. Cybersurfers have their own language, social customs, rules of behavior (called *netiquette* in cyberspace), and a strong sense of community. To date, many companies have attempted to market in cyberspace without spending any time trying to learn and adapt to this culture.

I've heard online service executives and Internet veterans speak with dismay about ad agency people and others who walk in with grand online marketing schemes, but who have never been online. Some don't even know what a Web server is, let alone what kind of people access it.

In these next few pages, I will present my observations about communities in cyberspace. I will suggest how to work with those that exist, and how to build communities of cybersurfers who are loyal to, and supportive of, your areas. But regardless of what I say, you won't fully understand online culture until you spend time there.

Just Regular Folks like You and Me

Over the past few years, I've spent many hours online. And I've met quite a few people in person who I initially met online. The way the media portrays typical cybersurfers, you'd think the only people who form online communities are nerdy guys with terminal acne, antisocial tendencies, and pocket protectors. Reality, however, is quite different.

Perfectly normal human beings—both men *and* women—with reasonably decent social skills, a family life, and friends develop incredibly strong online attachments. One of my clients remarked that "my husband has a completely different life online," and he doesn't fit the computer nerd image.

What differs about being online, and what spurs this bonding, if you will, is the environment and the way people communicate in that environment.

In many areas of cyberspace, you have color-blind, gender-neutral societies with few written rules. People can meet, work with, teach, and learn from others without getting caught up in the issues that can sometimes make dealing with people in person such a challenge.

Generational issues are minimal. People with hearing impairments or who are wheelchair bound are "looked" at no differently than anyone else because…well, no one can see them. People just see these individuals' words on a computer screen.

Take away all of these external physical elements and you get an environment where there isn't much to drive people apart and plenty of things that draw them together: similar entertainment interests, shared hobbies, or owning products from the same company.

Geoworks's Online Manager Steve Main put it this way. "Online you are one of the 'pixel people,'" comments Main. "All you see on the screen are yours and other people's pixels [the tiny dots computer screens use to form images such as letters and symbols]. Those other external things that determine who we are in everyday life don't matter online. Everyone's on equal footing."

I will say that this is more true in some areas than in others, but then, cyberspace isn't Nirvana.

Besides an environment that is conducive to drawing people together, there is also the way in which people communicate with each other. Unlike cocktail parties and company meetings, people online can't rely on a smile and a nod to participate in a discussion.

As Main states, "If you don't post [comments] you don't exist online. I found out that just being there smiling didn't matter because no one sees you, just your words. You have to use the keyboard to say something, and to acknowledge or respond to other people. This method of conversing changed me as a person."

It's amazing sometimes to watch. This different way of communicating does indeed change the way people relate to each other (for better or worse), and in many cases, it draws people closer together. Let me relate a couple of stories to illustrate my point.

Communities in Action

I read a story recently about a man whose teenage son spent a lot of time on the computer at home. At some point, the father noticed that his son was becoming more introverted, seemingly more depressed, and definitely more interested in being on the Internet than being with his family. However, the father decided not to push the issue with his son.

Then the son committed suicide, leaving his family numb with shock and unable to comprehend the "why" of such an act. The father partly blamed the computer, feeling that in some way, it contributed to his son's isolation and depression.

One day, he turned on his son's PC and managed to find his way to the Internet, determined to try to find answers to questions he wasn't even sure how to ask. He sent a few messages, describing briefly the suicide, and asking about his son, wanting to know if anyone could tell him something to help him understand his son's obsession with being online.

What started out as a trickle of responses soon became a flood of messages from hundreds of people from all over the world as word quickly spread about his son. They were from people with whom his son had met and bonded online, a community of people who knew his son and knew each other. They came together to offer comfort to the father and to each other, in much the same way as the community to which you belong would come together in a such a tragedy.

I'm still occasionally surprised by the intensity with which people bond and relate to each other within their various online communities. But if you are going to use cyberspace as a marketing communication vehicle, it behooves you to understand this sense of community. You should neither trivialize it nor abuse it.

One of our clients, Maxis (makers of SimCity and a plethora of other Sim titles) found they could leverage this sense of online community to be one of their big marketing strengths. Maxis's Print Artist is an example of a product that inspired a rather strong community of supporters.

Print Artist users started congregating regularly on Prodigy and AOL (with no encouragement from Maxis) to talk about the product and exchange artwork they created with the software. The Pixelitte Group, a small company that developed the program, became online Print Artist evangelists, as did another company that markets add-on products for the software.

This community started to feel so much like family that a group in St. Louis decided to host an in-person family reunion. People came from everywhere, including a woman who drove from Los Angeles and stayed with people along the way who she had met online. Everyone had a great time doing the typical reunion socializing that was topped off with a Maxis-sponsored dinner.

Some return-on-investment-oriented people may wonder how these activities impact Maxis's business. "It's hard to measure," states Maxis's Corporate Communication Manager Lois Tilles. "The goodwill we get, and the amount of interest and loyalty to the product, is great. We are building evaluation tools to judge our online activities more effectively, but a lot has to be taken on faith."

Consider that Maxis did little to generate this enthusiasm and sustain these customers' efforts besides provide product information and support online, and underwrite the cost of a dinner. Think about what it costs to build this level of product loyalty through advertising. Tens of thousands of dollars per month minimum!

Other companies also believe this sense of community online can be leveraged as a significant business benefit.

"Professionals who use CompuServe have a strong commitment to get online and help each other," observes SCO's Manager of Solutions Marketing Mark Riley. "We don't have the manpower to help all of our third party developers directly, but on our CompuServe forum they communicate with each other to exchange experiences and solutions to programming issues. This helps keep our business partners loyal to us, and frees our resources to impact other income-generating activities."

Building Your Own Communities

As you develop content and start brainstorming for cybermarketing ideas, you always want to think about community.

How will you build a strong community around your online areas? How will you guarantee a stream of returning online users? How will you foster frequent communication between you and your visitors that strengthens loyalty? And what about encouraging communication among the customers and prospects?

Look at this community building process as a form of brand marketing. For those of you not familiar with the term, *brand marketing* is the promotions, advertising, and so on you do to get people so loyal to your product brand name that they never (hopefully) switch.

Procter & Gamble sells millions of tubes of toothpaste which, when you really look at it, is similar to other companies' toothpastes. But P&G has built a "community" of customers loyal to their brand. If you think brand loyalty is a trivial concept, just think about what would happen if someone took away your favorite cereal, toothpaste, shampoo....

As you consider what kind of community you want to build around your online areas, be sure you understand the sense of community that already exists in a particular online service or area of the Internet. Be sure your community plans complement, rather than conflict with, the general environment.

Major Cyber "Communities"

The BBSs, online services, and the Internet are similar respectively to cities, states, and the world, though they're not all interlocked—yet.

Smaller BBSs can give you the feeling of small midwestern towns (or the *Cheers* bar) where life is simple and everyone knows your name. They know when you came in, when you left, and who you left with. Other BBSs are similar to the Big Apple where life is fast, entertainment is varied, and there's always something exciting going on day and night.

In most BBSs there's only one sheriff—that's the sysop—and this person's likely to be the Mayor and City Council too. If you're planning to do business here, you want to be nice to this person because if the sheriff doesn't like you, you're in big trouble.

The online services are similar to states. Once you get there, you've got a lot of little towns, some big cities, and everything in between. There are communities within the services focused around companies, special interests, particular demographics, and many other niches. Each community can have its own personality and regular group of visitors.

But each respective services also has a unique dynamic and personality as well.

CompuServe is a techie world and more conservative than some of the newer services. Many of these users have been around for years and they've got that "Old Dog" mind set—"What do I need with some new fangled graphical user interface." These folks are quite content with a text-based interface, thank you very much. (Note: Windows and Mac users can get software that gives CompuServe a more graphical look.)

America Online is more contemporary, generally consumer-oriented, and liberal, and there's a whole lotta socializing goin' on. AT&T Interchange is looking to be a leading-edge service, the epitome of high tech, with a highly graphical interface, and everybody hyperlinked to something or someone.

The Internet is the world, but with slightly less social and political upheaval. You can electronically visit practically any country on the planet. Some Internet sites, regardless of their geographic locations, seem like foreign countries. Some have open borders, while others have heavily guarded domains where they try to be selective about who can come in and access information.

If there are anything similar to alliances of nations in the Internet world, you would have to characterize them as the "Death to commercialism!" faction, the "Give me capitalism or give me death!" faction, and the "Don't bore me with either, I'm just here to (pick one) work/have fun" faction. The first two factions can be a bit extremist and definitely contentious, which can make for some good entertainment for those of us in the third league of cybernations.

Even with its diverse collection of often independent-minded citizens, the Internet does have an overall sense of community. You saw this community feeling come to the fore when the online services opened the gates to give their users Internet access. The reactions of many Net dwellers to these "newbies" were likened to a response to an invasion of Martians. A lot of flame throwers came to the fore.

Before you move on to the next chapter to learn more about the technical side of cyberspace, there is one more thing to consider when you're marketing to cybersurfers: the "fun" factor.

Cybersurfers Just Want to Have Fun

It's probably an accurate statement that many of us in business don't spend a lot of time on the "fun" factor, unless you happen to be in the entertainment or game business. You sell serious products and your customers are serious people. And heaven knows, when the financial people come blazing through the office yelling "bottom line," you get very serious.

Cybersurfers are serious people too, and they want to be taken seriously. But like most people, surfers like to have fun sometimes. Cyberspace, by luck or design, is a place where people can find fun things to see and do while they hunt for serious information, like stock quotes and annual reports. Some fun sites are incredibly popular, and I don't mean just the Playboy home page on the Net.

Cybersurfers are attracted to quirky things, such as the home page on a Web server in England that receives scanned images of the office coffee pot. People from all over the world drop by this page to see if there's any fresh coffee available. Surfers like to be entertained. Many of the people I interviewed have success stories about the popularity of games and contests.

Surfers love to meet the stars. AOL is probably the king of online celebrities. Stars of TV shows, movies, and soap operas, rock singers, politicians, and preachers have made appearances in AOL online auditoriums, and fans have packed the aisles.

Many surfers are sports fiends, too. Must be that heavy male influence.

Sun Microsystems set up a Web page with news from the 1994 Winter Olympics that was a far cry from the slick online presentations you hear so much about. But still over 70,000 people a day visited the site. When Sun hosted the World Cup soccer matches online (an effort truly superior to their first), over 300,000 people visited the site. Read more about it in Chapter 9.

So what should you do about all of these fun-loving sorts who surf the cyberwaves? Entertain them, of course. Do it whenever you can, as long as the entertainment doesn't overshadow your efforts to present valuable information that advances your business objectives.

Games and contests, when done well, are always popular. Sports tie-ins are usually a good bet. When those hundreds of thousands of people visited Sun's Web page during the World Cup, Sun also distributed lots of product material about their computers. Once in a while, you can even be goofy online, and still do business. Visit the Disney Studios Web site if you don't believe me.

But seriously, folks, fun works. Just be sure you do it right. Throughout this book, you will read stories about companies that are mixing business and pleasure with nice results. You should also subscribe to *Internet*

World magazine. Besides being a great source for useful Net information, articles often list some of the crazier sites that could be great inspiration for you.

Now, let's take a look at BBSs.

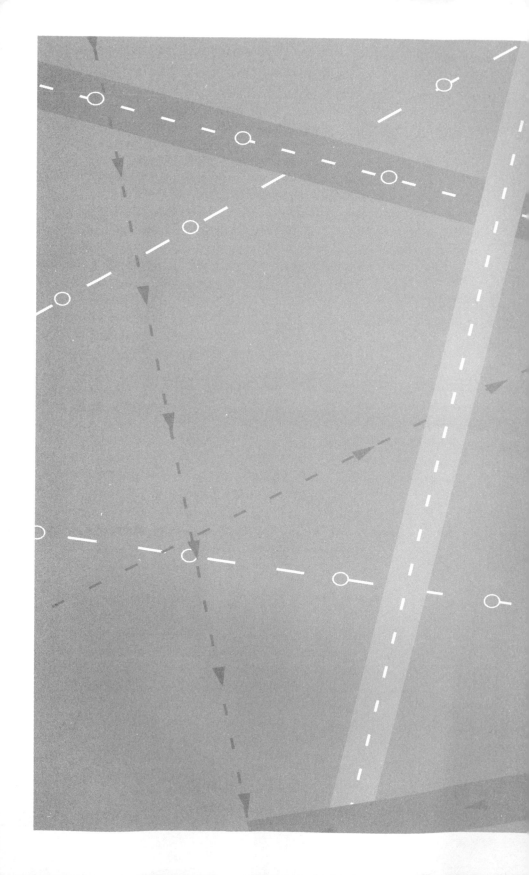

Chapter 3: Bulletin Board Systems and the Internet

As you develop your cybermarketing strategy, you need a good understanding of the lay of the land so you can better prioritize and focus your resources. This chapter addresses two of the three main areas of cyberspace, BBSs and the Internet. (The third area, commercial online services, is covered in Chapter 4.)

I talk about these areas of cyberspace separately, but think of them as tools to use collectively for cybermarketing. For example, having an in-house BBS that customers access via modem may make sense for distributing customer support information. However, if used in conjunction with the Internet, your BBS may serve a greater function by collecting research data or processing product orders generated by Internet traffic.

This chapter presents the marketing roles that BBSs and the Internet can play. I differentiate between BBSs that serve as distribution centers for your marketing materials and those that give you access to potential customers around the world. I show you which areas of the Net let you take your marketing message "to the streets" and which are the magnets that draw people to your information.

When you read this chapter, you will discover that there are disadvantages as well as advantages to using these areas. I offer advice throughout to help you deal with potential problems and better prepare to market yourself in cyberspace.

As you read about BBSs and the Internet and how they are used, start your subconscious working on how you can leverage these tools to work for you. Get those creative juices flowing, so you'll be ready to dive right into the discussion on a cybermarketing strategy in Chapter 5.

The Role of BBSs in Cybermarketing

BBSs can play two roles for you in cybermarketing. First, you can set up a BBS in-house to distribute company and product information, as well as provide customer service and support. This is a good strategy for companies of any size, in any industry, regardless of what you sell.

Your second option is to *attempt* to market through some of the 50,000 other BBSs around the world in what can be best described as either "guerrilla warfare" (if you're an optimist) or "trench warfare" (if you're a realist).

Developing an In-house BBS

A BBS can distribute text-based and graphical computer files, which you can make as fancy as you want. The problem is that most software for setting up a BBS doesn't allow you to display graphical user interfaces. People who modem in to your BBS will see text only, not the kind of flashy screens that they'll find at World Wide Web sites. This problem isn't major, however, because people can download your information onto their computers and get the full graphical impact of your message that way.

When you design materials to store on your BBS, take into account that most of the people who come to it will already know something about your company and are probably customers already. Either an ad or word of mouth has enticed them to dial you up, so they have some interest in being there. You therefore should focus less on catching their attention than on continuing to build interest in what you have to offer.

Campbell Services provides a good example of how a small company can use an in-house BBS. Lotus Development Corp., on the other hand, gives a large company's perspective.

Campbell Services   Campbell Services, one of our clients at Successful Marketing Strategists, markets a personal calendar and group scheduling software package called OnTime. Software engineer Ben Forta developed the company's in-house BBS primarily as a customer support vehicle, and also as a way to get evaluation software into customers' hands quickly.

Campbell Services' BBS supplements the company's telephone and on-site customer support effort with tech support files, demo software, and answers to frequently asked questions. It enhances marketing activities by giving prospects access to product brochures, instruction manuals, other printed materials, and live software.

Forta notes that "If a prospect wants to see OnTime, ideally you want them to install it as quickly as possible while the conversation is still fresh in their mind. Our BBS delivers a copy of OnTime immediately. If users want to buy a 'live' version of OnTime, they can download activation disks from the BBS with passwords provided by the salesperson."

Forta is a technology wizard who has been an avid cybersurfer since the early days of modem communication; you can trust his advice. He recommends that, if you're new to BBSs, "start off small, with maybe a two- to four-line system that can cost you as little as $3,000. Thoroughly research BBS software (magazines like *Boardwatch* are useful for this), since some are designed more for business and other packages are designed primarily for entertainment use. And don't worry too much about your initial setup. BBSs are fairly easy to modify to meet changing needs."

Lotus Development Corp.   On the other end of the spectrum is software giant Lotus Development, which has a few million more customers than Campbell Services does. Lotus markets Lotus 1-2-3, Lotus Notes, and other business software programs.

When Lotus first started its BBS, it was looking for a more convenient way to have customers pick up product information and software files with minor enhancements and bug fixes. Rather than looking for new sales, the company saw the BBS as a value-added service, something extra that customers didn't get in the box. The BBS also aided the customer support staff by reducing the number of incoming calls and the amount of time spent on calls that did come in.

Lotus sees a lot of value in having a BBS. Wayne Heitman, principal technical consultant of Lotus, says "you can tell how valuable this has become to customers and to us when the BBS crashes. People are rather quick to make their displeasure known when something goes wrong with that system." Lotus's maintenance team subsequently takes extra steps to be sure that the system stays up and running.

Upside, Downside   There are advantages and disadvantages to setting up your own, in-house BBS. Look at them carefully.

If your company is just starting out, you may want to set up your own BBS as a starting point to cybermarketing. Doing this could be less expensive than setting up an Internet site if you already have a computer system that's either idle or not used too much.

Another good thing about starting out with an in-house BBS is that it lets you work out some of the online marketing kinks, such as perfecting your customer response process, with a small, manageable audience. (Conversely, once you're on the Net, you're out there. If there are any glitches in your information or its delivery, a whole lot of people will know about it.)

Having the system at your location also gives you fast access when you want to change or update content. Smaller companies that have Net sites typically have them managed through an Internet provider. These companies have to rely on the provider to make and upload changes whenever it has the time—and sometimes, at a cost.

If yours is a service company with an audience narrowly defined by geography, age, profession, and so on, consider that a BBS can also be a good place to create a country club atmosphere. People like to feel that they belong to or buy from an exclusive club where the average Joes and Janes don't congregate.

Taking this concept a step further, you might create a section in your BBS for certain customers to come for information or services available only to them. You could also give preferred customers VIP access to key executives at your company via the BBS.

Don't overlook the practical consideration that a BBS can be a convenient way to communicate around the clock with field sales people, sales reps, or widely dispersed distributors or retailers. SCO's BBS, for instance, was originally set up to support 4,800 resellers and business partners. A BBS will spare you the hassle of getting these individuals on an online service or the Internet, since it's easier for some people to buy an inexpensive modem than sign up for a service with monthly charges.

Also keep in mind that, despite the hype, not everyone with a modem visits online services or the Internet. Some are quite content to go BBS hopping or communicating one-on-one with other computer users.

A BBS is also a good place to store lots of data that may not be useful to all of your customers but that nevertheless is important information that someone somewhere might need someday. This can be particularly true of consulting firms, large bureaucratic organizations that thrive on paper, and tech companies. Borland International is a good example.

Borland's BBS holds nearly 5,000 technical documents accumulated over six years. It's not that they expect a flood of people to stop by asking for this information; it's just that they don't want to send someone on a Indiana Jones hunt for the Hidden Document of Doom when a single customer does need it.

There are, of course, some downsides to a BBS.

One thing that can turn companies off about a BBS is that you have to learn how to use and maintain the software that runs it. This is okay if you have the time to acquire the expertise for doing this (or have someone else who will do it for you). But some find that paying an Internet provider to do the same thing is a better option.

A BBS also requires a significant effort to make its presence known. If you run direct mail and advertising campaigns, it's easy to add a few lines about your BBS and offer people incentives for visiting it. Otherwise, it's almost impossible to let people know that your BBS exists.

As developers create more BBS software with gateways to the Internet, you will at least be able to resolve this isolation issue. On the Net, people can happen to find you by randomly searching through cyberspace, or you can create links to every logical Net site that will take you in.

Finally, if you're doing business nationally or internationally, the fact that your BBS is a toll call for many people could dissuade them from accessing it. This is another disadvantage to BBSs, since most businesspeople try to minimize costs in getting information to prospects.

Now that you have a feel for BBSs as in-house communication tools, let's look at how you can leverage others' BBSs for your marketing benefit.

Reach Out and Touch Some BBSs

Leveraging the thousands of BBSs out there is easy in theory, but it can be a painful process when put in practice.

Earlier in the chapter, I referred to marketing through the myriad BBSs as "trench warfare" because this is a very tedious way to make a dent in the world. Part of the problem is that you have to contact each BBS individually: e-mail the sysop, present your case for uploading information, and wait for a reply. In many cases, you have to go through a sign-on procedure that includes paying money. It's usually a small amount per BBS, but this can add up.

If you get clearance to post your information on a sysop's system, you may have to go through several steps to track how many people actually access your material, or you may have to get the sysop to give you this data. This can really take its toll on your patience.

Sometimes, you're not allowed to post your information on a BBS. You have to send it to the sysop and trust that he or she will post it for you. You must also pay any charges for calling a BBS outside of your local area.

Now, this is not to say that the effort is not worth it. It's just a reality check so you can get a general idea of what you're in for. The following story, though, should encourage many of you—particularly if yours is a small-to-medium-sized company. It shows that, even in this unglamorous marketing trek, rewards come to those who fight the good fight.

In the Trenches with McAfee Associates   In 1989, McAfee Associates was a little California startup company with a software program that detected and neutralized computer viruses before they could harm a PC's data. It's fair to say that the BBS world was McAfee's road to fame and fortune.

Today, the company makes several million dollars a year, its product line has expanded to include several PC and network utilities, and it's even rich enough to buy other software companies—which it has.

When McAfee started, its people didn't do traditional marketing; there was no sales force and software retailers weren't knocking down the door wanting to carry the company's product. "We believed that if we built a quality product that solved a pressing need and provided exceptionally good support, people would not only buy it, they would become evangelists for the product," stated Bill McKiernan, former president and CEO of McAfee Associates. His team provided the quality and the good support. BBSs provided the evangelists.

As people started using the antivirus product, word quickly spread through cyberspace. "It was a natural phenomenon," recalls McKiernan. "Sysops from various BBSs contacted us to get our software, which they in turn used to draw people to their boards. We didn't have to pay or incent them in any way. We just let them copy the software freely and pay for it if they liked it."

Though many satisfied users did pay for the product, the real advantage was that these customers instigated grassroots campaigns that convinced entire companies and government agencies worldwide to standardize on McAfee's software.

McAfee's internal BBS also played a major role in this cybermarketing campaign. "We set up special forums for customer support, responded immediately to e-mail messages, and quickly incorporated user feedback into product enhancements, which reinforced our reputation for providing a quality product," continues McKiernan. The internal BBS was also used heavily to distribute products and upgrades.

Users coming from other BBSs knew right away that they had a place to go not only to find help, but also where someone would listen to them and their ideas. They also could find other users with whom they could exchange advice and tips.

This plays back to the issue I mentioned earlier about building a sense of community. Every one of the users who went back to his or her respective BBS would talk to friends and post favorable messages that were seen by hundreds of users at a time.

Now take a look at what types of companies can benefit from this cybermarketing trench warfare.

Types of Companies That Can Benefit from BBSs   McKiernan, who now heads an Internet software distribution company called Software.net, believes that people can duplicate his former company's success if they do many of the same things that McAfee did. The ability to deliver a product through a BBS is a key element, so you have an advantage if you sell software, music, videos, or other products that you can digitize.

Service providers who market information have an advantage, because it's effortless to deliver that information electronically. McKiernan's strongest emphasis, though, was on the value of developing a reputation for good service.

Companies that sell hard goods have a harder way to go unless they can offer something exciting that draws users to a sysop's BBS (maybe a software utility or a shareware game to which you attach a promotional message for your product).

These companies may also do well marketing to BBSs if they have a product that is particularly appealing to people who match demographics of online users in general or of members of a specific BBS. For example, gold desktop crosses could be a big hit in the several dozen BBSs that cater to the various Christian denominations.

John Seamster, director of electronic publishing at Borland, thinks that cyber trench warfare is recommended "if you have few or no other cybermarketing alternatives, you have a product that users can immediately see value in purchasing and its learning curve is zero. That was the great thing about McAfee's product, you just popped it in the computer, typed a command or two, and you were set."

BBS-to-BBS marketing can probably work well if you have novelty products like pet rocks, which tend to have short life cycles, a low cost of goods, and an insanely high sales rate.

For those of you not old enough to remember, some genius in the 1970s came up with this concept of taking a garden variety rock, putting it in a nice box with a penny's worth of tissue paper, and selling it for $5.00 ($15 in today's economy) as a pet. The pet rock's life cycle was a year or so, but stores couldn't sell them fast enough during that time. Create a similar kind of mania online and who knows where it will take you.

Probably the best use of the BBS marketing tactic is not to try to sell users but rather to inform, educate, and sometimes entertain them. Maybe your product has an underlying technology that potential customers need to understand before they can see the value of your product. Or perhaps you have a special way of making chocolate that produces the kind of flavor that a chocoholic would die for. Package up this knowledge, give it a good headline, and send it on its merry way.

My company's work with AT&T exemplifies this tactic of using a BBS to distribute "knowledge" and thereby getting people interested in your particular company's product.

AT&T's Global Business Communication Systems (GBCS) markets a product called PassageWay, which enables AT&T business phone systems to link with PCs so you can do lots of neat stuff that you can't do (or do as easily) with either phones or PCs alone. This is called Computer-Telephony Integration in high-tech speak, or CTI.

The problem with marketing a CTI product is that you have to make some pretty complex information easily understandable before someone says "Hey, I'll take one of those." So we wrote a short presentation paper on why CTI makes sense for a business.

Olgilvy & Mather, AT&T's ad agency, created a PassageWay game that gives people a fun way to entertain themselves and at the same time learn the value of CTI. We snagged this game, converted the presentation paper to ASCII text, and set up a person to upload this info combo to BBSs that appeared to have receptive audiences of business owners, professionals, and managers.

Though we have just begun to analyze the results of our efforts with AT&T there are some lessons that we learned.

Lessons Learned from the Trenches

1. This is a tedious process that probably makes sense only if you have a person to dedicate solely to the BBS effort, while you pursue other marketing activities.

2. Using software is a good idea, either as the main product or as a promotional tool, particularly if it's a game. However, its file size should be small (100–500K). Files that are much bigger than that take forever to upload and download. You would do better just to send a short blurb to BBSs telling sysops that you have software as a special offer for users if they request your educational information. Offer to deliver the software either online or by regular mail.

3. Trying to find out if a BBS uploaded your material and tracking the number of users who accessed it takes almost as much time as getting the information there in the first place. You have to go through many of the same steps. It may make more sense to just not worry about tracking results, other than to monitor calls to your 800 number and e-mail.

Given these issues to consider, you may be wondering if it doesn't make more sense to skip BBSs altogether and just go to the Net. Well, there are some points to consider before you write off BBSs.

BBSs or the Internet?

BBSs and the Net actually hold many of the same marketing advantages in terms of their ability to quickly and inexpensively distribute lots of information to many people. The Net does have an edge: You can link your site to other Net sites easily and inexpensively, and people can find you with less hassle.

Companies with general consumers and home office products may have better luck with BBSs, because most of the home users with modems tend to hang out at BBSs more than other areas of cyberspace. In fact, people whose home computers were bought before 1994 probably don't have modems with enough speed to make Internet access practical.

Broderbund is a company whose target audience is the home and general consumer market, and it is sticking by its BBS guns.

Although Broderbund is a large, well-known software company, the people there are still evaluating whether they want to move to the Net. They're unsure that the returns will justify the cost and effort, given the company's home market focus. Meanwhile, they plan to beef up their presence on BBSs and online services.

Later, I talk about specific strategies and tactics and show other situations that may justify using BBSs.

The Internet: The Whole World in Your Hands

The Internet is where the multitudes from around the world hang out. This is the apple of the media's eye that you can't stop reading and hearing about every time you pick up a newspaper or turn on the TV. And the books! The books about the Net are legion—just look in any bookstore.

This preponderance of publications is why I don't devote a lot of pages here to the technical aspects of the Net. You can read elsewhere about the particulars of setting up and maintaining Net sites. I just want to give you an overview of the component parts of the Net and describe how to use them as marketing tools.

As I discuss developing a cybermarketing strategy and tactics later, I reference these Internet components and the roles they can play in your specific strategies or tactics.

One thing I will say here is that, if you are not an experienced computer user, recruit some technology-savvy person to set up your various Internet areas. Though easy to explain, these Net areas are a righteous pain to set up.

When you finish this book, I suggest that you find another good book, this time about how to set up Web servers and other Internet sites. Even though you may not get into the nitty gritty of slinging computer cable and hacking software code, you will be able to use the Net more effectively if you understand the technology that drives it.

The Net's Dual-Marketing Role

The Net has two roles in your cybermarketing effort: (1) use it to proactively deliver information to people, and (2) use it to store information that users retrieve from you.

To keep this discussion manageable, I describe six elements of the Internet. Three of these—electronic mail or *e-mail*, Internet mailing lists, commonly referred to as *listservs*, and *newsgroups*—are communication tools that you can use to deliver information into Net surfers' e-mail boxes.

The remaining three—*FTP servers*, *gopher servers*, and *World Wide Web servers*—are the types of computer systems (usually UNIX workstations) on which you can store tons of information for people to access from their respective computers.

In an ideal Cyber Marketing campaign, you use all of these communication tools and servers together in a way that complements the strengths that each offer. Before I go into detail about that, take a look at each element separately.

E-mail, the Net's Main Attraction   The most universal communication vehicle within the Internet is e-mail. This is the extent of Internet access to which a majority of the purported 30 million Net users have.

E-mail is a simple concept, really. You get an e-mail account so you can create messages and send them to any other soul who also has a Net e-mail account. In some cases, you can get an account for $25 per month from an Internet provider.

This account is assigned an e-mail address, which serves the same function as your home or business address. It tells people where you are. Net addresses typically have a person's name, followed by the @ sign and a designated name for the Internet site where your account is located. Jane@company.com is an example.

An e-mail account lets you send messages and computer files and receive the same from others. You can also use e-mail to trigger certain Net sites to automatically send you computer files, such as product brochures or a newsletter. Some e-mail accounts are for individuals, and others are accounts for entire corporations.

If you don't do anything else, I suggest you get an e-mail account. E-mail serves a valuable communication function by enabling you to avoid telephone tag and reach people's computers regardless of where they are on the planet.

This book would have been more difficult to write and taken longer to finish had I not been able to send e-mail to ferret out the right people at different companies for interviews. Several interviews had to be conducted entirely by e-mail; otherwise, I wouldn't have gotten the interviews at all.

Obviously you don't have real-time communication with e-mail, but people can read and respond to your e-mail messages at any time that's convenient for them. A lot of useful dialog can go back and forth much faster than it would take to get busy people together for a conference call or a meeting. E-mail also tends to keep your discussions focused, and you use your time more efficiently.

Most of the online services have Internet access, so your screen name for the service that you use to identify yourself online is also your Net address. For example, [screen name]@compuserve.com would be a CompuServe member's Internet address. Of course, if your screen name is Honey Bunny or The Bear, you may want to consider getting a new name or a real Net address for business communication.

E-mail as a Marketing Tool   You can do mass e-mailings if you collect cybersurfers' e-mail addresses with the explicit consent from them to send unsolicited mail. You need to clearly explain to users how often and under what circumstances you will e-mail information to them. The best way to do this is to create an electronic form for users to complete that includes the necessary information.

In later chapters, I show ways to collect e-mail addresses that are interesting and fun for users.

When you do e-mail people, send them only useful information. New product updates are the type of material that many people consider important. But information such as annual earnings reports should just be posted online.

Receiving unsolicited e-mail may seem no more bothersome than getting junk mail in your regular mailbox. If you don't want it, you chuck it. But it's different with e-mail. Not many people come back to their offices after a day or two on the road and find 150 pieces of mail piled in their In boxes. But e-mail in this volume can be typical.

When you get this much e-mail, it's somewhat annoying having to clear out mail that you don't want and didn't ask for. Some e-mail packages don't let you read the sources of messages, so you have to open the messages to see what they are. Start piling these people up with what they consider junk e-mail, and you'll soon see bad will and a backlash. This is not a winning combination in my book.

There's another issue to consider that involves unsolicited e-mail. People online, particularly on the Net, feel that their e-mail address is a private thing. If you take it without asking and then sell it or use it, these people will resent you a lot. This resentment often starts *flame wars,* which can really hinder your ability to build a warm, community feeling in your online area.

Mailing Lists   Internet mailing lists, usually referred to as *listservs,* are collections of e-mail messages that address specific topics or interests. These are collected at a single Internet site, also called a listserv, and then mass e-mailed to users who subscribe to these particular lists.

You can have one person sort and direct (or *moderate*) this e-mail traffic and even screen out mail that does not fit the topic of the list. Alternatively, you can install software at this Net site that automatically manages the traffic. Listservs generated from this type of Net site are referred to as being *unmoderated.*

A word of warning: An unmoderated listserv is courting disaster. Though it's fairly easy to set up a listserv, you have to constantly monitor what's called *administrative e-mail.* Listservs are prone to system glitches that can block e-mail traffic; administrative e-mail alerts you to these problems and gives you clues on how to solve them.

Software that runs an unmoderated listserv has no way to respond to administrative e-mail. Your listserv could stop functioning altogether, and you would never know until someone brought it to your attention.

From my experience, what typically happens with the marketing listserv that I subscribe to is that someone posts a message and twenty people may respond to it. I get the original message, as well as one separate message from each of the people responding.

This can be a nice way to see what useful ideas come from various people. It can also produce useless drivel by the truckload every hour, particularly if you subscribe to more than one list. Be careful which lists you subscribe to.

From the standpoint of proactive marketing, listservs can be helpful marketing tools.

Listservs serve two valuable purposes.

You can dramatically shorten the time it takes to communicate with people by starting you own list. If you have information that changes frequently (financial quotes, product pricing and availability, research results, and so on), a listserv can broadcast these changes as soon as they occur so that people can receive them within minutes.

Listserv subscribers benefit because they automatically get information that they want or need delivered to their e-mail boxes. This is faster and easier than continually accessing your forums or Internet sites. You benefit by becoming more proactive and distributing information in a way that can shorten your sales cycles.

You can promote subscriptions through all of your online areas. Anyone who can get to the Net by e-mail can access your listserv. And by the way, in case you're wondering, companies do not charge for subscriptions to listservs. You may, however, want to consider including access to listservs as a part of a product service plan for which customers do pay.

Because of the chaotic direction that listserv discussions can take, you should control communication by setting up the listserv so that information is mailed only from your site. It's not necessary to have people respond via the listserv. Give them another response avenue, such as your main Internet e-mail address.

This is one case where it's okay to have one-way communication, as long as you have two-way communication in your other online areas. It's less hassle for you, and some of the people that I interviewed felt that there's little marketing value in trying to use a listserv to foster online conversation.

A second valuable use of listservs is in monitoring what's going on with your market or industry. You may have to shop around before finding a list that actually offers value, since some lists serve up more useless junk than pearls of wisdom.

Subscribing to listservs that address your industry also lets you see what people are saying about you—and your competitor. Actively participating in a listserv can provide you with even more valuable feedback.

Though you should take appropriate action if you ever see your company being maligned in a listserv, I highly discourage you from using listservs to attack competitors. And you don't want to toot your own horn, either. These tactics have a way of backfiring in the cyber world because people are often offended by them.

The next section covers newsgroups, which are a more structured vehicle for Internet discussions. You can still assert a certain amount of control over a newsgroup that you set up yourself, but two-way communication with subscribers is the norm, even with company-sponsored newsgroups.

Usenet Newsgroups   Newsgroups are part of a subset of the Internet called *Usenet* or *Usenet News*. Newsgroups originally started as a way for universities to carry on long-distance discussions involving research.

As the number of newsgroups increased, domains (category headlines) were created to classify newsgroups by general topics. Today there are over 9,000 newsgroups, and the domains have proliferated dramatically.

Similar to listservs, newsgroups are collections of e-mail messages that relate (or should relate) to specific topics or interests. Newsgroups can be moderated or unmoderated. Unlike listservs, though, newsgroups use *threaded e-mail.*

With threaded e-mail, someone posts a message that others respond to. Then the person who posted the message responds to these responses, and so on, creating a string of related messages that can become quite long. Anyone who happens upon this thread can literally go to the top of it to read every message posted in the string, and then add to it.

There is more structure around newsgroups than you find with listservs. The people who run and participate in newsgroups work to keep a coherent conversation going back and forth between users, rather than allowing the random postings that you find on listservs.

Another difference is the way that you access newsgroup information. While listserv subscribers automatically receive everything broadcast from a server and can read messages as regular e-mail, newsgroup users need special software called *newsreaders* to read newsgroup messages. You can get newsreaders for free from the Net if you look in the right places, or you can buy a more polished newsreader from one of several commercial sources.

Newsgroups are fairly easy to set up and do not require as much monitoring for technical problems as listservs do. However, you will have your work cut out for you when answering the e-mail messages, which can range from fewer than ten to dozens per day.

It's recommended that you respond to messages within a day, so give serious thought to the workload involved before setting up a newsgroup. Who at your organization is going to manage it? Will you need to hire someone to do this, and what are the pros and cons? Look at your Net options collectively before making a specific decision about newsgroups.

Making Newsgroups Work for You   Companies with Net accounts can restrict newsgroups that come into their offices and prevent employees from wasting time with nonbusiness information. Newsgroups about "Star Trek" and Barney the dinosaur may not make it past the corporate iron curtain.

Individuals at their computers can also screen out certain newsgroups. Users can go a step further, too, and get software that searches through newsgroups they receive to find specific messages of special interest.

These are reasons why the tactic of blindly sending ad messages to newsgroups, as described in Chapter 1, doesn't make sense. Companies and individuals with the software to do so will just filter out ads before they're read.

The best way to leverage newsgroups is to use them to distribute information. You can distribute the same kind of time-sensitive information that you can with listservs, but newsgroups generally have a "community" spirit that fosters more discussion. You subsequently can get vital feedback on current or future products, pricing, marketing ideas, and other aspects of your business.

As with listservs, scanning newsgroups is a good way to keep tabs on what other people in your market or industry are doing, and on what's being said about you and your competitors. Because you can filter out just the information you want, newsgroups are more manageable than listservs as research tools.

The November/December 1994 issue of *Internet World* has several good articles to help you better understand and use newsgroups. There are also newsgroups you may want to check out that will help you work newsgroups into your marketing campaign: **news.announce.newusers** contains articles that explain aspects of Usenet, and **news.newusers.questions** is where you can post questions about Usenet.

Now that you know how to "take it [your marketing message] to the street," it's time to take a look at where you store and distribute the bulk of your marketing materials, and where you—hopefully—conduct business transactions. Granted, e-mail, listservs, and newsgroups let you deliver messages to people's cyber doorsteps, but the full, multidimensional marketing impact of the Net comes from FTP, gopher, and Web servers.

Storing and Distributing Information

There are three areas of the Internet where you can store content for users to access: FTP sites, gopher sites and World Wide Web sites. Each plays a different marketing role.

FTP Sites   Even though Web sites get more publicity, FTP sites are veritable workhorses for many companies that want to distribute tons of information to the widest range of people.

Because of their technical design, FTP sites are reachable by almost anyone with access to the Internet. Businesspeople who want to make information about their companies available to the highest possible number of people post their content at FTP sites. You can post an endless amount of computer files with all types of information—text, graphics, or whatever.

Unfortunately, FTP sites do not allow you to set up a menu system so that people who visit your site can easily see what information is there. Users see only a long list of filenames, which are not very descriptive. Also, they cannot view files while at an FTP site; they must download them and read them later. This tends to discourage people who don't want to go through the trouble of downloading big files, only to find that the files are not what they want.

To work around this problem, have whatever materials you use to point people to your FTP site (brochures, ads, another Net site) describe what it is that you're sending people to find, as well as the specific filename(s). For example, "Be sure to get our latest price list at our FTP server in file **price.blahblah.blah**."

You can also post a file at your FTP site, which you name either "index," "contents," or "00_," that contains a description of all the files on the server. Visitors will still have to download the file and read it, but at least this document makes it easier for people to determine what's in your area.

If you want to see an FTP site that's laid out as nicely as possible given the technology limitations, get on the Net and FTP (*FTP* is used as a verb, too) to the following address: *oak.oakland.edu*. Someone in the Oakland, California education system did a good job of making this area user-friendly.

Because of their lack of menu structure and inability to display graphics, FTP sites primarily have a passive marketing role. You can store thousands of promotional and tech support materials, which is what many companies do, but you can't create visual promotions that draw people to specific information or guide users through the area.

Unless you specifically point them to your FTP site, people are unlikely to find you unless they use software that searches FTP sites for information that meets users' search criteria. This can be a laborious process for users and a hit-or-miss proposition for you.

To get the most from your FTP sites, all of your traditional and on-line marketing materials or promotions, sales people, and so on should reference these areas. If you set up gopher and Web sites, hyperlink these to your FTP sites. Some companies use a Web site to create a graphical directory of FTP site information. Users can easily see what's at the FTP site and then use the hyperlink to go right to the file and get it.

One proactive measure you can take with the materials stored on an FTP site is to have these documents end with a call to action, so people are prompted to do something after reading them. You should also include promotional offers (a free gift, a special discount) to increase responses and help you track the responses.

Gopher sites, though waning in popularity, are a step up from FTP sites in terms of marketing effectiveness.

Gopher Sites   By the time you read this, gopher sites might be a relic. I say that because the purpose for which gopher sites were designed is being superseded by the World Wide Web.

Gopher servers came into existence to make it easier for people to search for and preview Internet files before downloading them. Similar to FTP sites, gopher sites let you store any kind of text, graphic, video, or audio file that you want to distribute.

Gopher technology, however, also lets you build menu structures that allow users to navigate through your information hassle-free. Users can view documents on-screen and can quickly surf between gopher sites or between gopher and FTP sites.

The reason that gophers are losing popularity is that Web sites do everything gopher sites can do, and much more. Users can display graphics and motion video files at Web sites on their computer screens and play Web site audio files through their computers (if they have the necessary equipment) without having to download these files.

This ability to display multimedia presentations online lets companies do more creative cybermarketing than they can on gophers. Web servers also have technology benefits that give them better overall performance than that of gopher servers, plus you can easily access gopher and FTP sites from your Web site.

For companies that are new on the Net, it makes more sense to just go with a Web site and an FTP rather than incur additional charges setting up a gopher server. The Web site gives you all the glitz and glory (and greater marketing communication options), while the FTP sites let you reach the rest of the Net community that's not equipped for Web prime time.

World Wide Web Sites   Of all the Internet sites, the World Wide Web (WWW, or Web) is receiving the lion's share of the news covering cyberspace. Web servers offer greater creative potential than FTP and gopher sites; you can display graphics and video clips for people to view and audio clips for them to play from their computers.

Businesses, individuals, and even rock groups are flocking to set up Web home pages by the thousands. A *home page* is the initial information that users see when they arrive at someone's Web site.

From a home page, a user can click the computer mouse on hyperlinked graphics or words to access more information that may be at the same Web site or at any Web, gopher, or FTP server located on the Net. (*Hyperlinking* is writing software code that links an item in your online document with other information. Clicking on the item tells the software to transfer you over to the new information.)

The draw of Web sites is that you can be as creative as you want by combining visual and audio features, as well as hyperlinks to related information, to present your message. Web servers also let you set up transaction capabilities so that customers can order your products online. Together, these capabilities let you design a truly interactive marketing vehicle.

There is, however, a drawback to Web sites. They require users to have so much computing horsepower and *bandwidth* (the amount of data per second that can pass through the connection between users and a Web site) that the average person cannot access Web sites.

Only an estimated 3 million of the 30 million Internet users can actually browse Web pages. And not everyone's computer has the capability to play those video and audio files that you can store at Web sites.

So why set up a Web site?

One reason is for the potential growth in visitors. Every day, some company is releasing a better Internet connection or better software that will give more people access to the Web.

At some point the scales will tip in favor of universal Web access, and the Web will be swamped with visitors. You want to be in place and have worked out all of the bugs when this flood hits.

Another reason is PR. Actually, this is really compelling. No one writes about IBM or GM setting up an FTP site, even though FTP sites are accessible by everyone. They write about a company's nifty new home page or "xyz" information you can get by going to **www.whatever.whatever**.

The Web is sexy, and if you want people to believe that you're serious about being on the Net, you do need a Web page. The upside to this cyber showboating is that you can get home pages designed for as little as $500 (or less, if you're willing to learn how to do it yourself) and $10–$50 per month maintenance if you use an Internet provider.

I caution you, though, that if you want your Web page to be used by the greatest number of people, avoid the tendency for grandiose graphic design. The more elaborate your graphic file, the more bytes (computer space) it requires. This means that the average user has to wait longer for the graphic to materialize on-screen. If it takes too long, users get exasperated and move on.

When the bandwidth issue gets resolved and people can download massive documents in the blink of an eye, go ahead and knock yourself out with earth-moving, heart-stopping visual masterpieces.

I also strongly advise you to link your Web site to everything and be listed at every Internet site possible (I'll give you tips on how to do this in Chapter 8). There may be many millions of people cybersurfing, but there are also tons of Web sites. People faced with a sea of choices often will resort to directories and information search software to find what they want. Or they will just visit sites that they already know about.

Right now, users are so enamored with the Web that they'll spend hours wandering around. But later, when average people who see technology as just another business tool start logging on, wanderers will give way to people who just want to get what they need and move on. Good linking strategy will pay off by helping you to effectively address this shifting trend.

Putting the Pieces Together

I want to conclude with a scenario that shows you how to weave the six Internet elements together into a tapestry of awe-inspiring marketing communication.

Before doing that, I need to make an extremely important point. You will not be able to fully comprehend and appreciate the information presented in this book until you explore cyberspace firsthand. I talked to dozens of people about their Net activities, but their comments did not have the same impact as seeing things up close and personal.

Until you search through the endless Net directories looking for links for your site, it's impossible to know how much time you have to allocate to this exercise. Not until you sit stewing in aggravation waiting for a Net image to crawl through your 14.4 bps modem, will you appreciate the *KISS* axiom—Keep It Simple, Stupid.

You have to explore the Net to really understand the differences between listservs and newsgroups, or between FTP, gopher, and Web sites.

You need to see what your customers will see in the way that they will see it if you want to communicate effectively on the Net, or in any part of cyberspace.

You should subscribe to a couple of listservs and newsgroups. Post a couple of messages after you've been a member for a while. Few things can teach you the rules of *netiquette* (acceptable behavior on the Net) faster than seeing some poor soul crash and burn in a newsgroup's wall of flames.

So get out there and test the cyberwaves. While you're at it, here's my little scenario of one way to leverage all that cyberspace has to offer.

When you design your FTP, gopher, or Web sites, create ways to capture as many e-mail addresses as you can. Either develop an electronic form that users complete to access information (ask your Net provider to explore this possibility) or set up contests that require users to submit e-mail addresses in order to participate.

You also can include an offer in the promotional materials that users download that encourages them to enter their e-mail addresses in your database in order to receive information updates. Whatever you do, be sure that you get users' expressed consent to have you send them e-mail.

Once you develop the mechanics for collecting e-mail addresses, start a listserv for information distribution and a newsgroup for hosting general discussion, Q&As, and collecting general customer feedback. Promote your listserv and newsgroup on all of your Net sites, as well as in your conventional marketing materials.

You should post the basic materials that you want to distribute—brochures, price lists, support information—on your FTP, gopher, and Web sites. Even though the Web is where you turn your creativity loose, you want your information in places where the most people can get to it. Be sure that each site points to the other two, and hyperlink your Web site to your FTP and gopher servers.

When you launch your campaign on the Net, use e-mail, your listserv, and your newsgroup to proactively distribute information, promote your Net servers, and keep interest high in your Net presence. Then push your gopher and Web sites to their creative limits to attract people and (most importantly) keep them coming back.

You should now have a good perspective on the Internet's role in the cybermarketing scheme of things. Next, I move on to the commercial online services. While the Net gives you an outlet to reach the world at large, online services let you target your activities to more focused segments of cyberspace.

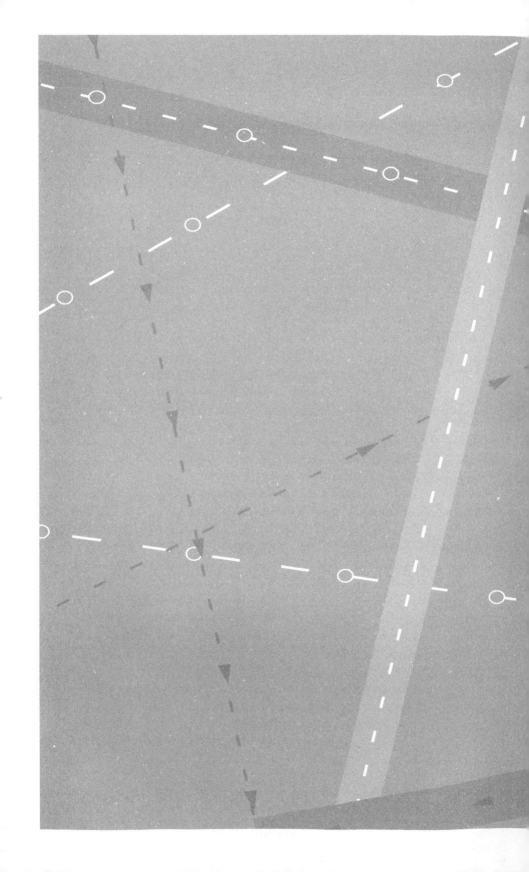

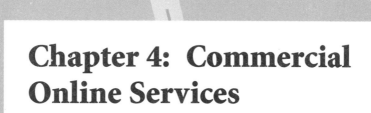

Chapter 4: Commercial Online Services

In this chapter, I describe the major commercial online services in detail. Keep in mind, though, that a lot of this information may change, so you should consult the online companion to this book to get the latest scoop on the services.

Matchmaker, Matchmaker, Find Me a Match

As you evaluate online services and look for features that meet your marketing needs, keep in mind that you want to develop a partnership that balances your needs against those of the respective services. This can be difficult sometimes, but do take the time to resolve the challenges that working with each service presents. The end result will justify your effort.

Commercial online services have staff dedicated to helping you set up your online area, develop content and promotional ideas, and manage some of the technical aspects of your areas. Most services will also train you to use their software tools to manage and maintain your sites.

Another issue to deal with is the fact that more companies are vying for space on CompuServe and AOL (America Online) than these services have available. So you not only have to think of how to develop partnerships with these services, but you also have to be aggressive and creative in order to beat out other companies for limited space. Alas, no rest for the wicked.

Matching Objectives

Your major objective when evaluating online services is to select those with fairly large memberships (over 100,000) whose demographics are similar to those of your target market.

Online services' bottom-line objective is to sign up as many members as possible and then keep those members online as long as possible. They're looking for companies with lots of customers who can be convinced to sign up with the services. The online services also want products or services—say, floral delivery or financial counseling—that will be popular with members.

To help you find audiences that are similar to your target market, the services offer measurable demographics so you can determine your marketing opportunities. You can also get a good idea of whether the services' environments are suited to your needs by getting membership accounts with those that seem to make sense for your company.

Online services typically offer generous trial offers; for example, ten hours of free usage before they start to bill you. Use this time to explore the various sections and features of the online services, see what other companies are doing, and meet with users of the service.

Finding the right services is easy compared to getting them to actually accept you. Your company size and market focus may be a key factor in getting yourself in the door of an online service.

Large companies and companies with great marketing ideas can probably find a home on AOL and CompuServe. High-tech companies of any size that are willing to make their forum areas highly user-interactive are welcome on AT&T Interchange. And companies from any industry that have medium-to-large customer bases should be able to get accepted by GEnie and Delphi.

Prodigy is a little different: It offers space to anyone who can come up with the $20,000–$30,000 per month to be there. This does beg the question: Why pay to post information on Prodigy when you can set up shop elsewhere for free? Especially considering that not only do you avoid these fees on the other services, but that some of the other services even share the revenues generated by users who come to your forum.

The reason that Prodigy charges this way is that it delivers more quantifiable analysis of who accesses your content than the other services do. Subsequently, it treats vendors as if they were buying ad space in a magazine. There are changes occurring in the way Prodigy views its business model regarding advertisers, however, so its pricing policy may change soon as well.

If you market products for the Apple Macintosh market, note that eWorld is starting to show some signs of life after its somewhat questionable start. eWorld is the result of efforts by Apple and other companies to create an online service exclusively for Mac users.

Also note that there are Macintosh user sections on the other online services where you can post your content, if that fits your marketing strategy.

Running the Gauntlet

All online services have procedures to follow before you are assigned an area. The process of getting accepted may seem in some cases like it's weighted against small and medium-size companies. But while it's true that larger companies have an advantage, this is still cyberspace. And in cyberspace, little guys have clout too.

Microsoft Network, Interchange, and GEnie primarily use Q&A sessions, both by telephone and at your office, to be sure that your business fits with their demographics. They also want to verify that you are committed to actively maintaining your areas and supporting customers. Practically any size company is on equal footing in this process.

AOL and CompuServe, though, are quite selective about who they assign space to, and their waiting lists are long. In addition, AOL charges a $10,000 setup fee. CompuServe strongly encourages that you run several specific promotions designed to get your customers to sign up with CompuServe; these promotions can cost you several thousand dollars.

With the rules of the game in mind, you may have to alter your information or product offering in order to meet some of the services' particular requirements and get your company approved. You can set up a forum on AOL with product literature, briefing papers, and an order-taking system, for instance. But GEnie may limit you to running a live RoundTable discussion group on a topic that fits your field of expertise.

As I mentioned, acceptance by all the services is easier if your company is well-known, you have a large customer base, and many of these customers are already online. So if your customer base is large, use this as leverage when you meet with the services' reps to negotiate for space.

Remember that you can also strengthen your bargaining position if you have a promotional idea that fits with the services' specific audiences and can generate a lot of traffic to your online area.

For example, software company Borland International worked with AOL to develop a particularly creative promotion that benefited everyone involved. Borland designed a special version of its SideKick personal organizer software just for AOL's Grateful Dead special interest area. The customized software, which users can download from AOL, contains a schedule of all the Dead concerts around the country. Since hard-core fans, called Deadheads, follow the group everywhere it tours, the software was valuable for them. Since there are quite a few Deadheads online, AOL made money for the time users spent downloading the software. Borland also benefited by getting a lot of people to try its software. And even if some Deadheads didn't buy the complete version of SideKick, they would tell their online friends that "this is cool software, dudes. Ya gotta check it out, man."

Another way to strengthen your bargaining position is with a promotion to get your customers to join the service; for example, by sending them software from the online services that they then use to sign up. (This is virtually a prerequisite with CompuServe.) A recruiting promotion to get your customers online can cost as much as $2.00 per contact, but think of this as an investment. Getting your customers online makes good business sense beyond just appeasing the services. (I explain why in Chapter 6.)

A final bargaining chip is your customers' loyalty. An estimated 30–50 percent of users who join a service log on a few times and then either switch services or stop logging on (often the result of shock at seeing the first bill!). Services have to replace these short-term users in order to maintain and grow memberships. Convince the services that your customers will regularly get online just because of you, and your value to them increases.

Other Options   Even after "running the gauntlet," if yours is a small-to-midsized company, you're likely to have a hard time getting accepted by some services. AOL and CompuServe won't accept you unless you have a very strong business case: that you have a product that people online can't live without, plus the marketing muscle to build customer demand. And even then, you may get only a small area of a larger forum—not the end of the world, but certainly a loss in your ability to attract casual cybersurfers who could find you faster on a forum of your own.

It's also possible that even with your best efforts made, the other services may not take you onboard. You still must present a compelling case with creative ideas and show a willingness to work aggressively to build user traffic.

You might use to your advantage the fact that the services have different user interfaces and structural designs that can put limitations on creativity in designing content. If you can design content or a promotion that capitalizes on the unique layout of a particular service, this will increase your value to them.

If you cannot get a forum, an alternative (or supplement) is getting retail companies located in many of the services' shopping areas to carry your products. Selling arrangements vary, and some require significant annual fees. However, online retailers may give you enough presence on the online services to compensate for not having a forum.

With most of the services adding Internet access for members, clients sometimes ask me if online services will eventually become mere gateways to the Net. If this does happen, why shouldn't companies post content once on the Net and then let online service users come to their Net sites? My answer is that, for now, businesses still should have online forums because there are communities of users who will hang out primarily in the services' respective areas and rarely visit the Net. Sometimes you have to go where the people are and make adjustments as circumstances change.

Next, take a close look at each of the major online services to get a better feel for what they have to offer and what you can offer them.

CompuServe

Founded in 1969, CompuServe now has over 2.7 million subscribers (see below). It provides forum areas that are available to the general public, as well as value-added forums for private business use. For example, Amway—which I cover in detail later—has a private forum that is used exclusively by Amway personnel and distributors.

CompuServe Demographics	
Total audience	2,700,000
Typical age	25-54
Female	8%
Male	92%
Average income	$90,000
Education	96% attended college; 69% college graduates
Occupation	90% professional/managerial (70% work in Fortune 500 companies)
Influence software purchases	39%

Demographics in this chapter were collected in February, 1995.

Vendors are not charged to set up shop on its public forums, but CompuServe does charge for setting up private forums. (When you read my section about Amway, you may or may not decide that a private forum makes sense for you.) CompuServe also has public "auditoriums," which you can arrange to use for major product announcements and similar events.

In addition, CompuServe offers members a number of information services that include news, sports, games, shopping, weather, stock quotes, and Internet access. It offers hundreds of databases, as well as gateways to more extensive information-retrieval services. You can use these services for public relations and research, even if you don't have a forum.

CompuServe wants to add companies to its forum tenant list that can bring 5,000 new users to the service in a short period of time, as well as companies with good promotional ideas. The service likes to "encourage" prospective tenants to set up content on CompuServe only, and not the other online services. Given the value of the other services, I advise clients to politely decline that request, but come up with major promotions that are exclusive to CompuServe.

You'll find that CompuServe's interface is not very graphical, which limits your creative design options. You can place endless amounts of content here, but there are precious few icons that users can click to access it.

Once users get past these few icons, they must rely on text-based menus to get through your forum. Text, graphics, and software files have to be listed chronologically. It's difficult to make this kind of an environment interactive, but CompuServe is working to make its interface more graphical.

Though CompuServe's forum structure may cramp your creativity, many members of the service are proficient with technology and are comfortable using text-heavy interfaces. Subsequently, they will still access your content. But if your customers are not serious computer users, you may have an easier time getting them to sign up for one of the other services.

Even if your current customers are more likely to choose AOL, CompuServe still offers marketing advantages. Its members are fairly affluent and many are business professionals and managers; 83 percent of these people use computers both at home and at work. If these are the kinds of people who can use your product, you want to be on CompuServe.

CompuServe offers another advantage if you market products internationally. It has the strongest international presence of all online services, although access in some countries can be a bit difficult. Improved gateways to the Internet should resolve this issue.

When you get approved to have a forum set up on CompuServe, be prepared to send the person who will be managing your online area on a trip to CompuServe's headquarters in Columbus, Ohio. Companies must have an employee trained by CompuServe's staff to set up and maintain forums and to use CompuServe's publishing tools (the software that you use to design and manage your forums).

If you cannot get a forum area in CompuServe, you can buy space in its Electronic Mall shopping area which includes over 100 retailers and catalogers. Users come here and browse through various graphics displays that companies provide (CompuServe does all the set up work after you give them the graphic elements). When they see something they want to purchase, they can select it and place an order by giving their credit card numbers and other pertinent information.

It costs between $20,000 and $99,500 per year to have a space in the Mall. CompuServe offers a package of options that include product listings and descriptions, space for graphics designs and photos, marquee banners, ads in the service's monthly magazine, and usage credits to give to users so they can browse your area for free. Price is determined by the number of options you take.

Prodigy

Prodigy, which has about 3 million members (see below), targets the American family. It is the service of choice for people who want basic information, simple communication, and an entry-level taste of the online world. Prodigy's user base appears to be quite loyal to the service, which combines general interest information, advertising, and transaction areas where users can order products or services online.

Prodigy Demographics (as of 4/94)	
Total audience	3,021,000
Median age	37
Female	42%
Male	58%
Average income	$57,000
Education	78% college graduates
Occupation	38% professional/managerial

Prodigy is the only service that displays advertising on its initial screens. It pioneered flat-rate usage fees for accessing all areas of the service, online advertising for vendors, market promotions, and classified ads. In 1993, however, Prodigy abandoned flat-rate pricing for three of its key services: bulletin boards, Dow Jones Company News, and Eaasy Sabre.

One vendor whose company uses Prodigy refers to it as an online magazine. "They don't look at us as a content provider, but as a full-page display ad. That's their business model." This seems to run counter to the rest of life online, so I asked this person (who wishes to remain anonymous) why the company stays with Prodigy: "Because we make money [with Prodigy]. That, plus the fact that Prodigy is making a shift in attitude to be like the other online services by getting rid of intrusive ads, developing more content-rich services, and being more supportive of vendors."

Working with Prodigy, for now, is similar to buying ad space in a magazine. Determining your options to get online with Prodigy is pretty straightforward. Call up an ad rep, get a price sheet, determine how much time you can afford, and then negotiate as well as you can for the best rate. If you can afford it and Prodigy's audience fits your target market profile, go with it.

Prodigy has a graphical interface, so you have a lot of options for designing your content. It can either be information-heavy or a series of print ads with an online, 3-D feel. However, for the time being, you get only five pages for your money. You therefore may want to be judicious with how much information you place in your content.

ZiffNet

Ziff-Davis Publishing operates ZiffNet, an online service with 250,000 users. ZiffNet contains the content of all Ziff-Davis PC publications, including *PC Week*, *PC Magazine*, *MacWeek*, and over a hundred other publications from other sources.

ZiffNet is technology-oriented in terms of its audience and content providers. Users who access ZiffNet tend to be high-tech professionals and consumers of technology products. ZiffNet offers news services, reference services, and areas where users have discussions by posting e-mail messages to each other.

ZiffNet also offers an Industry Partner Program that allows companies to post software updates, marketing materials, and tech tips, which is a good information distribution option for software companies of any size. Hardware companies are welcome, too, if they have information to contribute. There are no forums for companies like the ones you find on CompuServe, AOL, and AT&T Interchange, and no other typical trappings of commercial services, such as live chat areas.

ZiffNet has a text-based interface, and it is accessible through CompuServe, AT&T Interchange, Prodigy, and Microsoft Network. Besides being an outlet for your information, it offers a great PR vehicle through Executives Online. This is a week-long "talk show" style threaded e-mail discussion that is hosted by an editor from one of the Ziff pubs who interviews a high-tech industry executive. In a threaded e-mail format, people access Execs Online's interview dialog, post their own questions to guests, and read all e-mail between the guests and online users.

You don't have to be an industry giant or a top executive to be on Execs Online. It does help if you're announcing a new product that week, because the show's producers like to leverage the "late-breaking news" angle when they can. They also like it when you can offer users a special price on the software (if that's what you sell) that users can download from ZiffNet.

Campbell Services' president Don Campbell was a guest the week that his company shipped a new version of its OnTime calendar software. After Campbell's well-attended appearance, over 3,500 users downloaded OnTime, and the company then received the names and addresses of those buyers in a database file ready for mailing (with the users' consents, of course).

ZiffNet's new ownership intends to maintain its operating format. If you are a nontech company but offer something of value to technology-oriented professionals, you may want to develop a good promotional idea and give ZiffNet a shot.

AT&T Interchange

Interchange was to be Ziff-Davis' gussied up, ready for prime time, highly graphical online service that would complement ZiffNet. However, AT&T bought Interchange at the end of 1994, and now businesses and cybersurfers are waiting to see what Interchange looks like when AT&T rolls it out in 1995. What I describe here is what I've been able to find out about how the service will look.

Interchange's mission is to provide the most extensive amount of online information about high-tech products, people, and markets—and to have this information hyperlinked in every way possible. Interchange offers content from the same publications that are posted on ZiffNet.

The audience for Interchange will have the same demographic profile as ZiffNet's, since a lot of the audience will be drawn from Ziff-Net. The total number of Interchange users could conceivably equal or surpass the number of ZiffNet subscribers.

Interchange and, purportedly, Microsoft Network will have the most user interactive environments of the online services and will give you the most creative cybermarketing vehicle, next to the Internet's World Wide Web. The service will provide publishing tools that enable you to control every aspect of your online content development, including graphics, presentations, pricing, and advertising. You will have real-time chat rooms in your forums, as well as the ability to host threaded e-mail discussions.

One major difference between Interchange and other services will be its *universal linking* feature. This feature will let you link any piece of information in your forum to any other information on Interchange. These links will be represented with icons that users click on to jump to the linked documents.

Using this feature will allow you to easily link your forum documents to related articles, software files, or e-mail discussions. Someone reading an article about your product category, for instance, could see an icon there that he or she could then click to be taken to your specific product information. What's really neat is that you can imbed the icons for these links into e-mail and send it to other users on Interchange.

Here's a good scenario for how this technology can help your marketing: Create an e-mailing list of customers and prospects and then send them mail whenever you get write-ups and product reviews. Rather than having to clip and reproduce the articles for mailing, you can just send short messages with icon links. Recipients open the mail and click on the icons to go straight to articles. It's a much easier process for you and for those on your mailing lists.

America Online

America Online is one of the most popular and fastest growing online services, with about 1,500,000 users (see the next page). AOL offers services such as e-mail, bulletin boards, real-time chat areas, and a range of general and special interest publications from *Business Week* and *The New York Times* to *Woman's Day* and *Flying Magazine.*

There are also entertainment services provided by the major TV networks, business and financial information, educational services such as online classes, and transaction services such as travel reservations and shopping. A variety of computer firms on AOL provide services such as software downloading and computer-oriented special-interest groups (SIGs).

AOL's audience is a good option if your market is a broad spectrum of America. AOL's push to be a center of diversity is reflected not only in its range of online publications, but also in its special forum areas and the special events that it hosts. You can find hangouts for Deadheads and bikers (both motor and nonmotor varieties). AOL has hosted guest appearances by rock stars for the MTV crowd and by Billy Graham for the heaven-bound.

America Online Demographics	
Total audience	3,000,000 (and constantly rising)
Typical age	35–54
Female	15%
Male	85%
Marital status	Married with children
Average income	$75,000
Education	College graduate or some college
Occupation	Professional/technical
General	Many members are homeowners who have lived in their homes for three to ten years. They are interested in electronics, video games, music CDs, and investments, and a large number of members have purchased products through mail order.

Even though AOL users are intelligent and competent with technology, AOL tends to draw people looking for an enter taining online experience. In this vein, companies that host online seminars and product briefings in AOL's auditorium areas often use contests and giveaways to create a light air around the event.

AOL offers a graphical, fairly user-friendly environment, though it doesn't give you the opportunity to link information the way Interchange does. You do have the option to do what's called *double-pointing*, which means setting up your content in a forum that is listed in your main product category—say, Windows Software—and then duplicating this content in the Graphics Software section. This option appears to be most suited to high-tech companies, but if you explore the possibilities, who knows what "linking" opportunities you may find.

AOL's graphical interface and easy Internet access give users the ability to surf the Net easily and with minimal confusion. You can have forum areas or services in AOL with directions to your Net sites. And AOL is establishing its own Web sites where vendors on AOL can post information, further strengthening the link between the two cyber regions.

As with CompuServe, demand for space on AOL by vendors is intense, and the staff is backlogged with companies waiting in the queue.

AOL is particularly aggressive about distributing its sign-on disks, which allow users to quickly sign on and get hours of free initial usage. If you go to AOL with a promotion idea to distribute lots of their disks, you should get a better place in the line.

There are two things to keep in mind when evaluating AOL as a cybermarketing option:

1. It will cost you a one-time fee of $10,000 to set up on the service.

2. You will have to send someone to Vienna, Virginia for two days' training.

These can be inhibiting requirements for some companies.

Delphi Internet Services

Founded in 1981, Delphi has about 100,000 users. It originally positioned itself as an entertainment service and a quick information resource for businesspeople and the family. Though it still offers the typical online platter of entertainment, games, chat, news, and transaction-based services, Delphi is now repositioning itself as a full-on gateway to complete global Internet access.

Delphi puts an emphasis on creating special interest forums, called *Custom Forums*, where members go to post and respond to e-mail messages. These are similar to Internet newsgroups, described in the preceding chapter.

Your best avenue for entry into Delphi may be to offer to set up a forum around a topic that complements your area of expertise, or around issues that your product addresses. This is definitely an opportunity to leverage your weight with Delphi by going into your information provider role.

Delphi is a text-based environment that attracts more of a techie-oriented audience. It also doesn't give you many opportunities to create anything more exciting than text files.

If you do set up shop here, be very clear about the directions you give people to find you. Novice computer users typically have trouble navigating text-based online areas and can easily get lost. Even if it's not your fault, users won't necessarily associate your name with fond memories if they get lost trying to find you. Unlike graphical environments where you use a mouse to point and click over icons to navigate, DOS environments require you to type every letter and punctuation mark accurately to get anywhere.

Even though Delphi has a small audience and not very much excitement online, I recommend that you set up some kind of presence here because of the "Rupert Murdoch factor." Murdoch bought Delphi in 1993, reportedly as a vehicle to expand and deliver an interactive service where television, computers, and telephones converge.

I'm not sure what Delphi will look like when Rupert gets it where he wants it, considering what he's done with other businesses he's acquired, it's probably worth the price of admission to bet a few chips on the Mighty Mr. M.

According to the latest word from Delphi, Murdoch wants to position Delphi as an Internet-linked space that will bring users directly to the vast resources that the Web can offer. To that end, the Delphi interface is supposed to change its look so that its more like a Web site.

Delphi is also planning to offer several levels of "marketing communications" services to companies that come online with them, and Delphi will charge for everything. The least expensive Delphi service will be "classified ads." What this means to you is that getting space on Delphi eventually will be like buying space on billboards, TV, and in magazines.

Delphi doesn't readily provide demographic information, so I'm still waiting to see if anyone ever gets off the dime and sends me something. When last contacted, some dedicated soul at Delphi was trying his best to get me something I can publish.

GEnie

Founded in 1985, GEnie has about 400,000 subscribers. The service focuses on offering large amounts of information content that is geared toward business professionals, though it does have a shopping mall that has about 40 stores (see the next page).

A large portion of GEnie's information is provided through over 400 databases that cover a wide range of subjects and online publications; GEnie also gives users access to the Net. Opportunities for real-time discussions are offered through RoundTables (forums) that are built around particular special interests, hobbies, professions and types of businesses—but rarely about specific companies.

RoundTables typically consist of bulletin boards for posting e-mail messages, real-time conference areas with scheduled presentations, downloadable software, and a user-searchable database.

Companies big and small can participate in RoundTables whose topics complement a company's product or expertise. If you get assigned to an area, you will be required to run several scheduled, hour-long presentations

GEnie Demographics	
Total audience	400,000
Median age	39
Typical age	64% of users are 25 to 44
Female	23%
Male	77%
Average income	45% earn $50,000 or more
Education	61% college undergraduates or postgraduates
IBM PC users	74%
Usage	60% for entertainment, 42% work-related, 19% for education

each month, which are typically in the evenings. These events must complement your RoundTable's main topic.

You can ask GEnie to sponsor a new RoundTable if you can't find one that fits your area of expertise. But you probably should work with a third party who will actually manage the area. GEnie likes to keep direct commercialism out of its forums, so it resists company-sponsored areas. A good example of this scenario involves the Harley-Davidson motorcycle company.

A Harley customer convinced GEnie to let her set up and manage a Harley RoundTable, although GEnie was skeptical about the forum's prospects for success. It turns out lots of Harley bikers were very enthusiastic about blazing onto the Info Highway. The RoundTable became so popular and active that Harley-Davidson declared it the official association of Harley owners.

Granted, Harley-Davidson didn't initiate the site. But you can direct some of your customers in a similar effort if you think you have enough of them who will regularly visit the group. Just keep in mind that this area is primarily to build a community of supporters for your company. You can't play too active a role in distributing information. That will have to happen on other services.

GEnie's marketing people told me that their members tend to be rather opinionated. The service uses this characteristic to their advantage by running user surveys about three times a year.

Since their audience is open to surveys, you should conduct a few of your own. You can administer a survey online faster and less expensively than in the traditional ways. This is a good way to collect valuable market information, particularly for small companies who tend not to do much research because of the cost. You can distribute the surveys as part of your RoundTable discussion sessions.

Microsoft Network

Finally, we come to the big question mark—Microsoft Network.

What is Bill Gates's Microsoft Network online service and how is it going to affect the other services? What marketing opportunities will it offer businesses? Who will be on it, and should you be one of the first to sign up for space? Given its money and market clout, Microsoft is a presence to deal with.

Microsoft Network is the online service that is integrated into the company's new operating system, Windows 95. When you turn on your computer, Windows 95 appears on the screen with its rows of pretty icons. One of these icons will, when you click on it, automatically launch you into Microsoft Network. Sound familiar? Refer back to the Geoworks story in Chapter 1.

Rather than debating the opportunities or dangers of having the mighty Microsoft marketing machine meandering through the cyber waves, I'm going to tell you to just do it! Sign up today if you can find a place for your business! Why?

First, there's no charge to sign up (for now), so your risk is low. More importantly, though, Mr. Gates expects to have Windows 95 running on 60 or 70 million PCs. If only 10 percent of those people ever go into Network, that's a lot of people to potentially be drawn into your online area.

Network is highly graphical, and offers a lot of opportunities for companies to hyperlink their information, the same as Interchange does. Network has a number of special interest areas, comparable in that way to AOL, and offers Internet access.

Companies that meet Microsoft's selection criteria will get a forum area, which includes a chat area and a BBS where users can have threaded e-mail discussions with you or your representative and with each other. You can post snazzy, eye-catching graphics materials rather than just the straight, one-size-fits-all text that you are limited to in some of the other services.

Your forum also has a Download library where you can store content for users to access, including software files. Downloading happens in the background, letting users do other tasks while their PCs receive this information.

Users can also upload files to this area. A word of caution, though. You want to monitor these uploaded items to make sure that you're not getting copyrighted materials, computer viruses, or other little nasties that can make life difficult for you or your customers.

Microsoft Network also offers users e-mail capability, access to numerous chat rooms for real-time discussions, and the ability to read files on-screen without having to download them first. You can design electronic forms that you can use to collect information from people for market research or order processing.

You have the option to charge for any activity that takes place in your forum, at whatever price the market will bear. You can charge users to download certain information, charge admission to certain events that you host in your chat area, and even charge them just to access certain "premium" areas of your forum.

However, I think you shouldn't be too zealous with this option. If users feel that they can get the same or better information elsewhere for free, that's what they'll do.

Since access to Microsoft Network is provided to everyone who buys Windows 95, the demographics of your audience will match the Windows 95 customer base. I hesitate to predict its demographics.

With a good overview of the look and marketing options of the major areas of cyberspace, you can move on to my discussion on developing cybermarketing strategies and tactics. As I talk about these issues, I give numerous examples of how companies are using BBSs, online services, and the Internet to reach various strategic and tactical objectives.

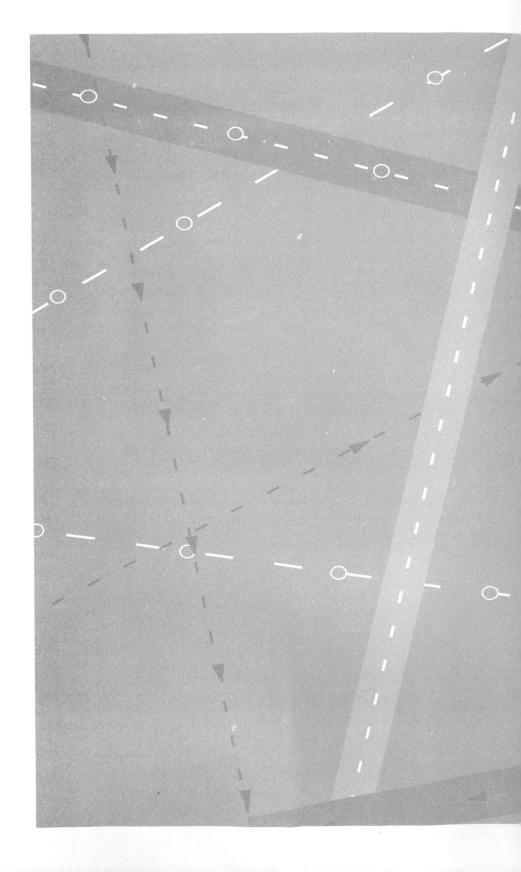

Chapter 5: The Four-Dimensional Strategy to Cybermarketing Success

It's time to dispel a myth that's preventing many companies from reaping the real value of cyberspace, a myth perpetuated by media hype about cyberspace and people unclear on its concept: that the primary purpose of cyberspace is to sell products.

In their quest for the "Holy Grail," companies are missing the pot of gold. Every day, I read about people working feverishly to build security-laden business-transaction computers and software so that companies can sell products online. Companies are saying that, until these transaction systems are in place, their businesses won't go online. Unfortunately, these companies are missing the point—and a great opportunity to impact their bottom line.

How? They are not looking at cyberspace for what it is: a great communication vehicle that decreases the costs and increases the effectiveness of your marketing efforts.

This chapter tackles the cyberspace myth. I explain why a multidimensional cybermarketing strategy—rather than a "sell, sell, sell" approach—is what you need to reap all the marketing benefits that cyberspace holds. Most importantly, I show you how to cost-justify a multidimensional strategy and how to develop such a strategy to meet your specific needs.

I present the four-dimensional strategic approach that I recommend our clients take. I look at important issues related to each dimension and then show you how to prioritize the dimensions and weave them into a coherent, balanced strategy. You will have the foundation for creating your own cybermarketing strategy statement, as well as a good starting point for developing specific cybermarketing tactics.

One point before going on: Even given the great opportunities that cyberspace offers, cybermarketing is not a replacement for conventional marketing such as direct mail, advertising, and whatever else you do to generate sales. Cybermarketing is a process in which you use cyberspace as a communication tool to complement conventional marketing.

Cost-Justifying the Four Dimensions

When I meet with clients, I tell them that they're likely to be disappointed if they focus exclusively on trying to generate new business through cyberspace. Cash might not flow forth from the cash registers like a mighty, rushing stream. And even if they do generate sales, new business is but a small portion of cybermarketing's benefits. If they limit themselves to this approach, they will leave a lot of money on the table.

I say this not only because cybersurfers are sales-pitch aversive. Another real issue is that many people are not comfortable with ordering products electronically; they worry about credit card information getting hijacked en route to vendors.

Also, humans are creatures of habit. Doing transactions from a computer just hasn't worked its way into the public subconscious the same way that using ATM cards has. Remember that when ATMs first started, people had a hard time kicking the habit of dealing with a live teller. Changing that habit took a while, but once people accepted the idea of getting their money anytime from any ATM machine, ATM cards became a way of life.

Every expert that I interviewed fervently believes that the glory days of online transactions are still in the future. But that hasn't prevented *them* from working cyberspace with a vengeance—and with significant financial gain.

So, if not for direct sales, why set up online at all? What's all the hype about? Where is the cost justification?

The cost justification comes from the benefits of the following four-dimensional approach to developing a cybermarketing strategy. Remember earlier, when I said you have to change the way you think about this new communication medium? When you do sit down to lay out a strategy plan for marketing in cyberspace, here's the way you should be thinking.

Dimension One: Contact Customers for Less Money

Use cybermarketing to help you market more effectively to your existing customer base.

If you have at least 10,000 to 20,000 customers with whom you communicate at least once a year and you have new products or product enhancements to sell, consider this scenario. A typical direct mailing to 10,000 people can average $1.00 per person when you factor in postage, design and production of the letter, a brochure, a response card, any other direct mail goodies, and the assembling and mailing of the piece. That's $10,000—plus it will take anywhere from three days to three weeks for delivery, once you drop everything off at the post office.

Alternatively, 10,000 e-mail transmissions of that same information may cost you at most a few hundred dollars, depending on the speed of your Internet connection, and the transmissions will be delivered within a couple of hours from when you send them. You have the expense of writing the piece, and maybe some graphic design work, but that's pretty much it.

Another great thing about this medium is that, whether you mail to 10,000 or 100,000, your incremental increases between these numbers are negligible. Buy access to high-speed transmission lines, and the increases are irrelevant when you consider what you're saving. But let's take this from the hypothetical to the real world.

Broderbund, which markets education and game software, annually publishes a catalog of its many software products that it sends to a few hundred thousand customers. "Our online version of the same catalog costs one-fifth as much to deliver to users as it costs us to have the print catalog designed," remarks Jason Everett, the company's online marketing coordinator.

Everett continues: "When you factor in production, mailing, and other costs of getting the printed catalog to customers, you can see why electronic information distribution is the way to go. The real commitment is time when working online. That's the real cost. What money you do spend is still much less than developing traditional marketing materials."

If you don't want to worry about transmission costs, consider what DEC (Digital Equipment Corp.) did: It set up a couple of Internet servers, and some tens of thousands of people (many of them customers) visit the servers every month to pick up an average of 20,000 pieces of marketing literature and technical support information.

This is not to say that by having your own Internet servers you eliminate the need to develop *marcom* (*marketing communications*) materials. Broderbund still has a sizable number of customers who prefer to get information the old-fashioned way. What you *are* doing is generating savings that can go into other areas of your business. Not only that, if your e-mailings are for the purpose of selling upgrades and add-on products, the money you earn from these sales is above what you will save over conventional mailing.

Significant cost savings in cybermarketing can go beyond the area of direct marketing to that of investor relations. Sun Microsystems, a UNIX workstation manufacturer and publicly traded company, estimates it saves about $250,000 each year by placing its quarterly report online and on a fax-back system. The company used to produce glossy documents that were mailed to stockholders.

With these examples, do you feel the first dimension of my strategy alone cost-justifies your entry into cyberspace? But wait! There's more!

Dimension Two: Support More with Less Money

Use cybermarketing to provide service and support more cost-effectively.

Here's what Wayne Heitman of Lotus Corp. says: "On average, we can respond to ten people on CompuServe for each person we support by telephone. When you factor in what it costs us to keep our online systems maintained and staffed, that ratio averages out to four to one."

How much will it affect your bottom line if your existing customer service staff can respond to four times as many people with the same resources that you currently have?

If you market software, you will appreciate this story. Claris Corp. markets Windows PC and Macintosh software. The company estimated that it cost $13.00, including the phone call, materials, shipping, and so forth, every time they sent a customer a software upgrade disk with some important changes and bug fixes. When Claris enhanced File Maker Pro for the Macintosh, the company put the new files online. There were 3,734 downloads in less than three months. You can do the math to figure out the savings there.

Being in cyberspace makes sense (and saves dollars), even if you're not in the high-tech business. Take Amway for example.

Amway is probably the king of multilevel marketing (one person recruits ten people to sell products for that person, and each of those ten people recruit ten people, and so on). Its products are a far cry from high tech, but Amway nevertheless discovered an enormous value in providing support to distributors through its own private CompuServe forum.

Before CompuServe, an Amway distributor with a $10,000 order had to spend over an hour with an Amway operator going through a tedious and complicated ordering process. This wasted both the distributor's and the operator's time. Now, that same process requires the distributor to spend just a few minutes online to do the same task, without the help of an operator.

There are many aspects of your service and support operations that can benefit from your presence in cyberspace.

Do you get dozens—or hundreds—of people calling your company to ask the same questions over and over? Have you ever shipped a lot of product units, only to discover afterward that the product has a problem that you need to tell customers about? Maybe you have a lot of field sales people, manufacturer's reps, or retailers who need support from you on a regular basis.

In each of these scenarios, communicating through cyberspace could dramatically cut your support costs. Not only can you answer more people faster online, but once you post an answer, literally thousands of people can read it. Many of these people subsequently won't be tying up your support staff on the phone.

So, how much do you think it's worth *now* to take your marketing online? But wait; there's more!

Dimension Three: Contact Prospects for Less Money

Use cybermarketing to market more effectively to prospective customers.

That's right, even though you are in the business of providing information, you can still make a buck picking up new customers without getting flamed.

However, unless you're a new company, consider this dimension as icing on the cake after successfully achieving numbers one and two. As time goes on, and more people get comfortable with ordering products online, generating new customers will become a more prominent part of cybermarketing.

The cost justification for using cyberspace to generate new business is the same as for cybermarketing to existing customers; the cost for reaching 10,000 prospects electronically (or having them reach you) can be the same as that for reaching 10,000 customers that you already have. Sometimes cybermarketing is a cost-effective way to indirectly build a customer base.

The Disney empire and other movie producers use cyberspace to build prerelease excitement for movies through a series of online promotions and giveaways. When the launch dates come, ticket sales at theaters get a great running start.

Through online promotions, product announcements and controlled discussions through forums, mailing lists, and newsgroups prior to shipping new products, you can start ripples in the market that pay off in waves of sales. These are all relatively inexpensive and can cost much less than the traditional advertising and promotions that precede some product launches.

If yours is a young company, needless to say you need to focus heavily on generating new business. Since you have no reputation, little or no market presence elsewhere, and few customers, you have to work hard to develop quality content and draw attention to yourself. But that's "sweat equity," rather than cash outlay.

Even if you're new, your efforts to generate customers should be supported with online after-sales support to customers and with communication to keep customers coming back for more. It's easier and less expensive to work these elements into your online areas when you're starting out.

Later, after business picks up, you will probably be busier. You may find that making changes to your online areas later will cost more time and money than designing customer support features at the outset.

Dimension Four: Give Conventional Marketing More Clout per Dollar

Use cybermarketing to supplement your traditional marketing (and vice versa).

Nothing in marketing should happen in a vacuum, and cybermarketing is no exception. If you spend a few hundred (or a few thousand) dollars to set up an online presence, then protect that investment by promoting your online areas in brochures, during sales presentations, to the press, and so on.

Being online gives you great opportunities to really tell your story about why people should buy your product or service. Cyberspace picks up where your other marketing activities leave off. No matter what you do, you can't tell the whole marketing story through conventional marketing as inexpensively as you can in cyberspace.

For a case in point, look at Wonderware Corp., a southern California company that sells client server software tools. The company's magazine ads and product promotion literature include its Internet address where people can go for more product information.

Vicki Stowe, who handles Wonderware's marketing, says, "We don't want to leave any method of marketing untapped. We're going to use every mechanism at our disposal. Besides, this doesn't cost more than a line of text." Wonderware just started running ads with its Internet address a couple of months before the time of this writing, so the company is still analyzing the impact this is having.

The numbers are in for Compaq Computers (a major PC manufacturer), though. Compaq noted a significant increase in traffic to its online areas once it added messages to its ads and brochures, directing people online for more information.

Gary Gluck, of Open Market, Inc.—which provides several services and products to help companies launch businesses on the Internet—sees cybermarketing as the top of what could be called a *marketing progression*. He says, "Billboards, when done right, put out a message that catches people's attention and presents a general image. TV and radio ads try to present a longer message, though that mission often gets compromised in the attempt to arrest people's attention. Print material gives much more information, but in a fairly passive mode. Prospects read it, then either respond or not. In cyberspace, the opportunities to communicate are vast. This is the next dimension."

From a cost standpoint, the beauty of this fourth dimension of my strategy is that it doesn't necessarily require spending more money. You just have to incorporate information about your online areas in materials and ads that you are already developing. If your materials are already designed, then you will have to incur costs for developing inserts or for modifying some artwork.

The Fifth Dimension?

Some would say that there's a fifth dimension to consider—using cyberspace to have fun. When you look at some Web sites or hear catchy names that people give their cyber outposts, it's obvious that the people designing the names had fun while still being serious about business. Claris, for instance, refers to its internal master Web server as "Planet Claris."

I leave it to you to determine how or even if you want to pursue the fifth dimension, but I will say this: If you're trying to create a sense of community and make the people visiting you online feel like they're coming to a special place, allow for the wildly creative. People, even the stodgiest of corporate types, like to be entertained and to laugh.

Just be careful that the fun dimension of your online areas doesn't divert attention from or obscure your primary business mission.

Developing Your Four-Dimensional Strategy

So now you have a better feel for the cost benefits of a four-dimensional strategic approach to cybermarketing. But how do you actually create such a strategy, one that's just right for your company?

When we at my company work with clients who want to know how they can get the maximum benefit from cybermarketing, we begin by focusing their strategic thinking. The next four sections of this chapter will give you a framework of questions and issues to consider that will help develop your strategic focus.

Since cyberspace is changing almost daily, and every company has a unique set of marketing needs, I don't attempt to give you a formal process; I let you decide which questions are applicable to your company. You can work through them either by yourself or with your management team, in a brainstorming and group planning session.

Not all of the questions and issues that follow will apply to every company. You may want to omit a few or add some of your own. When you finish, you may decide that some dimensions are more important than others. That's fine. You will still benefit by evaluating all the opportunities.

Also, as you answer the questions that follow, be prepared to uncover operational issues that you will have to address. Some may not be the kinds of issues associated with traditional marketing planning, but you should know now that once cyberspace becomes a significant part of your business, the way that you do business will change.

I suggest that you set up each of the four dimensions as a key marketing mission. For example, "My key mission is to market more effectively to my existing customers." From this discussion point, work through a series of questions that lead you to an overall strategy and, ultimately, a tactical plan.

Now take each dimension separately, and you'll see what I mean. (Chapter 6 shows you how companies are actually tackling these dimensions; reading it will help increase your understanding of the following points.)

Marketing to Your Existing Customers

If you intend to cybermarket to your existing customer base, what kind of information do your customers need, and in how much detail, before they buy new products or product upgrades? To get an idea, look at the literature that you're currently mailing out, as well as at the questions that your sales and customer support people get asked every day.

Do customers need technical specs, nutrition information, product features, or directions for placing orders? Are they curious about your company history or your board of directors?

A related question is, what kind of information can you provide that customers may not ask for but that will help them be more loyal customers? Customers may not ask for financial reports, but reading them (if the reports are good) can make customers feel more confident about doing business with you.

What kind of information can you provide that may have nothing to do with your product or service directly, but that will be very popular with your customers due to their particular demographics? Consider the example I gave in an earlier chapter about the pizza parlor that provides sports information because many pizza buyers are demographically disposed to being sports fans.

The kind of information that you provide may be dictated by what you plan to sell to your customers. Are you going to sell add-on products to existing customers, such as headlights and water bottles to bike owners? In that case, you could e-mail information to customers about your add-on products once or twice after selling the main product. If you sell supplies that have to be replaced, such as paper for copy machines, you may want to send regular reminders to restock.

Maybe you want to sell customers additional products from your product line. In that case, you probably have to provide the same kind of information that persuaded them to buy the first product from you.

Along with the question of *what* you plan to sell is the question of *how* you plan to sell your products. Are you going to rely on online transactions or telephone sales? If you're selling online, your content must give people all the information that they need to make a purchase decision, and it must also guide them to the area where the online transaction will occur.

If selling by phone, then you want your online promotions to get people to call a special "Favorite Customer" 800 number.

What kind of community environment are you going to build for your customers? You should have special areas and exclusive promotions just for them which create the environment that you want.

How should you design your online areas so that they project a warm environment, a business center atmosphere, or maybe a zany zoo image? The kind of graphics that you use and promotions you create should reflect the answer to that question. Effectively stimulating communication between your company and its customers will tighten the community bonds that form.

In some cases, the environment that you create may be dictated by your existing market position. Take Silicon Graphics, for example, a company that markets computer workstations that produce incredibly high quality graphics and animations. Given the company's product and its market—companies that rely on designing good graphics—Silicon Graphics had no choice but to create a Web site with spectacular graphic images. Otherwise, customers would have been disappointed, regardless of how good the marketing materials were.

As you ponder the answers to the preceding questions, you'll start to see which areas of cyberspace make sense as places for your company to set up shop. You must also review customer demographics in order to figure out which areas of cyberspace are likely to make your customers feel most at home. If your audience is made up of working parents, for example, then America Online and GEnie may be ideal, whereas setting up a BBS and going on CompuServe and Interchange make sense if you sell products to techies.

One question that is fundamental to marketing to existing customers is, how do you get customers online who aren't there already? This question is likely to open up other marketing or business operations issues, such as how to pay for the cost of moving customers online.

Assuming that your customers already have basic PC equipment, you must decide whether to provide them with modems or Internet e-mail accounts as part of a customer support package or the initial product sale. This can be an expensive loss leader, but then, what is ongoing business from each customer worth? Maybe you can even convince the online services to help you bring customers online with a joint promotions campaign.

In addition to the efforts to get customers online which may be cost intensive, what are other avenues at your disposal? Consider promoting your online areas in newsletters, direct mail pieces, trade show appearances, and other conventional marketing activities that you may already have planned and included in your budget. (More on this when I focus on the fourth dimension.)

By now, you should have the foundation of your strategy for selling to existing customers and be ready to move on to customer support.

Giving Your Customers Service and Support

To those who feel that customer service and support are not marketing functions: Nothing is further from the truth. Recently, while scanning a new client's AOL forum area, I went into the client's message board and found this message from a disgruntled user who got bad service: "Howdy! Still not answering our messages I see. No doubt it's because [competitor's product] handles [function] much better and [prospect's product] will be unlikely to survive the next two years. Let me know if you disagree."

If a few hundred people wander through and read a message like that and then go out and tell a few friends who tell more friends, you'll have a nasty cyber tidal wave washing over your business. And then you *definitely* will have a marketing problem on your hands.

So what does it take to turn online customer support into a strong, positive facet of your cybermarketing strategy? Walk through a question-and-answer session similar to the following one until you develop the foundation of a good approach to the support and service question.

First, what role will your customer service and support staffs play? Ideally, these staff members will work with you to create content and communication procedures that will make support and service easier to deliver. Before making grand proclamations to the market about your great online support, have everything in place to deliver the correct information and ensure that customers' problems don't slip through the cracks.

What kind of information will you need in order to maintain high levels of support? Is your product complex, or is it fairly easy for customers to understand? The easier your product is to use, the more support you can handle online; with complex products, you'll find that online support will take customers only so far before they need direct human assistance.

One software company that I'm familiar with classifies support calls into seven tiers, ranging from those that require minimal time to solve, to problems that demand extensive help. The company hopes to create online procedures to help customers in the lower four tiers. Customers whose problems fall into the upper tiers will be directed to telephone support staff.

Do you market a line of products with distinctly different service and support needs? If so, you may want to create distinct sections for each product in your online area so that you don't confuse customers more than help them. Also, when you determine what resources to commit to content development, you need to know how much tech support material you're going to need.

What is your current volume of customer service and support traffic, and how well is your staff handling that traffic? If they are already overworked, what's going to happen when you set up on four online services—and the Internet? Even though cyberspace lets you communicate with many people while using few resources, there is a transition period and learning curve that can put a strain on the support staff.

Let your support and service people help you determine how fast and extensively you set up your online presence. Go to bat for them to get more people, if that's what they need to make sure that your online service and support activities don't implode the company.

Does your company plan to release a series of new products or services in the upcoming months? As your new products enter the market, do you have to continue supporting the old ones? It's difficult enough to keep on top of all the support issues regarding current products without getting bogged down with questions about old products that you haven't sold in a couple of years.

Determine whether older products will receive personal attention from service people or whether you can archive support materials for these products in your online areas. If you want customers to keep coming back to buy new products, it's wise to make sure that they always get good support for items they bought a year or two ago.

People online expect fairly quick response to their problems and inquiries; are you prepared to provide 24- to 48-hour turnaround on service questions? If you think that your online activities will generate more work than your support people can currently handle, consider developing software that automatically traffics e-mail between customers and the appropriate staff.

Some of the companies whose representatives I interviewed have over 20 products, and several online areas that attract thousands of visitors a day. But these companies need only four or five people to manage their online areas, because they developed software that sends and tracks customer questions through the proper channels in their companies. The software also has a feature that ensures accountability for resolving problems.

Should you find that your company is too small, or not properly structured, to handle advanced-level support, are you prepared to lower customers' expectations? Perhaps you should start with just one online service or a small Web site until you staff up to support a bigger effort.

Another option is to create an online environment that fosters customers helping each other, which you should do whether you're a small or large company. For example, Geoworks is a small company (125 employees) that relies on a team of volunteers, which they call "GeoReps," to help other customers. And Borland has nearly 2,000 employees, but they also have a volunteer support team—the "Borland Maniacs"—composed of both retailers who sell Borland products and their customers.

Questions like these may cause your business to do some soul-searching. One reason is that online support involves more than just the marketing department, and that's where you can get into that ugly *P* word—*politics.* If your departments are a bit territorial, or they will need more personnel to make online support happen, you may need a strategy just to market cybermarketing within the company.

Another question regarding support concerns salespeople, field staff who do sales or training, and third parties such as retailers and business partners whose products or services support yours. Do these people rely on you for "support" in terms of marketing materials, data to support sales presentations, price sheets, product specs, and so on? You can support them faster, better, and less expensively in cyberspace.

You can extend this question of support to others within your organization. Quite often, the people within a company need as much or more support than customers.

People who are new to the company require product training, as well as knowledge about the company, policies, and procedures. Product development staff need support in the form of market research. Consider whether there are areas within your organization that you can support with your online areas; if so, add that fact to your case for cost justification of going online.

If you're wondering whether the questions ever stop, just remember the seven Ps: Proper previous planning prevents pitifully poor performance. Good questions lead to good planning.

Now look at how you can market to new customers.

Marketing to Your Prospective Customers

When you've progressed in your strategy to the point where you're ready to think through the issues associated with generating *new* customers, you'll find that some of the ground in this area has been covered already. You have to ask many of the same questions that you asked about marketing to existing customers—though the answers may be different.

For instance, the kind of materials that you need to market to prospective customers may be different; you may have to offer more information about your company, how your products are made, and who is using them, than you do to existing customers.

As you start developing this part of your cybermarketing strategy, you should ask some finance-oriented questions, such as, have you overplayed the income potential of generating business online? It's better to sell the cost-saving aspects of marketing to existing customers than to get into trouble from expecting or promising more new customers than you can get.

If people are willing to order your products online, can you still make a profit while keeping prices, delivery times, and service consistent with users' expectations? For instance, people who order products by direct mail have come to expect delivery in three or four weeks, but cybersurfers expect instant gratification. If you can't deliver products in a few days, you may create disgruntled online customers—something you *don't* want to happen.

Are you willing to partner with companies who can extend your online reach and enhance your credibility among people who are not familiar with your company? It's possible to partner with the online services or service providers in some joint marketing efforts, as I mentioned in my earlier story about Borland and AOL. These co-marketing options can definitely impact your strategy.

Are you a small company, or does everyone know your name? If you're still an unknown, are there competitors with high name recognition online? The smaller you are, the more creative you have to be to make people aware of your online presence. And if you're planning to make a long-term commitment to building a business, you have to go beyond creating awareness to developing strong business relationships online.

So roll up your sleeves. As Software.net's Jim Hogan observes, it's a mistake to think that just setting up a Web page immediately brings 30 million people to your door. He says, "That would be like walking into a crowded room, taping a piece of paper on the wall, and expecting everyone to stop to read what it says. Few people will notice until you do something to catch their attention. Then you have to keep their attention."

Another question that you need to ask while developing this dimension of your strategy is whether you can find a way for people to experience your product or service online, even if it's not a direct experience. For example, if you are a service company, deliver a portion of your service online as a trial. If you sell hard goods, show pictures of happy customers using your product. This "show and tell" approach can compensate for being new on the block or can give you a better shot at leveling the playing field between you and bigger competitors.

The next question is so obvious that I almost forgot it: What is your company's strategy for building new business in the traditional marketing arena? Your online selling strategy should complement your current marketing strategy; otherwise, you could cause complications within your company and confusion in the marketplace.

Are you relying on direct marketing, selling through retailers and manufacturer's reps, or a combination of the two? Be careful that you don't offer online promotions that put you in competition with your resellers. Conversely, you may want to set up online promotions that drive cybersurfers to your retailers.

This leads us to the fourth dimension in this cybermarketing strategy: using cybermarketing to enhance your traditional marketing activities.

Integrating Cybermarketing with Your Conventional Marketing Plan

Cybermarketing for smart companies is not a process unto itself; it's a process that is integrated with the entire business operation.

Probably the first question when evaluating this last dimension of your strategy should be, are you willing to make the commitment to integrate cybermarketing into your company? If so, you may have to educate and sell this new medium to upper management, finance, product development, the sales team, and, of course, the rest of the marketing department. This isn't a commitment to take lightly.

Along with this internal marketing effort, you should consider how you plan to make those people who interact with customers (customer service, the sales department, and so on) "cyber-literate." Can you get them Internet e-mail accounts or online service subscriptions? How do you train and provide incentive to actively promote your online presence to customers and prospects?

What are the best ways to ensure that all of your printed materials, advertisements, and other marcom activities promote your online presence? Will you have to change the way people approach the marketing planning and budgeting process? If this presents too many political hurdles, you may have to find ways to work around them.

Before you begin to execute your cybermarketing campaign, you can put procedures into place to develop materials simultaneously for conventional marketing and cybermarketing. The core information will stay the same, but its presentation will be different in cyberspace than in other media. You have to be sure to keep the messages consistent between the two worlds.

Take press relations, for instance. When your PR department or agency develops press releases for conventional mailing and faxing, be sure that the people there create an electronic version of the same release to post on your online services' forums and Net sites. And they may be able to add video and audio clips to the online release that they can't include with the printed releases.

When developing the company's overall marketing plans, can you play one medium off the other? For example, run a contest using print media to promote it, but place some of the contest clues in cyberspace. The print ad will catch people's attention and pique their interest. Embedding clues in your content will get people to access your online areas to read your material.

Having explored the four dimensions of strategy separately, you will next see how to integrate them into one strategy.

Putting It All Together

I have asked you a multitude of questions, and you should be starting to see what kinds of issues await you in cyberspace. You should also start to see a strategy forming within each of the dimensions. You may not find that all four work for you, at least initially. For many companies, size may dictate which dimensions are applicable.

Smaller companies, companies with uncomplicated products, and many service companies may have little interest in providing customer support, although service questions are almost always an issue. For example, "I ordered such and such, and I didn't get it yet," or "This is the wrong size." Small companies and those with minimal marketing budgets obviously won't be worrying about the fourth dimension as much as larger companies will.

But assuming that all four dimensions do work for you, you need to work the strategy for each into one overall cybermarketing strategy. As you do this, you may find that you heavily emphasize one or two dimensions.

I find that companies with a significant customer base (20,000 and above) develop strategies that focus heavily on marketing to existing customers. They then leverage that initial effort to generate new customers.

Many high-tech companies have a heavy focus on online customer support, but they are increasingly changing their emphasis from support to that of marketing to existing customers. They see both dimensions as taking on an equal role within the cybermarketing process.

It's logical for small companies to focus heavily on generating new business, though they do need to pay attention to existing customers, as well as to service and support, as their companies grow. I believe that if small companies lead off with service and support as their main focus (that is, "Buy our product, and we'll offer service second to none through our online presence!"), they will grow faster.

Remember the lesson from McAfee Associates (in Chapter 3) and others. Provide exceptional service, and word of mouth will spread like wildfire. Customer loyalty will be intense.

The Cybermarketing Mission Statement

When you get down to the final analysis, what you decide on as your final cybermarketing strategy will depend on three things:

- Your specific company and its specific marketing needs

- The answers to the questions (or similar questions) in the preceding sections

- Available resources—people, time, and money

I have given you the "questions" part of the equation; *you* must supply the first and third parts. But there is one last item before concluding this chapter: the cybermarketing mission statement.

Similar to any business or traditional marketing mission statement, the cybermarketing mission statement is a concise sentence or two that sums up where you plan for this effort to take you in 6, 12, or more months. The mission statement is a clear way to communicate to your entire organization the purpose of your company's presence in cyberspace. Let me give you an example of how a company might develop its mission statement.

Suppose a marketing department determines that its company makes most of its profit by selling add-on products to existing customers, rather than selling to new customers. Customers continually buy from the company because they like its service. But due to budget constraints and upper management myopia, the marketing department can't increase conventional marketing efforts to these existing customers.

After working through the questions presented in this chapter, the marketing team determines that cybermarketing would be a great way to reduce marketing costs and increase profits. After determining how the four dimensions will work in their overall strategy, the team's cybermarketing mission statement might read as follows.

"Our cybermarketing objective is to reduce marketing costs by 20 percent by putting 50 percent of our customers online. We will spend $100,000 of our conventional marketing budget to direct our customers online, and we will build superior online service to keep customers online."

As you see, the mission statement should be the sum and substance of whatever roles the four dimensions will play in your cybermarketing efforts. You won't necessarily fail without a mission statement, but I believe that you will market more effectively if you have one. At the very least, a good mission statement provides some measure by which to evaluate the success of your campaign.

This chapter should have given you a framework for determining how to make cyberspace pay off as a marketing communications tool. In the next chapter, I present stories from companies that are putting the four dimensions to work. There are valuable lessons to learn, as I use these stories to clarify the points I made in this one.

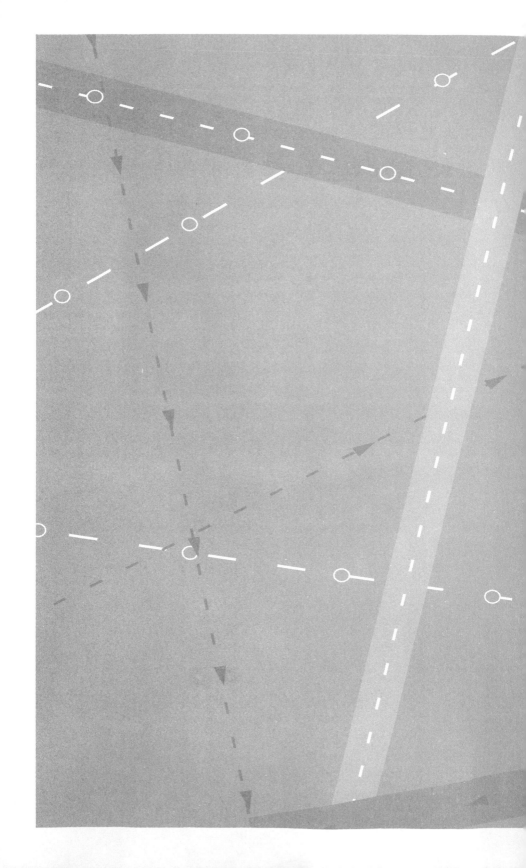

Chapter 6: Putting the Four Dimensions to Work

In the relatively short time that it's taken to write this book, new developments, software, and alliances that will impact the way you market in cyberspace have emerged. In this ever-changing marketing climate, the best that I can do is give you a general framework to work with and then show you what others who use a similar approach to cybermarketing are doing.

I have collected several stories that represent a cross section of companies, industries, and situations, hoping that at least some are similar to your company's position and needs. But regardless of that, I believe that you can learn something valuable from each story.

You will learn the most from these companies when you go online to see what they are actually doing. By inviting you to visit their respective sites, these companies give you an excellent opportunity to explore and examine the work of pioneers who have blazed a path through the new world called cyberspace.

Cybermarketing Veterans on the Four Dimensions

The four-dimensional approach to cybermarketing that I presented in the preceding chapter may leave some a little skeptical; so much is being said about cyberspace that it can be difficult separating fact from fiction. To help sort things out, read what some of the online marketing masters have to say about the value of using the four-dimensional approach to cybermarketing.

Hans Gomez, Adobe Software:

"These points are pretty much on target. To be successful in online marketing, you have to have all of these. If you think cyberspace is only good for providing technical support, you're missing the big picture. People need education about product benefits; they want answers to sales questions. You also have a great opportunity here for getting customer feedback so you can understand how to provide better products and services."

Wayne Heitman, Lotus Development Corporation:

"This four-dimensional approach makes sense because it covers everything you need to address in cybermarketing from a strategic perspective. You hit every possible area for even bothering with any kind of electronic business."

Rob Doughty, Pizza Hut:

"This is absolutely a good approach. We're looking at other uses for online marketing besides just taking orders. Our Web site will be used to distribute lots of information to existing customers, and we will also use it for some of our traditional sweepstakes and similar promotions."

John Duhring, WAIS:

"You're on target. This approach offers a good structure for supporting your online marketing objectives."

Marc Stobs, Claris Corporation:

"This definitely works as a thinking model to use as you prepare to develop your strategy. The first point is particularly good. As it becomes harder to compete, you have to focus on selling more products and different products to your existing customers."

Jason Everett, Broderbund Software:

"I totally agree that this four-dimensional strategy is a good place to start. This approach in cyberspace can be a great way to extend the life of a product."

Pizza Hut: Going Where the Dough Is

When you think of Pizza Hut, you probably don't think of it as a company on the leading edge of high tech. But beneath that dough, tomato sauce, and pepperoni-covered public image resides an innovative team that is heavily involved with computers and has a large MIS department to support it. This is a group primed for the siren call of cyberspace.

"We have a mission of putting our pizzas within easy reach of customers, regardless of where they are," states Ron Doughty, in corporate PR at Pizza Hut. "We're in malls, hospitals, hotels, and just about every other place you can think of." And now, cyberspace.

"When we first thought of the idea of going on the Internet, we didn't expect too much in terms of actual sales. It's actually easier to order a pizza by phone. But when people are spending long hours online, it's easier to jog over to our Web server site and place an order rather than to stop what they're doing, log off, phone in the order, then log back on."

Even though its Web site is accessible worldwide, Pizza Hut limited ordering to a test site in Santa Cruz, California, since this is a college town with lots of people who frequently access the Net and who also eat lots of pizza. The company will eventually do several more tests in other college towns and then will roll out the program region by region.

When customers access the Pizza Hut Web site, they get a preset menu of different pizzas. Users can click on the menu to get a description of each pizza and then click again if they want to see a picture of it.

At the end of the menu, users get an option to create their own pizza by indicating what size, type of crust and toppings they want. Then they can order their pizza and a drink, if they wish. The Web site tabulates the total cost with tax and then asks users to confirm the order.

The Pizza Hut Internet setup is fairly simple, particularly since every Pizza Hut site has a UNIX workstation running the SCO operating system. The Web site sends the order to Pizza Hut's headquarters in Wichita, Kansas, where a server links the entire nationwide chain of stores.

The server in turn picks up the order, processes it, and dispatches it to the Santa Cruz Pizza Hut. The computer in Santa Cruz prints one order for the chef and one for the delivery person. This entire process, once the customer places the order, takes just seconds.

Because Pizza Hut has a computer network that already sorts and routes telephone orders, it did not cost the company much to add Internet capability. "We only had to place two orders a week to break even, regardless of the size of the order," comments Doughty. "We're actually getting eight orders a week."

Imagine what's going to happen when hundreds of their stores go online. Says Doughty: "Our site currently gets at least 100 e-mail messages a week from all over the world, many asking when this service is coming to their area."

It almost goes without saying that Pizza Hut's strategy is focused heavily on marketing to existing and new customers (dimensions one and three). However, the company plans to incorporate dimensions two and four of the four-dimensional plan into their cybermarketing strategy as well. "Pizza Hut believes there's a big future in cyberspace for us," states Doughty.

Pizza Hut's customer service department currently gets many calls and letters from people asking for nutritional information about the company's pizza, history of the company, materials for students' class projects, and so on. Its Web server will store a lot of this information, providing quick responses to customers and cutting down on mailing costs.

Pizza Hut currently runs various sweepstakes as part of its marketing campaigns; in the future, the Net site will become a significant communication tool for these activities. The company also plans to use the Net to conduct its regular, nationwide focus groups involving everyone from eight-year-olds to adults.

Pizza Hut is a good example of a company that is heavily involved in research and planning in order to be sure that it has the correct ingredients on hand to meet the online challenges it will face in the future.

CUC International Does It All

CUC International is one of the cybermarketing pioneers that I discussed in Chapter 1; it has various shopping clubs that offer customers a wide range of products at affordable prices.

CUC actively employs the four-dimensional strategy to guide its cybermarketing efforts. "We put a heavy emphasis on selling to our existing customers," says Lew Bednarczuk, product manager of interactive marketing. "If you have a lot of customers who are already online, you can streamline aspects of your business to do things smarter, such as respond faster with the appropriate product offers to meet shifting customer needs."

The company does a lot of cross-selling online of its different membership services. "If we have customers who have discovered the value of using Shoppers Advantage, it's fairly easy to get many of them to try our other shopping clubs," observes Bednarczuk. He also tests a significant number of new services and sales offers with existing members. Once he finds what works, Bednarczuk uses these offers to recruit new customers. He then supplements these efforts with online advertising (through Prodigy), sweepstakes, and contests.

To facilitate customer service, Bednarczuk created a massive database that's located in CUC's facility in Connecticut and uses a gateway to link with the various online services. This system catalogs manufacturers' data in such a way that not only does it find the best product prices, it also calculates the various vendors' shipping times, shipping charges, and respective state taxes.

Customers subsequently get their products in the shortest possible time given the price they're willing to pay for everything, including shipping. The system is totally interactive, so customers can manipulate the variables if they want to trade off, say, delivery time for lower taxes. "This level of service is what keeps our customers loyal," Bednarczuk says.

It also helps to have a support team whose members have extensive PC skills and are dedicated to helping online customers. Bednarczuk comments: "Often we get calls about problems, not with our product, but with customers' modems or online service. Rather than push these problems back to the modem company or online service, we handle them on the spot. The extra effort on our part pays off many times over in the good will that we generate."

Bednarczuk is constantly looking for ways to integrate his online operation with other marketing avenues. He says: "We strongly believe in providing and promoting 800-number lines for ordering products and for customer services. No matter how much easier and faster people can do things online, they will still want to interact with another human being at some point."

The company will soon have its business up and running on the Net, though Bednarczuk wasn't ready to reveal more details at the time of this writing. He did say that this venture will integrate nicely with CUC International's other activities in cyberspace.

Planet Claris: Covering the Four Corners of Cyberspace

Claris, an Apple Computer spin-off with 600 employees, markets Claris Works, Claris FileMaker Pro, and several other Macintosh and Windows software packages. Claris is good to observe as an example of a company employing dimensions one and two of the four-dimensional strategy, both marketing online to existing customers and providing online service and support.

Claris has a BBS, forums on online services, Web servers—one for the world, one for internal communication—an FTP server, and a gopher server. (These people have more servers than a Beverly Hills–catered wedding!)

Claris initially turned to cyberspace to provide more effective customer support. "We set up an internal BBS to handle simple uploading and downloading of software files between us and our customers," comments Claris's online team leader, Marc Stobs. "At the time, we were launching our first Windows product. We wanted a way to offer patches [software bug fixes] that saved on materials and phone calls, and provide another easy way for customers to communicate with us."

Claris later augmented its BBS information with FAQs (frequently asked questions), trial software, templates from customers and Claris staff, and self-running software demos. It received requests from BBS sysops for fun software and demos to attract users to their respective boards. While Claris supported these sysops, it didn't make a specific marketing effort to reach other BBSs.

The company added an FTP server that contained the same information as its BBS, and it set up a gopher server with a database of 4,000 technical articles about software bugs and how to solve different business problems using its software. To support third-party trainers, consultants and template publishers, Claris set up private forums on CompuServe and AOL.

For managing general business and marketing contacts with customers, Claris's presence on the online services is stellar. The company has regular forums on CompuServe, AOL, eWorld, and Applelink (soon to be rolled into eWorld). Each month Claris gets 28,000 visits on AOL, 8,000–10,000 on CompuServe, and 3,000 in the eWorld/Applelink areas. That compares with 600 visits per month on its BBS.

What's interesting to note is that Claris generates few new customers relative to the volume of its online traffic. Its AOL forum, for instance, generates about 50 orders a day, and many of these are from existing customers who buy upgrades. What are Claris's views about the the ability to sell in cyberspace?

Stobs says, "The commoditization of products makes it hard to compete selling to new customers, so you have to look to selling more and different things to existing customers. That's why we're heavy into add-on business, such as specially designed templates for small business, education, and other vertical markets. These meet specific needs of our customers. Cyberspace is an effective medium for marketing add-on products."

Like Pizza Hut, Claris is looking toward the future and looking forward to reaping the rewards of selling to people who actually buy products online. "Online purchasing hasn't come into its heyday yet," says Stobs. "People paying hundreds of dollars want something they can hold and look at before they buy. Also, for now, some things can be purchased for less through direct mail catalogs."

But Claris will be ready when that heyday of online shopping arrives. "We see our Web server as the future online platform for product sales and distribution. We plan to tie the server into Claris's existing IS system for credit card verification and order fulfillment," says Stobs. "The internal Web server will link our various departments so we operate more smoothly. Because doing business online is critical to us, we're building these servers and systems to support them internally. We want this particular expertise in-house so we can have more control."

In the meantime, Claris will continue to leverage cyberspace as a great marketing communication tool that keeps it in front of customers day and night.

Maxis, Model Community Builder

Maxis's story, some of which I highlighted in Chapter 2, is a good example of how to build a strong online community of customers for your existing products and leverage that community to market to new customers. Its story is particularly applicable if you market games and entertainment products or other products that rely heavily on word-of-mouth to generate sales.

Like Claris, Maxis initially developed its online presence to support customers, and it placed this operation under the direction of Maxis's tech support staff. When my company went to work for Maxis, it was supporting its flagship SimCity software and other simulation software through a BBS, an Internet site, and forums on CompuServe and AOL; it was also planning a forum for AT&T Interchange.

SimCity is software that lets you build a city and, through simulation, deal with interrelated factors such as taxes, population growth, business expansion, and natural disasters. Decisions made to raise taxes, for example, would impact other aspects of your city's development, such as businesses leaving or services increasing. Once you create a city, you can save it in a computer file to modify later or to show off and trade with your friends.

Maxis's marketing department took notice of the fact that online SimCity users were enthusiastic product supporters. Many visited Maxis's forums frequently, and these users weren't shy about expressing their opinions to Maxis and to each other. There was a lot of city trading happening, as well.

The marketing folks wanted to harness this enthusiasm and turn it into an online marketing tool, not only for SimCity, but also for products that Maxis was releasing that were not simulation games.

My company's cybermarketing plan for Maxis included several contests calling for users to design cities with SimCity, artwork with Print Artist art design software, and scientific experiments with Widget Workshop (a children's software program). These creations would be displayed online and reviewed by a judges' panel, with awards going to the best works.

If you create promotions that get people to use your product—either online or off—and then display online the end result of their work with this product, it really gets people talking to their online buddies about what you're doing. Once word of the promotion gets out, folks who aren't customers will still come to your online area to see what others are doing.

In Maxis's case, customers were already exchanging samples of their work with SimCity, so we recommended giving people prizes or incentives to do good work as a way to increase the level of participation and really show the company's products in a good light.

Our marketing plan also included recommendations to redesign Maxis's forum layouts to better present product information and entice more users to access that information. And we showed Maxis how to *seed* (distribute) its product demos and information into other online forum and special interest areas whose users were prime Maxis prospects. These two activities can significantly increase online awareness of your product. Numerous companies have interesting products, but dull online areas with subsequently few visitors; if you create an online area that reflects the uniqueness and appeal of your products, you will have great crowds. And seeding works because it builds enthusiasm among people who may not otherwise hear about you.

Create a core of enthusiasts for your products as Maxis has, and those enthusiasts will become a de facto marketing force for you. With such people hanging around your forums and other online areas, you always have someone there saying great things about you when prospects visit your area. What's more, since these cybersurfers are voluntarily saying nice things about you, what they're saying doesn't come across like a sales pitch.

As I mentioned, Maxis wanted to market new products to customers who already owned Maxis software. Be careful that when you market new products to customers, you don't confuse the marketing messages for your respective products. Each Maxis promotion was designed to be distinct from the other so that the company could clearly position its respective products. For example, some were targeted to kids, while others were aimed toward both kids and adults. If you're launching several new products within months of each other, as Maxis intended to do, communicating clear messages is particularly important.

I also think it's important to convince people to buy one product before you try to get them to consider another, especially if either product is typically an impulse purchase. If you hit them at once with two products and two different sales messages, you may confuse prospects to the point where they respond by buying neither.

And don't forget to make sure that your customer service and support teams don't get caught off guard by the new efforts that will boost your online traffic. Maxis's tech support crew, for example, had its act together and was aware of everything we were planning ahead of time, so it wasn't caught by surprise with the new promotions. But if you're just starting out online, field test your support procedures *before* cranking up promotions. It does more harm than good to throw a great promotion if you can't adequately support the people you attract. Your more vocal online customers will be quick to express their displeasure if service isn't up to par. Remember that cybersurfers generally have high expectations about online service, and customers who are avid supporters of your products expect even more from you in return for promoting your products to their friends.

Now that Maxis has strengthened its position in its respective online services' communities, the company is preparing to make its presence felt on the Net.

Amway on the Info Highway

Amway's use of cyberspace is a good model if your company has a two-tier distribution system composed of resellers who buy products from you to resell to customers. The primary objective of Amway's cybermarketing effort is to improve the efficiency—and reduce the costs—of supporting and servicing the people who sell their products.

This story demonstrates one effective way to plan and implement online support for third parties with whom you may work, such as distributors and manufacturers' reps. It touches briefly on some of the business issues that companies need to resolve in order to get people who are new to computer technology to use cyberspace.

Amway is a multilevel marketing operation that sells everything from household cleansers to auto supplies. More than 2 million people worldwide, called *distributors*, sell products directly to family, friends, and others. Distributors usually sell in their spare time and typically through personal networking. A distributor's goal is to recruit a lot of people to sell for him or her and then to have each of these people recruit others, and so on.

New distributors get their start in Amway by initially buying all their products from another distributor who has been in the business for a while. When new distributors get a large enough army of people selling products for them, they become *direct distributors*, meaning that they now can order directly from Amway.

An order from a direct distributor that is for $10,000 worth of products may require that person to spend at least an hour on the phone with an operator listing each item in the order. The operator during the phone call has to find the items in a catalog; verify details such as availability, stock number, and so on; and read all of this information back to the distributor.

As the number of Amway's direct distributors began to grow rapidly in the late 1980s, so did the strain on in-house resources that the company needed to support the distributors. Then Amway decided to explore cyberspace as a place to ease this growing burden.

The company conducted three surveys to find out how many distributors owned PCs. The surveys uncovered the fact that 82 percent of direct distributors and 48 percent of regular distributors owned PCs. And 62 percent of those without PCs said that they planned to buy one within a year of the survey.

Amway next contacted the online services to find out who could give them a *private online forum* (meaning that only Amway staff and distributors could get to the forum) with international access. After learning that CompuServe had what they needed, Amway assigned to Gary Hunt the task of taking the company online.

Amway did a pilot test of its CompuServe forum (which they named Amway Business Network, or ABN) in 1989 with just 100 direct distributors. The company used a simple menu system that let distributors place their orders. A phone operator then downloaded this information and filled the orders.

Only when Amway was certain that its electronic ordering system worked properly did it let distributors do everything online: completely process orders and get the orders ready for shipping. Distributors now can access stock and invoice numbers, product availability data, and important messages from Amway. The ordering process that used to take an hour for that $10,000 now takes as little as three minutes.

But Amway's online efforts go far beyond order fulfillment.

Before ABN, Amway sent regular mailings containing items such as PC diskettes with price information and charged distributors $60 per year to cover the overhead; now that information resides on ABN. The company posts daily news flashes on its forum about new products, prices, and so on, thus communicating more information faster and with much less expense.

Another improvement: Amway used to mail a million newsletters each month in the U.S. alone, and a large number of newsletters went out of the country as well. Now Amway distributes these newsletters online and has seen its postage bill drop significantly as a result.

Not all Amway distributors use ABN, but in an on-going effort to convince these holdouts to go online, Amway operators regularly refer distributors to the forum. Eight out of ten questions called in are already answered in the online newsletter. When the same question that is not in the newsletter is called in by at least three people, this question is automatically posted online. Everything in these areas is keyword-indexed for rapid retrieval.

ABN is also a great research tool for Amway. Hunt says, "Instead of using 25 research people to survey distributors by mail and phone, surveys are posted to ABN for distributors to complete and return. In addition, everything posted and distributed through ABN is trackable, so we know where people are spending time, which promotions work or not, and what materials are popular."

Distributors can post messages online using an electronic form, and Amway guarantees them a 24-hour response. As an example of its commitment to rapid response, Amway has a team of operators who can take phone calls and answer distributors' online questions simultaneously. Messages are time- and date-stamped so that Amway can track distributors' business patterns and improve service to them.

CompuServe's strong international presence is a major benefit to Amway's road warriors. Many distributors travel regularly to foreign countries, and they take their laptop computers with them to access ABN from the road. For the road weary, Amway holds regular online conferences for distributors to meet with top management, product marketers, and others attending whom distributors would otherwise see only at Amway's annual convention.

For all of its accomplishments, getting distributors to go online took a lot of effort by Amway, and only in 1993 did the company see ABN use really take off. "We learned not to expect changes overnight," says Hunt. "Distributors, like many people, can be resistant to change. You have to get them to trust the technology."

He continues: "It really helped when Tom Eggleston, our chief operating officer, insisted that everyone he deals with use ABN. He also started a weekly online column just for direct distributors, which has become very popular. If the people at the top didn't see the value of the system, we couldn't have sold it to the rest of the company. It also helps having so many people coming out of college who expect to use nothing but PCs. They really push the veterans to adapt to the new way of doing business."

Another factor that slowed progress for Amway's online effort was training. A lot of distributors own PCs, but many are occasional users rather than experts. These are people from every walk of life, and most work for Amway only part time. It's necessary for Amway to give a lot of training to people who don't have a lot of spare time.

"We run plenty of training classes, and we train people who go out to the field to teach others. But it still takes a while to get people up to speed," says Hunt.

He believes that, regardless of how popular your online areas become, there will still be people who want to do business with you by phone, mail, and fax; you have to be patient and accommodate these people.

As a side note, Hunt said that theoretically the Internet could provide the same benefits as CompuServe's private network, but that not enough distributors have the technical expertise or inclination to tackle the Net. He's waiting for advances in software and other technology to give the average person a much easier way to use the Internet.

Let's Go to the Movies with UA

United Artists (UA) launched a promotion for its action adventure movie *Tank Girl* that is a great example of how to combine conventional marketing with an aggressive cybermarketing campaign targeted to new customers.

Tank Girl is based on a comic book series by the same name. This is one of those futuristic shoot-'em-up movies that's set in the year 2033, when the earth is a devastated wasteland due to some cosmic disaster. Our heroine (Tank Girl) appears on the scene to do battle with the forces of evil in one action adventure escapade after another.

UA went all out, leaving few stones unturned in either the "regular" world or cyberspace. A key element of its overall marketing campaign was its Internet Web site.

The Tank Girl Web site used color, still graphics of scenes and characters from the film, and narrative that was written in a style to reflect the characters in the movie. The site included general and behind-the-scenes information about the movie, the history of the *Tank Girl* comic book and video and audio clips from the soundtrack. There was also a complete listing of theater locations where the film played.

United Artists included the address for the Tank Girl Web site in selected advertising for the film, including newspaper and magazine ads and television spots. Promotional items handed out at colleges during spring break and a line of licensed Tank Girl fashions also had the Internet address prominently displayed.

At the Internet site itself, UA conducted a promotional essay contest that was sponsored by D.C. Comics, which publishes the *Tank Girl* comic book; the first place winner of this contest will experience everlasting fame as a character in one of the comic book issues. UA gave away additional prizes during the promotion, such as Tank Girl survival kits with dog tags and CDs of the film's soundtrack.

UA hyperlinked its Tank Girl Web site to various Net locations, including Digital Campus; Hot Wired (*Wired* magazine's Web server); and The Lion's Den, which is MGM/UA's corporate Web site containing information about all upcoming releases. There was even a link to the unauthorized Tank Girl Web site, which was established by devotees two years ago in London.

Not to be caught resting on its Web laurels, UA brought the online services into the picture. America Online, CompuServe, and Prodigy members got to chat online with stars Lori Petty (who plays Tank Girl); rap singer/movie star Ice-T; and Stan Winston, who designed special effects for the movie. Users could also access posted production notes, bios on the stars and filmmakers, and interviews with director Rachel Talalay and star Malcolm McDowell.

And accepting the award for Best Cybermarketing Supporting Role is D.C. Comics. The comic book publisher hosted its own Tank Girl promotions and directed people to the UA Web site from D.C. Comics' AOL and CompuServe sites, as well as from its site on Times Link. (Times Link is a joint online service provided by the *Los Angeles Times* and the *New York Daily News*.)

MGM/UA's executive vice president of marketing, Gerry Rich, certainly believes in the union of conventional and cybermarketing. "In the future, interactive campaigns will be the standard and not the exception. Interactive media demands a symbiotic relationship between publicity, promotions, distribution, and merchandising for an overall campaign."

You've read several examples of how companies are putting the four-dimensional cybermarketing strategy to work. Now it's time to develop specific cybermarketing tactics to help you implement your own strategy.

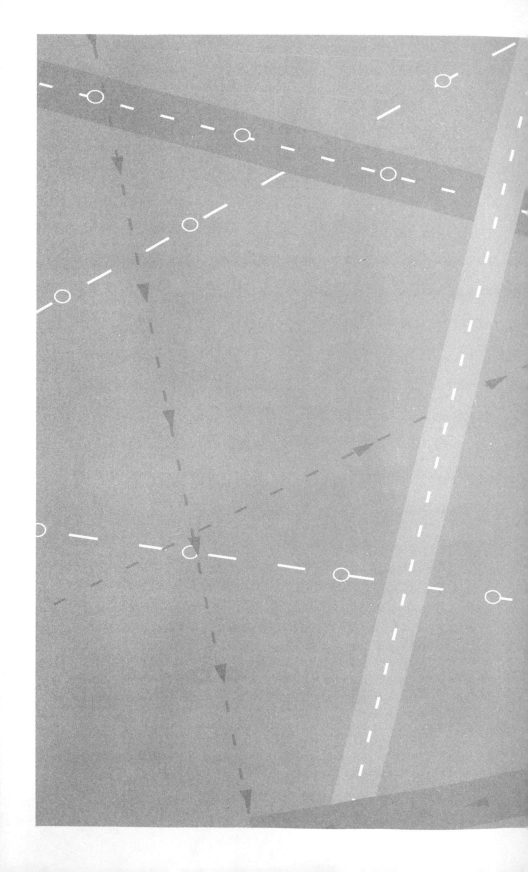

Chapter 7: Developing Your Own Cybermarketing Tactics

You've come to the really fun part of the book: developing the tactics you need to execute exciting and awe-inspiring cybermarketing campaigns of your own. You can now take what you already knew about conventional marketing, plus everything you've learned about cyberspace—and will continue to learn—to the stage where you can let your creative juices flow.

People use the word *tactics* in several ways; here I define it as specific activities that help you reach your strategic objectives. For example, a tactic may be running a contest for a free trip to Hawaii for every customer who accesses your forum, or hosting an open house at your Web site to launch your new customer service program.

There is probably no tactic that hasn't been tried, can't be tried, or won't be tried in the realm of cybermarketing before the final chapters are written on the subject. What I *don't* try to do in this chapter is give you a list of cybermarketing tactics, because the list would be endless and you'd be overwhelmed. Also, I couldn't prepare a list without some knowledge of your company, products or market, as well as your marketing strategy and available resources.

What I do give you is a framework with reference points for developing tactics that meet your specific needs. I sometimes refer to this framework as The Big 7 of Cybermarketing—the seven areas of conventional marketing that cybermarketing can potentially impact. You can use this list to focus your thinking, concentrate on each area individually, and let ideas for specific tactics come to you easily. After you think through these points and generate a list of tactics, also use the Big 7 as the framework for an outline to incorporate your tactics into a written plan that you present to your company for implementation.

The Big 7 of Cybermarketing

As with the four-dimensional strategy I discussed in Chapter 5, you may find that each of the areas in the following list apply to your own cybermarketing efforts with varying degrees of significance; some may not be applicable at all. The Big 7 of Cybermarketing are

1. Building brand awareness and loyalty

2. Direct response promotions

3. Market education

4. Product demonstration and distribution

5. Public relations/press relations

6. Research and product development

7. Service and support

Although the areas on the list are numbered, they have no set order of priority. You may arrange their priority for your own situation, depending on your product or service, your marketing objectives, and so on, and you may delete some areas altogether. I present the seven areas as an inclusive list that you can modify as necessary and use as a framework to develop your tactical plan.

Building Brand Awareness and Loyalty

I alluded to building brand awareness and loyalty when I talked about building a community around your online area. It's important to build a community of customers who are loyal to your product (brand). In addition to customers, you want as many cybersurfers as possible to know what your product and company have to offer; they may not be customers today, but who knows about tomorrow.

Keep in mind, too, that surfers who come to your online areas will potentially meet hundreds or thousands of others elsewhere who do not know about you. You want everyone who does know about you to spread the gospel in listservs, forums, newsgroups, and so on; "Hey everybody, you gotta check out the 'xyz' forum! They have some great stuff there."

Companies typically spend millions of dollars on traditional marketing activities such as ads, promotions, sponsorships, and merchandising to build brand awareness and loyalty. You can spend much less online and achieve the same results.

Your brand marketing tactics may consist only of promotions and creative sponsorships, but they can also include aggressive hyperlinking of your Internet information with other sites and seeding BBSs with product information.

Direct Response Promotions

It may seem like splitting hairs, but there is a difference between promotions that help build brand awareness or loyalty and promotions that induce people to take a specific action—preferably *right now* (buy a product, pick up literature, and so on).

The key difference is short-term versus long-term objectives. I've talked about providing information providers and building communities, but many businesspeople also need to generate immediate results.

You may need to recover your cybermarketing investment sooner rather than later, or you may need to get people off your back who are constantly asking you, "Are we making money yet?"

A company like Maxis has the luxury of using contests to generate sales indirectly, making sure people buy future upgrades, and getting users to say nice things about its products. However, if yours is a new company with immediate cash flow needs, you may be more inclined toward "buy one, get one free" offers or giveaways that induce swift action.

You do have many options for direct response promotions. For example, the online services can work with you to develop promotions that get people either to sign up with the services or spend time downloading your materials (similar to the Borland/AOL promotion discussed in Chapter 4).

Many direct response tactics that work in conventional markets—such as free trips, discounts, and special offers—will also work online. Just make sure that these tactics are consistent with your online image; you don't want to have a classy forum marred by a tacky promotion.

Another reason to use direct response promotions is that, as the number of online vendors increases, you may have a greater need for this type of promotion in order to rise above cybermarketing's increasing noise level.

Right now, businesses are generating some sales transactions online, but most companies use direct response tactics to get people to visit their areas and download information. In the future, however, expect to see direct response promotions generate more cash as online transactions become more prevalent.

Market Education

Educating your market goes beyond just making people aware of your brand. It also includes giving customers and prospects an in-depth understanding of your product or service, your company, or your industry. Many people are more likely to buy a product when they fully understand how it (or the company behind it) works.

You don't have to sell high-tech products in order for market education to make sense. If your product is complex in its design or application, and if explaining this complexity helps you close sales faster, market education tactics will benefit you. GE Plastics, for example, uses its Web site to educate people about the chemical components and various uses of its industrial plastic products.

Maybe your product is not complex, but you have an elaborate design process that enhances your product's quality. Explain to people how the process works, and they will see the value of your offer. This tactic works whether you sell industrial plastics or cakes that are prepared according to an "old family recipe."

Do you offer customized service plans that differentiate you from your competitors? Then let the world know.

If you stop and think about it, there may be a dozen things about you, your staff, product, company, or industry that, when explained to prospects, will convince them to buy from you. Regardless of the particular angle that you choose to take, when you need to "educate 'em to sell 'em," cyberspace offers some great opportunities.

For example, you can educate people with briefing papers and other hard-copy materials that they can download. You can turn your online areas into learning centers for people who want to know more about developments in your industry or about the type of technology that is at the core of your product.

The online services offer venues such as "live" seminar rooms, auditoriums, and special forums for educational discussions that you can sponsor or lead. The typical cybersurfer is information hungry, so feed that hunger and gain a new customer at the same time.

Product Demonstration and Distribution

Market education is an effective way to build people's comfort levels so they'll be more inclined to buy your products or services. And one of the best way to educate prospects about your product or service is to *demonstrate* it. You'll derive even greater benefits from this tactic if prospects are able to demonstrate your product or service themselves.

Distribution goes hand in hand with demonstrating products because, if you can demonstrate your wares online, prospects should be able to receive them right then, when they're highly motivated to buy. If you can't physically deliver what you're demonstrating, at least have a system in place so that a customer can place an order and then receive confirmation that the order has shipped.

The technology that makes communication in cyberspace work is also the mechanism by which companies with digitized information (software, music CDs, videos) and services can demonstrate, deliver, and receive payment for a finished product. If you sell this type of product, online users can download—or view directly from your online areas—samples of the type of information that you offer in order to determine its value.

If you don't market digitized information or services, you still may be able to create demonstration and distribution tactics. See Chapter 11, where I describe an ingenious tactic that a computer hardware company used to deliver for demonstration a $50,000 piece of fully functional equipment into people's offices via the Internet.

Also in Chapter 11, I show you how to demonstrate some very nontechnical products in cyberspace. Making the tactics I describe work for you is not impossible whatever your product, but if you market something like power saws, your creativity may be tested to its limit.

Public Relations/Press Relations

Public relations activities are those you engage in with the press in order to produce coverage that shapes how the public views your company and products; PR also includes direct action you take with the public to get press coverage that shapes your public image. Cyberspace presents many opportunities to implement these tactics.

Many journalists who may be the target of your PR efforts hang out online communicating with companies and looking for information. There's also a multitude of magazines and newspapers that publish online; though some take advantage of the new medium to enhance their formats, many do not use cyberspace to its full potential.

If you use the tactic of working with both the online journalists and publications to help them better leverage cyberspace, you can get coverage for your company as well.

You can also influence your public image by the way that you deal with people in cyberspace. Unlike the regular world where the press (TV, print, and radio) plays the key role in shaping public opinion, in cyberspace, cybersurfers themselves play a major role in shaping public opinion through word of mouth.

What's more, public opinion in cyberspace can have a very significant impact on your public image *beyond* the online world. When you read Chapter 12, you see why this is particularly true if you either own or are part of a large, well-known organization.

Research and Product Development

One of the most overlooked benefits of cyberspace is its research potential. Feedback from customers, the market in general, others in your industry, and even your competitors can make the biggest difference in your company's profitability. Cyberspace can deliver more feedback than you know what to do with.

The right information, received quickly via cyberspace, can alert you to a problem that you need to solve before you start losing market share. Or it can uncover a new market opportunity that will make you lots of money if you seize that opportunity before your competitors do. *Market information* is the tool that helps entrepreneurial Davids of the world compete toe-to-toe with the GM, IBM, or Microsoft Goliaths—and win.

Small companies—those who often need it the most—tend *not* to do research because it's costly and time consuming. Large companies do research, but their size and bureaucracy often cause that research to take months to complete. Cyberspace is the answer to these problems for both small and large organizations.

Cyberspace is an excellent avenue for getting quick, meaningful, and inexpensive feedback from customers and prospects regarding new features for existing or upcoming products. Cybersurfers are opinionated and love the opportunity to put in their two cents' worth. You can post a survey online today and get hundreds of responses by tomorrow, especially if your online areas are heavily visited.

Discover market trends as they're breaking by tapping into the thousands of Net listservs and newsgroups, as well as the hundreds of extensive online databases. You can design *data capture systems* to suck up reams of appropriate data daily—or by the hour, if you wish. You can analyze this data and then respond with the appropriate marketing tactics within days.

Service and Support

I included the area of service and support as one dimension in the cybermarketing strategy discussed in Chapter 5, because this area significantly influences strategic business and marketing issues. At the tactical level, however, service and support includes such activities as special offers that you might use in order to shift customers from telephone to online support, or incentive programs for customers who regularly volunteer to help others online.

As a support tool for your field salespeople or resellers, cyberspace can make sales presentations both easier and more effective, especially if you have an extensive product line with regularly changing prices. Rather than lug around tons of marketing materials, salespeople can modem in to your online area during a presentation to access the data that they need.

Many of your prospects will be impressed with such high-tech wizardry, and their comfort level with your salespeople will rise when they know that they're getting up-to-the-minute data or that information that is being customized just for them.

Online service and support can often facilitate other marketing tactics, as well. With the right systems in place to manage e-mail traffic, you can use cyberspace to enhance service for particular promotions or seasonal increases in customer volume (for example, the Christmas holidays) rather than add more staff whom you have to let go during slow times.

You can use your support areas to collect ongoing research with short surveys that users complete when they get service. You can also use these areas as distribution points for information about new products.

Cybermarketing Veterans on the Big 7

Now read what industry veterans have to say about the Big 7 of Cybermarketing.

Robin Harper, Maxis   "This sounds pretty thorough. Obviously, each company has to set their own priorities based on their overall strategy. To come up with the best tactics in each of these areas, there are a number of questions you have to ask yourself about each area, such as how do they mesh with your marketing goals, your marketing mix, and available resources."

Lew Bednarczuk, CUC International   "This seems to be a pretty complete list. We've gone through a lot of this stuff ourselves. Building brand awareness is definitely the piece that sits on top of all of these points. If you don't build brand awareness, you won't go too far too fast."

Hans Gomez, Adobe Systems, Inc.   "These points are pretty much on target. You have to have all of these to be successful in cybermarketing. People need education about products, not just technical support. If your PR staff isn't online, you can have situations that get out of hand and turn into bad publicity for the company. You have to provide frequent promotions, particularly for existing customers. Many companies forget them because they're busy pursuing new customers. The companies that are successful are doing lots of research work."

Michael Lehman, Day-Timer Technologies   "These points definitely seem logical and complete. They speak to the issues people are facing today as they try to determine how to use this new marketing channel. We see the first point as particularly important to us because we can use our online areas to build the Day-Timer brand, and simultaneously position the company as time management experts."

Gale Grant, Open Market   "This is a good list. There is, however, something else that's critical to any discussion of tactics. As you implement these tactics, you have to constantly focus on keeping everything new. You won't get very many people in your area if you only update information once every five months. Companies often have just one *What's New* document, but you need one for every segment of your area—product information sections, press section, support sections, and so forth."

Making the Big 7 Work for You

So how do you use the Big 7 to lay out your tactical plan? Well, for starters, bring out that old standby that has worked for decades: the brainstorming session.

The Brainstorming Team

Get marketing, customer support, PR, and other appropriate people together someplace where you won't be interrupted. Break out a few six-packs of your favorite beverage, lots of markers and paper, your cybermarketing strategy, and a computer that can access the areas of cyberspace where you plan to set up.

It helps if everyone at the session is up to speed with your strategic plans, what your main online marketing themes are, and so forth. I recommend that everyone in the room read the next seven chapters before arriving at your brainstorming session. They can then better help you decide which points apply to your company and jump-start some of your brainstorming ideas.

It will also help to have had these people log on to a couple of the online services and the Internet, assuming that they aren't already cyber-surfers. Everything I describe in this book makes more sense once you actually experience the online environment. If anyone in your group still hasn't gone online, do a brief presentation of the online areas before you begin brainstorming.

Then, working point by point, turn the session into a creative free-for-all, where no idea is criticized, discarded—or immediately accepted. Standard brainstorming rules do apply here. To guide you along, I provide in the following sections questions and issues that your group may want to consider.

Running the Brainstorming Gauntlet

With your team members primed for cybermarketing creativity, stimulate and spark the imagination of one another with questions and issues such as these suggested here. If you start with brand awareness, you might ask what brand-marketing activities you are currently doing that can be implemented online or supplemented with online activities. Are there areas of cyberspace, besides your online areas, where you can find people who are prime prospects for your marketing messages?

Moving to market education: Will your product or service require a lot of explaining? Are there aspects of your product development or delivery process that can influence how quickly prospects make buying decisions? If the answers are yes, you have a strong case for developing market education tactics. What conventional marketing activities are already working for you to educate the market? Do you have projects in place, such as a seminar program, that can be modified for online use?

Will the people who pick up your information online have to sell your product or service to others within their organizations? If so, how will you provide them with as much background information as possible about the company, products, and anything else that makes it easier for them to convincingly present your case?

What kind of visuals do you use for sales presentations? How can you adapt them to online market education?

If you determine that online PR is going to be an important part of your cybermarketing, ask your PR people: Where does your company currently stand with the press? Does it make sense to set up information centers exclusively for journalists and industry analysts? (We've set up press centers for our client, Symantec, at their Web site and other online areas. Content in these centers was designed to meet the needs of journalists for specific types of information.)

When you move to the area of online research: What kind of market information will help your company be more competitive? Does this information reside online? If you can get to it inexpensively, ask your MIS people or a software consultant: Can they develop an automated process for retrieving this data?

Are you good about asking your customers for feedback? How can you best use your online areas to regularly capture feedback?

Do you currently conduct conventional market research? How can you use special offers that motivate people to respond to conventional surveys or focus groups to generate responses to online surveys?

Finally, as you focus on service and support tactics: Is it practical to offer online access as part of your customer service contracts? Do most of your customers have a modem and an online account? Ask your customer service and support staff: What kind of incentives can you offer people to use your online areas more and the telephone less?

Can you manage and support your salespeople more effectively online? (Doing so will help leverage the content for your online areas.) How will you manage the logistical issues of equipping salespeople with everything they need to link to your online areas? How can you best provide them with link-up technology and train them how to use it?

After working through the Big 7, you may need to ask additional questions: What constraints do you have on people, time, and money resources? If you don't have the resources you need, how will you prepare yourself for the efforts to win over top management? Is management already a part of your brainstorming session?

While contemplating winning over the big guns, consider corporate culture and the way your company conducts business: Will these factors facilitate or hinder your ideas? Does your management typically wait until new technology is deemed "safe" before buying it? If so, how will you sell cybermarketing to management?

Fine-tuning Your Plan

Once your brainstorming group has asked all the questions you can think of and exhausted its creative energy, weed out the obviously bad and absurd ideas. Next, shorten your list to make it manageable relative to your resource constraints.

Refine ideas based on how well they conform to the rules of netiquette, the technical constraints of cyberspace, and general practicality. Some really great ideas may have to be discarded because of the graphical limits of cyberspace and the inability of some PC equipment to access online areas. For example, an eight-color brochure that automatically unfolds on-screen is great in theory, but people with 9,600 bps modems—what most users have—will die of old age waiting for the image to materialize on their screens.

For all of the seven tactical areas, determine how traditional marketing activities such as direct mail, advertising, and press relations will complement or directly support your efforts. Whenever possible, create synergy between traditional marketing and cybermarketing, given that you can first build market awareness and interest in your company with conventional tactics and then satisfy that interest fully in cyberspace.

You will find that some of the tactical areas also support one another. For example, direct response promotions can attract interest not
only from potential customers, but also from editors who are drawn to
special "media" centers in your online areas; direct response promotions
can also increase responses to customer surveys. Or you can design research surveys to gather information that you can also use to develop online product demonstrations.

Finally, adhere as much as possible to the points I brought up in
Chapter 2. Develop tactics that provide lots of information, build strong
community ties with the people who visit your area, and incorporate a
lot of interactive features for users. If you do these three things well, you
will produce spectacular results from your online areas.

The Written Tactical Plan

Now that you have a list of tactics and your troops are psyched up to
conquer the realms of cyberspace, you need to give your group a written
plan that will guide them once you've launched the campaign. I don't
recommend that you spend too much time creating a document that
looks like a Harvard MBA thesis; if you spend days "dissertating," you'll
miss some great opportunities.

I give you a general outline as a framework for writing a tactical
plan. Plans that my company develops for our clients, though not Harvard dissertations, are more extensive than the following outline because
clients usually want a very detailed document. You can fill in your own
details to whatever degree you wish.

Outline

Title the first section of your plan "Objectives." This will include the cybermarketing mission statement that you created at the end of Chapter 5,
along with any specific objectives that you want to list.

The second section of your plan should be called "Target areas in
cyberspace." In this part, describe the areas of cyberspace that you want
to use for cybermarketing. If you don't have the resources to immediately tackle all of the areas that you'd eventually like to, prioritize your
list. Maybe you'll want to start with an internal BBS, set up a forum on
Microsoft Network two months later, and then set up an extensive Net
Web site in five months.

Call the third section of your outline "Tactics." Here, list the seven
tactical areas that we covered in this chapter (or however many apply to

your company) and then place each item from your final list of specific tactics under the appropriate area.

The fourth area of your outline should be titled "Content." In this section, outline the following three points:

1. What content your area will have, along with brief descriptions of your content

2. What marketing promotions you will run online

3. Who will develop and deliver the content to whomever runs your online area

The technical design and limitations of some parts of cyberspace will determine how your content will look, so be sure that your content section addresses these issues.

Call the fifth section of your outline, where you will describe your resource needs, "Resources." In this section, you need to address several issues: How many people will need to be involved with content development and managing your online areas? Will these people be dedicated solely to this task, or will they have to split their time between this and other company responsibilities? How will you manage information flow between visitors to your online areas and appropriate staff? What outside resources will you need, such as Internet providers, Web site designers, writers, and so forth? How will you budget for these and other cybermarketing needs?

Finally, call the sixth section of your outline "Timeline." No good plan goes without a timeline; different people may have different ideas about how detailed these should be. I recommend that you plot specific dates on a calendar as milestones for key elements of your cybermarketing campaign. For example, dates for content completion, promotion launches, online seminars, and so on. For your list of milestones, you can be as detailed with dates and events as you feel is necessary.

Now that you have a good idea of the written tactical plan that you're working toward, move on to explore the seven tactical cybermarketing areas in more detail.

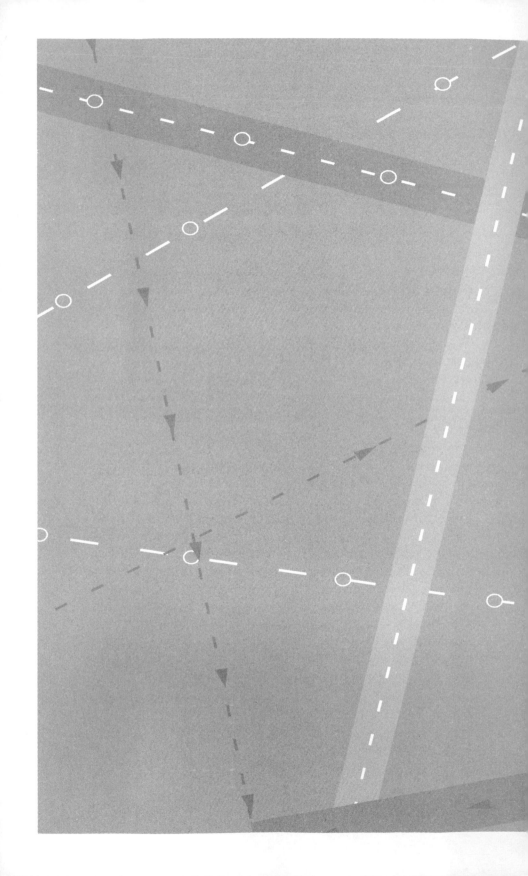

Chapter 8: Building Brand Loyalty the New-Fashioned Way: One Customer at a Time

Steve Yastrow, vice president of resort marketing for the Hyatt Hotels, is a cybermarketing pioneer within the hospitality industry. Yastrow has put his organization in the forefront of cyberspace by setting up an extensive Web site to market the Hyatt's many worldwide properties. Here's what he has to say about brand (product name) loyalty and cyberspace: "Today's consumers are skeptical of traditional advertising, because they are much more aware of their unique needs. They're saying, 'I'm different from everyone else. This ad can't possibly be speaking to me because it's directed to a mass audience.' Consumers are also skeptical because they don't trust institutions."

It's hard to blame consumers for being skeptical; businesses seem to be doing everything they can to build barriers between themselves and their customers.

Ads give people less, rather than more information. Layers of resellers and mail order houses stand between buyers and manufacturers. Managers and executives meet endlessly with each other, but rarely with customers. And stories about navigating the customer service voice-mail maze are legion.

If you want to build a competitive edge rather than barriers between yourself and customers, cyberspace holds the answer.

Yastrow continues, "People say that brand loyalty is disappearing. But that's only when the brand is obscured by mass marketing. People are as unique as fingerprints, and they expect to be treated that way. Cyberspace facilitates building one-on-one dialog with customers. Here, you can build brand awareness and loyalty one customer at a time."

Creating Brand Awareness: The First Step

If you want to convince cybersurfers to be loyal to your brand, you first have to make them aware of your presence online. This is definitely easier if you have a popular product and an established customer base.

Recruiting Customers as Soldiers for the Cause

With the proper actions from you, such as aggressive advertising, direct mail, and special offers, many of your customers will follow you online. But the objective isn't just to draw customers there; once they arrive, you also want to boost their loyalty and leverage them to become de facto salespeople for you throughout cyberspace.

Why is this important? Because a large, vocal group of customers in cyberspace can be an awe-inspiring marketing force that's worth its weight in gold. Word of mouth is powerful online, and nothing spreads good word of mouth faster than satisfied customers.

So how do you recruit this army of potential evangelists?

Every piece of your marketing literature—ads, brochures, direct mail—should trumpet your online presence. You should even consider doing a direct mail campaign just to entice your customers online.

Some services, such as AOL and CompuServe, will provide sign-up disks for your mailing campaign that customers can use to set up an account. Most of these services also offer free initial hours of connect time; you can suggest to customers that they sign on and then spend that free time to see your online areas.

If your area hooks customers with good promotional offers or by demonstrating how much easier it is to communicate service requests online versus using the telephone, these customers will probably become frequent visitors. And if you really want to be aggressive about creating legions of online champions for your product, Mark Riley at Santa Cruz Operation suggests that you consider promoting a "boxed" offer that includes Internet or online service access, a modem, and some kind of service package.

An example of a promotion might be to offer free product support online if you typically charge for providing that support by telephone. Another option is to offer a particular service the customers can't get otherwise, such as special previews of new products.

Whether yours is a new or established company, every new customer that you get through conventional marketing should be directed to your online areas. Your sales, customer service, technical support, and any other staff that comes in contact with customers and prospects should be preaching the gospel of going online.

Also make sure these people are thoroughly briefed about where you are online and what information you have posted there. If you can, get each of them online to see your materials so they can speak more effectively about this information to customers.

Of course, you need to supplement your efforts to draw existing customers online with aggressive activities that increase brand awareness among cybersurfers who are prospective customers. You'll find ideas for doing that in the "Building a Loyal Following" section, later in this chapter.

Here a Link, There a Link, Everywhere a Link, Link

As soon as you set up shop in cyberspace, I advise you to develop a burning, ceaseless drive to post and link your information to every part of cyberspace that you can reach out and touch. If this isn't something that you can or want to do personally, someone in your company definitely should.

Posting   Duplicate your content *everywhere*. It's not good enough just to have a Web home page; you also need a gopher site and an FTP site. These sites should have the same information as your BBS and your AOL, GEnie, and other online services forums. Duplication is good, because cybersurfers who miss you at one site may visit another.

If you can find a way to post some of your forum info into forums of companies with products that complement yours, do it. Of course they will ask you to return the favor in kind, and this may seem like a lot of effort, but hey—few rewards worth achieving come without a price.

Amy Roberts directs the online marketing efforts for Farallon Computing, Inc., which markets network connection products. She describes her efforts to place Farallon's information into some of the far reaches of the online services: "On the commercial online services, we post product announcements in the What's New areas where they can be seen by users that do not normally go into our forums. The promotional piece is written in very general terms to appeal to as many users as possible. This is not easy to do if your products are targeted at a very small portion of the mass market, but I look at it as a good exercise."

Linking   When you finish duplicating and posting, link like mad in every way that you can. Every BBS of any consequence should have at least a blurb that tells people where your information is.

You should be hyperlinked to or listed in every Internet directory of Web and gopher sites that exists. A good starting point is a site called Yahoo, which is run by people who are doing their darndest to list and catalog every Net site there is. Because Yahoo is such a comprehensive directory, millions of people access it every week.

To get started with Yahoo, first, get yourself listed in its free What's New listing; once you're there, some of those millions of Yahoo visitors will read about your site. Next, do an information search on the word *directory*. Yahoo will respond with hundreds of directories from which you can either select additional places to link to or post information about your Net sites. (Some of these directories' owners will charge for being listed in their What's New listing.)

Your Web site should have hyperlink tentacles from everything else of relevance on the Net. This includes companies whose products or customer demographics are similar to yours and any entertainment, information, and government site that attracts people who are likely prospects. Of course, every site that builds a hyperlink to your area will also want you to build a hyperlink from your site to theirs.

Reach out and touch a few newsgroups and listservs, as well. Even if you create your own, there are existing newsgroups and listservs that may have some interest in your information. However, proceed with caution: Linking with Net sites is okay, but if you approach newsgroups the wrong way, there could be trouble in paradise. Remember that many of these groups are highly sensitive—and negative—toward anything that smells like straight advertising.

If your online service, such as Microsoft Network, has hyperlinking, then hyperlink till the cows come home. All of your forums should also direct users to your Internet sites. In cyberspace, you can never have too many friends, and you definitely can never have too many links. Besides, other than the time needed to create them, hyperlinks are usually free. (Some Web sites that receive a high number of visitors will charge you to have a link from their site to yours.)

Since hyperlinking requires using software to imbed a few lines of information into your (or the other sites') content, the time required for linking can begin to pile up. Also, it usually takes a few days before other sites approve linking their sites to your areas or listing you in What's New. Consider these time factors when you schedule the launch of your online sites or a particular cybermarketing campaign.

A client asked me early on in the planning of her company's cybermarketing strategy, "Is there a way to find some college kids who'll be more than happy to plant themselves in front of a PC screen and do all this duplicating and linking?" The answer was—and is—but of course.

There are people who can think of no better life than to be paid to surf the cybers with a free reign to hook up with whatever looks promising. They'll even post and link your information while they're at it. The great thing is, some will do it for next to nothing if you throw in free online access for the times when they're not working for you. You don't even have to use college talent; lots of high schoolers will jump on this opportunity, too.

Take some precautions, though. Be sure that the person to whom you're entrusting this responsibility understands what it is that you're selling so that he or she can figure out what it makes sense to link with. Be adamant if there are places where you don't want your content. It may be hard to maintain an upstanding image elsewhere if your content is posted in the "I was abducted by space aliens" forums—unless you sell fiction books.

Also make sure this person represents you online in a professional manner. When anyone works under your company banner, this person *is* your company. You don't want them to be rude, crude, or socially unacceptable, and you probably want to limit their access to your vital data. Most students are trustworthy, but just as with dealing with people in general, there's no need to open yourself to needless risk.

Building a Loyal Following

Before deciding which tactics to use in building a following of cybersurfers, ask yourself what you want your company and product *positioning* in cyberspace to be. That is, when cybersurfers see or hear your company or product name, what kind of image do you want them to have?

Positioning: The Battle for Cybersurfers' Hearts and Minds

When you think of *Hertz*, you probably think "the number one car rental agency"; this is the positioning that Hertz has worked to achieve and reinforce in people's minds through advertising, promotions, and other marketing activities. Because of its position, many customers will be loyal to Hertz for years to come.

Effective positioning is the first step to building brand loyalty.

If you already have a position established outside of cyberspace, determine whether you want to maintain that position online or develop a new one? If you are developing a new position, what are the sales messages that will create it and contribute to its image?

I highly recommend that you read *Positioning, the Battle for your Mind,* by Al Ries and Jack Trout (Warner Books, 1981), if you are unfamiliar with positioning as a marketing activity. This book does a great job of explaining why positioning is important and the various ways you can position a product or company. They present examples of large companies, such as IBM and Burger King, that had great successes and of small companies that became large ones—all because of creative and effective positioning.

You also need to determine *how* you want to position your online area. For example, GeoWorks's Lee Llerano says that, besides influencing the average person's image of your area, "it's important to create an online personality to impress the opinion leaders [editors, analysts] who go online. We did this when we started our online areas years ago, and it's still important for us to maintain that image today."

Here's an example of positioning an online area. Our client Day-Timer Technologies incorporated features of the Day-Timer paper-based day planner into a personal information-management software package. We helped set up areas for the company on CompuServe, AOL, and the Internet. Eventually the Day-Timer parent company will bring online its catalog of paper systems and related products.

Day-Timer's market strength is that they sell one of the most widely used time management systems in the world; what's more, the company conducts time management seminars. In determining how to position Day-Timer, we decided to play off of this strength, positioning their online areas as time management centers.

Our staff wrote several briefing papers and tip sheets on time management for Day-Timer; we expect the company to use its AOL and CompuServe forums to deliver some of their standard time management seminars.

The content that Day-Timer is including in its online sites creates an image (or positioning) of the company's area as being "the ideal place to stop if you want advice, services, and products to help you manage your time more effectively." It satisfies cybersurfers' eternal quest for information and for people who want to improve their time management capabilities, it interests them enough to make them want to come back regularly.

When we succeed in our positioning campaign, Day-Timer Technologies will get lots of user traffic, and we expect a number of surfers to buy products as a result of subtle promotions that we incorporated into the online areas. Bringing a large portion of the parent company's four million customers online also will definitely add to the success of these areas, while providing more troops to spread the gospel through word of mouth.

Establishing a position for your online area can be more difficult if you have widely divergent products that do not fit into one category. In this situation, you may have to draw people to your area based on the strength of your company name or the brand awareness that you develop for each product.

Community Building

You should launch several online promotions that help you develop the strong sense of community in your online areas that I spoke about in Chapter 2. For example, contests and sweepstakes can really work well. Some of the biggest and best brand-marketing companies in the world, such as Proctor & Gamble, use these marketing tools with great success.

The most effective online contests for community building are those that entice people to use your product, exchange tips and other information with each other, and display online examples of work that customers create using your products.

Maxis's Lois Tilles says, "We try to create a community from the beginning for our new product launches. In addition to our contests, we distribute newsletters, software demos, and screen captures online, as well as press releases and general product information. What we constantly look for are items that have pass-along value among users."

Tilles also advises that, whatever promotions you develop, you must be committed to being original and changing these promotions regularly. If users see that your content doesn't change, your online marketing momentum will slow down. Once word gets out in cyberspace that you have a boring area, user traffic will drop significantly.

One tactic to spur frequent visits—though it may take extra effort—is to create short blurbs that change daily or weekly, such as Tip of the Day, Quote of the Week, and so on. This material by itself attracts regular visitors, but for maximum benefit, at the end of these blurbs you should direct people to other information.

And whatever you do, remember that brand loyalty in cyberspace is a double-edged sword: The people whose word of mouth builds you up can turn on you in a moment if you go stale or simply forget to tell them when you do have something new. Hell hath no fury like a cybersurfer disgruntled. Just ask Geoworks.

"We learned from early mistakes that the online community expects to be notified early about new products, changes in policy, press releases, and other news from the company," says Geoworks' online manager, Steve Main. "Our forum on AOL is usually the first place we post company news, then CompuServe, GEnie, and our own BBS. Customers on these services often spread the word for us to other areas in cyberspace."

Word-of-mouth communication among online visitors can also work for you in areas that aren't usually classified as marketing but that have tremendous impact on the amount of brand loyalty you generate, such as service. For example, Bill McKiernan of McAfee Associates, whom I spoke about in Chapter 3, constantly emphasized the positive impact that good service has on your word-of-mouth marketing.

Community building doesn't stop at creating strong rapport among cybersurfers; it also includes building strong ties between these cybersurfers and your company. One way that you might do this is by adding little perks to your online customer service. For example, you might give away useful or fun shareware utilities such as screen savers to show people how much you value their business. Even if you don't sell technology products, your online customers all have computers. So why not give them something to use *with* their computers?

Another giveaway idea is to supplement the information or product that customers receive from your company with valuable add-on products or services, even ones that you don't market. Make these add-ons easy for customers to obtain; cybersurfers appreciate everyone who makes their online experience more efficient and enjoyable.

Sponsorships: A Brand-Marketing Workhorse

After implementing tactics to build your online community, a good way to build both brand awareness and brand loyalty is to take another page from the conventional marketer's playbook, the one on *sponsorships.*

Sponsoring something—preferably valuable information—is similar to Firestone's sponsoring the Indy 500 or Texaco's sponsoring Saturday afternoon opera during the earlier days of radio. When people watch or listen to these events, they get a subliminal message to buy Firestone tires or Texaco gas.

These conventional sponsorships usually carry a hefty price tag, but online, you have sponsorship options that often require more time than money. For example, Sun Computers did a sponsorship deal during the 1994 Winter Olympics that paid off nicely for the company—though it did tick off IBM just a little.

Let the Sun Shine In   What happened? During the Olympics, IBM paid a nice chunk of money to be the "official computer company of the Winter Olympics." This meant that IBM was the only computer company helping to sponsor the Olympics. In return for its corporate largess, IBM had its name visible all over the ski slopes and ice rinks, not to mention in TV ads. Everyone who watched the Olympics was likely to see Big Blue. IBM also got to stamp the Olympic logo on its ads (a little prestige by association, if you will).

Sun, on the other hand, had no interest in the Olympics. The company didn't even have a Net presence beyond a small Web home page that three employees had set up on their own. However, Sun's Norwegian distributor, Skrivervik Data, and its Internet provider, OsloNet, did happen to set up a crude Olympic information center on a Web server in Norway.

The Norway site included wire newsfeeds about events and summaries of Olympic results. The Norwegian group took photos of their TV screens during events and scanned these into their site. It wasn't pretty (it was pretty ugly, actually), but the results were beyond everyone's expectations. The site was immediately swamped with visitors.

The distributor then called Hassan Schroeder, who managed the home page in Sun's U.S. office. Schroeder quickly duplicated the information from the Norwegian site onto the U.S. site to pick up the access traffic (called *mirroring*, in Net speak). He worked with the Norwegians to update the site's content every 15 minutes. With virtually no publicity, the U.S. site had over 70,000 accesses, or *hits*, a day.

Midway through the Olympics, Sun started getting widespread news coverage about its Web site. That's when IBM's legal crew came to rain on the parade. but the only consequence was that Sun had to remove its name from the Olympic information.

In the meantime, Sun's marketing department saw what a great opportunity the Web site provided, and posted product materials on it before the Olympics were over. Great idea! Even though Sun was not an official Olympic sponsor, the marketing impact was the same. Net surfers accessed up-to-the-minute coverage of the Olympics, courtesy of Sun, and Sun directed interested parties to information about Sun's products.

What's more, Sun received great press coverage for being on top of Olympics news. All this for peanuts compared to IBM's cash outlay. The sequel to this story, though, is truly awesome.

Remember that one thing about being online is that once you create a presence, you also create an expectation from cybersurfers—and Sun had certainly created a major presence with its Olympic center. When Sun became the official sponsor of the World Cup USA soccer tournament later that same year, "We knew that people were expecting us to set up another information center, only they expected it to be much better than our Olympics effort," says Schroeder.

Within three weeks, Schroeder and his team put together background information on the World Cup, team photos and rosters, general soccer information, terms, and rules. A map of the U.S. used cool animation to point people to the different locations around the country that were hosting games on any particular day. And besides its in-house Web site, Sun had mirror sites in Los Angeles, Japan, the United Kingdom, Norway, and Germany.

Mirroring such as this does two things. First, since Web sites allow only a finite number of hits, mirroring increases the volume of traffic that you can handle. Second, when you're communicating with people worldwide, a mirror site reduces the distance that users in other countries have to "travel"; people get information from your site faster because the site's closer, and Net traffic overall is reduced.

"Our sites collectively got 300,000 accesses every day of the World Cup, and Sun overall got great publicity," says Schroeder. "Similar to regular sponsorships, online sponsorships are hard to measure in terms of sales. But we can see that, as a result of this promotion, more CIOs (chief information officers) now know us as a major computer supplier."

With a little legwork, you can find ways to "sponsor" events by providing information concerning those events. Sporting events are especially popular, given the large percentage of males who are online. You can post schedules, player and team stats, and a gazillion pieces of trivia that TV sports announcers traditionally bore us with game after game. You can do this for national, college, or local level sports. And for events like soccer that receive hardly any TV coverage, you might be able to set up a way to do online game "broadcasts" or post-game wrap ups.

If you're not sure that sporting events are the right thing for your company to sponsor, take a careful look at a particular sport and its fans. Ask yourself whether these fans are people who are likely to buy your product. If so, sponsoring this type of event could be a winner for you.

If you decide that sporting events aren't appropriate, consider sponsoring other events, such as town meetings to discuss local or state election campaigns where interest is high and developments change frequently before coming to a close. Let your creative mind flow. How about sponsoring Paris fashion shows, music award ceremonies, or new book releases?

And you can sponsor more than events. If you market beauty supplies, for example, you can "sponsor" an information center with beauty tips that users can access. You might even set up an online chat session with a famous model to share her beauty secrets. If you market food products, sponsor a nutrition analysis center.

What will work for you depends on what you market, but keep in mind that it's possible to create many types of sponsorships and give as much consideration to the silly as to the serious. Also consider information that is not created by you; find organizations that are looking for outlets for their information. For example, the local transit authority may have carpool procedures and other materials for the public, but no online presence. Create a win-win situation by posting this type of information online, "brought to you by *XYZ* Car Stereo Outlet."

Other Branding Tactics

As you develop tactics for building brand loyalty online, look for ideas in what works in conventional merchandising. Activities such as giving away novelty items with your company name or logo printed on them can attract people to your online area, even if these giveaways are distributed through regular mail. If you typically give away things like key chains, sunglasses, mugs—a lot of cybersurfers are coffee drinkers—or T-shirts, these same incentives may get people to download materials and even order products.

If you market products that people eat or frequently have to replace, other merchandising tactics may work; for example, distributing electronic coupons. This might seem impractical since you can't keep people from endlessly duplicating electronic information, but if your coupons are redeemable for a discount only when people buy something, do you really care if thousands of people have "unauthorized" coupons?

And while you're linking your information all over the online world, try to find companies with complementary products to yours and then do cross-promotions. If you sell gardening supplies and Company B sells home improvement books, for example, set up a promotion in which customers buy a book and get one of your products for free or at a discount.

Cross-promotions work for services, too. Say that I provide marketing services and you provide financial management services; we could set up a cross-promotion in which anyone who downloads your tips on effective budgeting also receives a copy of my tips on effective marketing.

Just keep the thought in the front of your mind that "anything is possible in cyberspace!"

Another way to enhance brand marketing is to create logos or other graphic elements that you want people to identify with your products and company. And if you already have company or product logos, whenever possible keep them consistent online so they'll reinforce recognition of your company.

Some online services, BBSs, and some areas of the Internet make it impossible to reproduce your logo online in its original color and glory because the technology does not enable you to display full-color graphic images. You have to adjust for this, so you may need to design graphic elements that you use only online.

Even if you can't use your logo, keep your tag lines and slogans consistent (for example, Nike's "Just do it" and Allstate's "You're in good hands with Allstate"). And if your business will be primarily online, you have the flexibility to design your graphic elements specifically to meet the criteria of cyberspace.

In general, the online services, BBSs, and the Net can all be worked into a brand awareness campaign; just keep in mind each respective area's pluses and minuses as I detailed them in Chapters 3 and 4. Determine which area to focus your efforts, based on your product, strategy concerns, and the resources you have to commit.

Meeting the Needs of the Individual

I've saved the most important, and possibly the toughest, challenge to building brand loyalty for last: meeting the needs of the individual.

I started this chapter by saying that one of the major benefits of using cyberspace is the ability to build brand loyalty through one-on-one rapport with individuals. Though communicating directly with visitors online helps you to develop this rapport, there are actually four ways to break down this strategy in order to best build a sense among people that you will address their unique concerns. I recommend you incorporate all four into your cybermarketing efforts:

1. Provide enough content on your online areas to answer all or most questions that anyone might have.

2. Make your online areas interactive enough for cybersurfers to easily navigate through your content and find what they want.

3. Implement surveys and forms that solicit visitors' ideas, suggestions, and general comments.

4. Put your company's executives and staff online to meet "directly" with customers and prospects.

There's Never Enough

When you determine what content you will post, think of every question that you, your sales team, and your customer support staff have been asked, regardless of how minor. Then try to think of every question that hasn't been asked, but conceivably could be, and add those to the list. When your list is complete, you will have the framework for developing your content.

If people can get all—or even 90–95 percent—of their questions answered, they will feel that your content and your company meet their individual needs. You can answer these questions through FAQ (frequently asked questions) sheets, press releases, product fact sheets, customer stories, or whatever creative acts of genius flow from you and your staff.

Posting sufficient content does more than just build brand loyalty; every question that is answered online moves a prospect one step closer to buying. And each question answered is one less question to tie up sales and customer support staff on the phone.

See Ya Later, Navigator

Hand-in-hand with answering every question comes building a good system to help people navigate through your content. Providing answers for every conceivable question usually results in creating lots of content, and the more content you develop, the more attention you have to give to helping people find what they need.

To help visitors navigate your online areas, you need to develop a guide or directory at the beginning of each area to give people a clear road map to all your content. Respective elements of your content need to be put into logical subgroups, such as for product information, customer support information, and company information. Whenever possible, create hyperlinks between related pieces of information, and always have links back to your road maps so cybersurfers can keep their bearings.

Your navigation procedures should not only be logical, but should also take into account that cybersurfers will not always follow *your* concept of what is logical. Without creating too many hyperlinks, try to allow for individuals' random searching methods. There's no established rule for doing this, so rely on trial and error—and customer feedback— to determine what works.

It Takes Good Form(s)

One of the best ways to know what content meets individuals' interests and to build a tight feeling of community is asking visitors to your areas what information they'd like to see.

Many companies blow an opportunity to make their areas really popular because they don't post survey forms asking about buying habits, demographics, and other basic old-world marketing stuff.

Cybersurfers tend to dislike typical surveys and often complete them only if by doing so they can get something for free. You may get names for a mailing list from this kind of survey, and possibly demographics, which offer limited value. But don't expect to get long-term loyal customers this way.

The way to win with surveys is by asking people how you can enhance your content to better meet *their* needs. Many of them will tell you just what to do, so how can you go wrong? You don't have to guess what information or services to add to your online services because people will tell you exactly what they want. And when these people see you incorporate their ideas at your sites, they'll develop a personal attachment to your areas because they helped to build the sites.

If you ask people for ideas on how to enhance the products or services that you sell, they will regularly visit your area to see what happened to their ideas. You don't have to use *every* idea that you receive; just acknowledge that you received it and say why using a suggestion is or isn't feasible. Most people will appreciate that you care enough to respond, and will in turn develop a stronger sense of loyalty to your area.

In Chapter 13, I cover in detail how to create and implement effective surveys that help you develop better content and build a tight community in your online areas.

On the Firing Line

Now is the time for all good executives to come to the aid of their companies' brand-marketing efforts.

As companies become more isolated from consumers and suffer the pains of decreasing consumer loyalty, yours can gain a competitive advantage by bringing its executives "face to face" with the people who ultimately pay their salaries—consumers. On chat areas, online conferences, bulletin boards, newsgroups, and listservs, your executives can build a depth of loyalty that many companies only dream about.

When consumers can express views, share ideas, and shape decisions by interacting directly with the "powers that be" at a company, those consumers become committed to that company. People want to have some control over things that impact their lives, including the products and services that they buy. If your company gives people this sense of control, they will repay it with loyalty.

Of course, there is a downside to getting close to the public: Executives might not hear what they want to hear. Dissatisfied customers can get "in your face" online, which is a very public gathering. PR pros may cringe at the prospect of turning execs loose in such an uncontrolled environment. But often the gain is worth the risk, because customers think better of executives who can respond well to the bad as well as the good.

So your company thinkers may have to consider carefully the best ways to deploy your executives online. Here's one scenario that might work. Let whoever manages your online areas handle regular communication with cybersurfers. Then, if a problem arises that requires executive-level intervention,—a complaint from someone threatening to go ballistic, for example, or from a major customer—bring an executive online. And once a month or so, put product managers online to talk about each of their respective products.

Depending on the size of your company and the schedules of the top executives, you may want to save these big guns for a quarterly appearance or for an online presentation that coincides with a major new product announcement.

Larger companies may be more inclined to have their top execs make few online appearances because of time commitments or the fear that larger companies are damaged more than smaller ones if a CEO performs poorly or gets skewered by the masses. Small-to-midsize companies' executives, on the other hand, may be more willing to get out there and take an active lead establishing their organizations' online presence.

Upcoming chapters address market education, research, product demonstrations, and customer support, giving additional ideas that you can incorporate into your tactics to build one-on-one rapport with customers and prospects. Some may seem tedious and time-consuming, but keep in mind that your company will definitely benefit from them in the long term.

With an understanding of building brand awareness and loyalty, now move on to the next tactical consideration: direct response marketing.

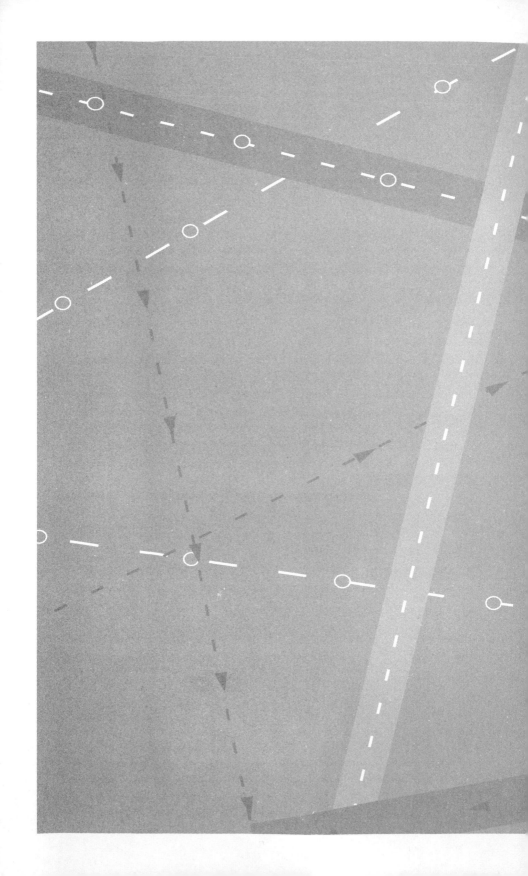

Chapter 9: Direct Response Marketing: Get It and Get It Now!

Brand awareness and direct response marketing overlap in some ways; many of the same tactics can be applied to both, such as contests, cross-promotions, sponsorships, and general merchandising. But what separates brand awareness from direct response marketing are their objectives.

When creating brand awareness, you're working toward the long-term objective of building loyalty to your product and company. If your tactics in this area don't generate immediate responses—such as having people download information or buy products today—it's OK, as long as you eventually develop a strong market position.

Direct response marketing, on the other hand, has the short-term goal of generating results today, *right now*. You want people to come into your areas in droves and immediately download background papers, product brochures, samples of your products, and so on.

The concept behind direct response marketing online is that the faster you can entice people to read your information, the faster they will be motivated to buy. The ideal direct response tactics are those that motivate users to order your products or services before they leave your online area.

Now, I know that I've preached a gospel up to now of "don't sell, inform," and this is still my position. But if yours is a new or small company, generating sales may be an issue that you can't ignore. In this case, I advise you to use direct response tactics that sell, but do this carefully—within the bounds of what's considered appropriate online behavior.

To illustrate my point, in this chapter I profile two companies that use direct response tactics to sell products online, but they are sensitive to conforming to the culture of cyberspace: Roswell Computer Books in Nova Scotia, Canada, and Software.net in Menlo Park, California.

Later in the chapter, I discuss how many companies use direct response tactics just to distribute as much information as possible, as quickly as possible. Some—for example, Borland and Sun Systems—get tens of thousands of people to download information daily. For these companies, a successful direct response promotion results in every visitor taking something away.

If your products or services typically have high price tags or long sales cycles, you can pursue direct response tactics to spur fast and furious information distribution. Then follow up to move the contacts towards purchases. It's highly unlikely that someone online will send you his or her American Express Gold card number for a $5,000 purchase. (If they do, I want to know about it—and so, probably, does the FBI!)

Regardless of whether you're trying to generate quick sales or speedy information distribution, the next two stories offer valuable lessons in direct response marketing online.

Book 'Em, Roswell

Roswell Computer Books is a small Canadian company that went on the Internet in 1993, when there was hardly any commercial activity on the Net. Roswell's online site generated so much business initially that the company almost went *out* of business responding to it, but soon the company gained control of the situation, and learned several valuable lessons from the experience.

Roswell sells computer books to customers who either visit its retail store or phone in orders. The company keeps $75,000 worth of inventory in stock. What makes Roswell special, though, is not the dollar value of its inventory, but the uniqueness of it.

"We're a specialty store with a lot to offer," says owner Roswell James. "Besides a selection of general computer books, we have books in stock that people can't find elsewhere." These books may include guides for using obscure programming languages or software programs that are no longer being sold.

In 1992, James was surfing the Net when it occurred to him that it might be possible to sell books using this medium. Looking for a way to take his business online, he contacted NSTN, Inc., a Net service provider in Nova Scotia.

At that time, NSTN happened to be exploring the possibility of setting up companies to do business on the Net, but it needed a test case to prove the Net's commercial viability. Roswell and NSTN struck a mutually beneficial deal whereby Roswell would be the test case, and NSTN would set up the Net connection and give Roswell space on a gopher server.

Roswell had an order-fulfillment process in place that was fairly easy to replicate on the Net. The store maintained a computer database of information about what was in stock and what books were available from sources that the staff could access within an hour or so. When customers came in or called the store for a book, the staff would either get the book off the shelf or find it through the database. Call-in customers were given availability information, plus the price and shipping options. When these customers confirmed what they wanted, their books were shipped the same day.

NSTN set up Roswell's database on a gopher server. They created a system that let customers search by category and by full or partial title. The search brought up book titles (with no description) that matched the requests, and users selected the books they wanted.

Users next went to a screen with an order form that they had to save to their computers as a file. Customers then had to copy the file into their e-mail, fill it out, and send it back to Roswell's server. Although this is an arduous transaction process, gopher sites were the best option in '93.

Within 30 days of Roswell's site "going live," the company had 7,000 inquiries that practically overwhelmed its small staff. The workload was almost more than they could handle.

"We had no idea what to expect," says James. "We were only planning to support Atlantic Canada, but we got requests from all over the world. I had to spend an extra three or four hours every day typing up order processing forms." There was no way to dump the data from e-mail requests directly in to Roswell's in-house computer system.

To take some of the pressure off his staff in the short term, James added descriptions to the book listings so that users could find more information on their own and not contact the staff with questions. This significantly decreased everyone's work load.

Then, for six months, James studied the online system before deciding what else to do: "I wanted us to take our time and not respond too quickly with modifications that made things worse, not better."

After this review period, James decided to make a few changes to the existing database and add two more databases—one for book descriptions and one for third-party book reviews. He also developed some direct response tactics that worked pretty well.

For example, James put into practice his belief that the company had to make an extra effort to be responsible Net merchandisers. "We worked hard not to be an irritant on the Net," he says. "We thought we were the first bookstore on the Net, so we had NSTN send messages to several Canadian newsgroups and other newsgroups that we felt would be interested in what we offered. We didn't want to indiscriminately send messages everywhere."

James added an automatic signature line to his e-mail system, so that all messages going from the company included two lines at the bottom telling people about Roswell's gopher site and its customer mailing list, which people could join to get Roswell's monthly newsletter.

How effective have these tactics been? Roswell now adds at least two people a day to its mailing list. Says James: "Every time we respond to someone, they find out about the mailing list. When they willingly contact us to be on the list, it's OK for us to send them our newsletter with a list of new book releases and other information."

Many mailing list subscribers generate additional customers. "It seems word of mouth keeps new people coming to us. I find out from customers that they pass our newsletter around to a lot of their friends," James says.

Another tactic that James uses is putting his e-mail signature to creative use in the newsgroup section of the Net. He regularly monitors newsgroups to find those for which he thinks his company's information will be relevant. When he does find one, James joins it, follows the e-mail threads for a while to understand what's going on there, and then contributes to the discussion without saying what he does for a living. But, the signature line shows up in the newsgroup along with his comments: People see it—and respond.

James says, "In the context of the discussion, the two lines are insignificant and do not offend anyone. And because I always make a sincere effort to contribute valuable [not self-serving] comments, no one complains. However, every time I post comments, I get an increase in the number of people who want to order books or find out more information."

Another tactic that James discovered to be effective was inviting customers to write reviews of the books they buy. He posts the reviews in his database of book reviews for others to access. "This project keeps customers coming back because it involves them in the company, makes them feel their opinions are valued and adds a personal touch they don't find in a lot of other places online," says James.

Roswell is now designing a Web site to offer customers a better order-processing system. James found that, even though it's not perfect, the Web is easier for customers to use than the gopher server. He's still working out some of the details, but by the time you have this book in your hands, you should be able to drop in to the new site and check it out.

Software.net: Putting Customers' Names Up in Lights

Bill McKiernan, former CEO of McAfee Associates, is out to make his mark again in cyberspace, this time with a new venture: Software.net.

Software.net is a company that distributes software over the Internet. It currently carries over 6,500 software titles, a number of which are from small developers whose products are not carried in traditional distribution or retail channels.

Software.net's basic strategy is to let people browse its software titles, read and post product reviews, and download software demos. This content creates a good learning environment that helps people make more informed decisions and forms a tight community between customers and software vendors.

When McKiernan was putting McAfee Associates on the map, the network of BBSs was his primary online communication vehicle, but today, he advocates the Internet all the way. Software.net went live near the end of 1994, and within a few months, McKiernan saw his company's direct response tactics paying off both in the high number of daily accesses to his server and in product sales.

"One thing that has worked very well for us is posting hyperlinked announcements about Software.net in the What's New sections of other Web sites that have heavy user traffic," says McKiernan. "We get spikes [sudden increases] in our sales every time our announcements appear on these sites. What's gratifying is that, when these surges drop off, sales never drop below the level where they were before the spike. Usually the post-spike sales volume stays above that level."

Of the What's New sections that McKiernan mentions, two are particularly popular. One is in the National Center to Supercomputer Applications' (NCSA) Web site; this is the group that developed and distributes Mosaic, the "browser" software that enables you to navigate and view Web sites. The second is in O'Reilly & Associates's Global Network Navigator (GNN) Web site. Both organizations charge a fee for appearing in their What's New section.

On the day that I interviewed McKiernan, 22% percent of the people visiting Software.net (the largest percentage to come from one source) came directly from NCSA, and that was a typical day's traffic for Software.net. As you can see, hyperlinking to *NCSA* can provide a valuable source of online traffic.

Another tactic that works for Software.net is an old direct marketing standby: the T-shirt and coffee mug giveaways. McKiernan says that people are always eager to visit Software.net to fill out forms or download information so they can acquire one of these "treasures."

Elaborating on the giveaway tactic, Software.net developed a contest that it runs each month, giving away different prizes to encourage feedback on products, service, and so forth. People's names are put into a hat—literally—and someone from the company draws the winners names, which appear in flashing lights on Software.net's server. Check it out. Maybe you'll get to see your own name in lights.

Software.net also has an e-mail message board on its server, where customers can place reviews of the software that they buy (a tactic also employed by Roswell Computer Books, as mentioned earlier in this chapter.) McKiernan says, "We did this to leverage the Internet culture of sharing ideas with the community. We plan to make this area more interactive so customers can talk to each other in real time, and our product managers can do online seminars."

McKiernan finds that much of what apparently entices customers to place orders are the value-added features that his company offers. For example, giving people the maximum number of ways to order products increases sales: "We'll accept checks, cash, money orders, phone calls, faxes, online transactions, or any other way customers can think of to pay us for an order, as long as it's legal," he says. "It's always best to give customers as many options as you can."

And while the press reports that online transactions are hampered by poor security on the Net, McKiernan says that 90 percent of Software.net's online orders come from customers who use their credit cards. He says, "We explicitly explain the risks of online transactions to them before they order. Maybe it's because we take the time to describe the process that people feel comfortable enough to place orders this way. It's definitely more convenient for them to order right then while they have all the information they need."

Software.net will soon offer customers the option to *encrypt* their credit card information before sending an order. (Encryption is an electronic process that scrambles data to make it unreadable by anyone except the merchant who provides the encryption feature.) McKiernan says, "We don't get too many requests for encryption, but it's another option for our customers that we want to make available."

McKiernan reiterates the advice he gave in Chapter 3: "You have to give customers value and a reason to visit. Then you have to give them a reason to visit again. The best way to do this is to give them something that they can take with them when they leave your area. Your ultimate goal is to get people to add your online site to their Hot List."

The *Hot List* is the section on Internet browser software where people can list their favorite places to visit on the Net. Anytime they go online, users can just click on any of these names to be immediately transported to that site. Once someone puts you on a Hot List, it's highly likely that he or she will be a regular visitor to your area.

CompuServe and some of the other online services have a feature similar to Hot Lists in their online navigation software. CompuServe's equivalent of browser software, called WinCIM, has "Favorite Places," where users list areas that they like to visit.

To encourage users to add Software.net to their Hot Lists, the company included a section in its Web site called Free Stuff. Here you can find all kinds of goodies, such as free software and those highly coveted T-shirts and mugs that I mentioned earlier.

McKiernan predicts that future direct response tactics will require delivery of information in formats such as video and full multimedia presentations. For example, a tire company could have a video of a car using its tires in the Indy 500 car race. Web sites can deliver this kind of presentation today, but many people's PCs don't have the necessary technology to view them.

Six Lessons Learned

Of the lessons to be learned from the Roswell and Software.net stories, six in particular will help you to develop direct response tactics that get people to place orders. Even though both companies are on the Internet only, these lessons are applicable to any online areas that you may use.

1. First and foremost: learn everything you can about the culture of cyberspace. I know, I've said it before, but repetition is the mother of learning—and learning prevents flaming.

   Follow the example of Roswell James who continually goes out of his way to understand the Net and be an active member of its community. He thinks through each of his tactics carefully and makes sure that all conform to proper Net behavior.

   James mentioned that he's seen some people join a newsgroup and then add random comments to the discussion, apparently just so everyone could see the 10–20-line blatant ad in their signature line. The results were quick, direct, and negative for these poor, misguided souls.

   Also learn from McKiernan, whose earliest experiences with the culture of cyberspace are reflected in his overall approach to cybermarketing, as well as in some of the specific direct response tactics that he uses such as having people write and post software reviews. Software.net's ability to produce results in a short period of time validates McKiernan's tactics.

2. Develop tactics that motivate people to contribute something to your area, such as James' and McKiernan's respective book and software reviews. And be sure that contributors' names are posted with their respective contributions because everyone loves to see his or her name publicized.

   You might be surprised how many of the experts I interviewed for this book were excited about having his or her pictures included in the online portion of this book, but it makes sense. People who work hard and have creative ideas appreciate public recognition of their talents.

3. Keep your online areas fun and interesting. No matter how staid a company may be, there still should be a little fun and excitement associated with its areas. This is what will keep people talking about your areas to other cybersurfers, encouraging them to visit, too. A person is more apt to part with his or her money while having a good time.

4. Remember that direct response marketing is not just a one-time event; it's a series of activities that keep people coming back to download information, which they'll read and pass on to others.

   James and McKiernan are continually thinking of new promotions and value-added offers so people continually visit their respective areas. "If you don't add value, people won't come back," remarks McKiernan.

5. Don't overlook whatever traditional marketing activities will work for you.

   James started by taking his order-processing system, which he knew worked well, and duplicating as much of it as he could in cyberspace. And after he watched the system operate online for a while, he modified it to better suit the medium. And McKiernan uses some of the most basic traditional direct response tactics with great effect.

6. Reaching out is key. As with building brand awareness, reaching out to link up with every practical online site is critical to the success of direct response marketing. You can create promotions with great selling power, but if no one knows you're out there, you've wasted your talent.

   Also reach out to customers. For example, James got his idea to solicit book reviews from customers after conversations with people who came into his bookstore. McKiernan built part of his marketing strategy around proactively collecting customers' feedback and then quickly implementing their ideas for new products, services and promotions.

Your online customers will be some of your best marketing partners—if you regularly communicate with them.

Getting Down[loads] with Direct Response

It's important to get people to download some of your information, whether it's promotional materials about your products or educational information (covered in the next chapter.) By getting this information into their hands, you keep your company name in front of them long after they've left your online areas. Plus, they can pass this info on to others, and increase the number of people who learn about you.

I spoke with Gale Grant of Open Market, Inc., about her ideas on direct response activities that encourage people to download information. (Open Market offers software and consulting services to help companies do business more effectively on the Net.)

Grant says, "You need to offer people something interesting, something with a unique hook to catch people's attention. Once people come in and start to look around at things you have to offer, other promotions can entice them to download specific information."

Direct with Directories

Consider, for example, setting up a directory in your online areas to help people search for a particular type of information in cyberspace. Open Market has a directory of commercial Internet sites that users can easily search through to find their way around the Internet maze.

Say your market is optometrists; you could set up a directory of eye care supplies and equipment providers. Or say your prospects do a lot of work with the federal government: set up a directory of government information sources (various government agencies are quickly popping up online). Directories like these can do a lot to generate frequent visitors.

Catch Frequent Online Fliers

You also might draw frequent visitors by developing a promotion similar to the airlines' frequent flyer programs. With the right kind of tracking program, you could assign "frequent visitor points" for each visit and also for downloading specific documents. You could then offer a gift or special award when visitors collected a certain number of points. Such a program assumes, of course, that you have a lot of information to distribute and that you will change that information regularly; there's no real challenge or fun for visitors in collecting points if they can collect only 10 or 15.

List Lists

Grant suggests increasing the value of information you offer by including listings of items, of events, or facts that people can't easily get elsewhere. There are people who can't seem to get enough lists; look at how books like *David Letterman's Top Ten* and *The Book of Lists*, are big sellers. As one idea, Grant recommends creating month-long TV show listings to pull in TV junkies; these could have an advantage over printed TV guides which list only a week's schedule at a time.

Palo Alto, California, posts on the Internet the schedule for commuter trains that make stops in the city. How much traffic could you draw to your online area with public transportation schedules for your city, or with some similarly enticing list? Just remember that, whatever category of list you choose, you change it on a weekly or biweekly basis—stale listings are worse than no listings.

Get Wacky

The wild and wacky can also draw direct responses from visitors, as Grant relates in this interesting story: "An office in the U.K. set up a Polaroid camera in the room with their coffee pot. They engineered a system to take frequent pictures of the coffee pot, digitize them, and scan them into the company's Internet site. People at their desk can go to the Net site and see if there's coffee in the pot before they walk over to the room."

Not exactly *my* cup of tea, but once word got out around the Net about this site, cybersurfers started dropping by for visits. Grant reports that some surfers sent messages to the office that its camera was apparently broken because all they saw at the site was a dark screen.

Actually, the camera was fine. The site looked dark because the office crew turns the light out before they go home at night, but the system keeps on producing online snapshots of the coffee room. If you want to see if you can get a cup of joe to go, surf over to http://www.cl.cam.ac.uk/coffee/coffee.html, but good luck—the pot was empty the day I stopped in. This is just the sort of wackiness people love to find on the Web, so start thinking about how you can do something like this to draw people to your area.

Build Anticipation

Another tactic for getting people to download your info is to orchestrate a few online activities that build anticipation for a particular product release or event. The anticipation should focus people's attention on taking some specific action at some specific time, resulting in a high volume of traffic in your area when the event finally does happen.

As an example of this approach, GeoWorks Online Manager Steve Main recalls how his company used it to launch a new product. (Their goal in this case was to generate product orders, but this tactic can be used just as effectively to increase information distribution.)

Main says, "When we released version 2.0 of Ensemble, we pre-announced it in our AOL forum. To reinforce this message, we also sent postcards to our customer base. The AOL announcement gave our online customers an 'early bird' chance to place their order for the new version before it was available elsewhere."

There were additional benefits to this "early bird" tactic. Continues Main, "It allowed us to start taking orders immediately (which is good for cash flow). It also spread orders out over a slightly wider range of dates, which reduced the workload on our operators."

You can adapt this technique to your own situation by 158 158announcing that something specific will happen on a set date (for example: "Don't miss the grand opening of our new chat room on September 1!"). By regularly promoting the event and the date, you should have people lined up outside your "doors" waiting to see what's up.

An alternative way to build anticipation is through the uncertainty of a "mystery tease and deliver" campaign. Hollywood studios often use this tactic to promote their movies.

How do you do this? Post teaser messages in your online areas to this effect: "Be here June 1! Something special and exciting will happen! You don't want to miss this!" Of course, whatever you deliver had better be worth the anticipation that you build. You can imagine what'll happen if you disappoint people.

In a similar way, you can tie direct response promotions to seasonal events such as Christmas, Easter or Father's Day. As specific holidays or particular dates draw near, the pressure to respond should build.

"Just ten shopping days left to take advantage of our special Christmas sale. Download our catalog today!"

"Order our special Mother's Day bouquet. That special day is just five days away."

"Winter's almost over. Have you taken advantage of our special ski vacation package?"

Get a Little Bit Conventional

Another way to generate a lot of responses from people is to combine conventional marketing tactics with your online tactics.

Grant mentioned a recruitment agency in Boston that uses radio ads to direct people to its Internet address for more information. You could do something like this: "Hey out there in radioland! This is C.J. your D.J.—turn your computer dial to Monster.com to keep on top of the ever-changing career landscape!"

There are numerous possibilities for using this marketing angle; one is to have both your ads or other traditional marketing materials and your online content contain a puzzle that people try to solve to win prizes.

For example, your ads or brochures can have clues—hidden or otherwise—to a mystery, and you can scatter answers to the mystery throughout your online areas. Your traditional marketing materials will have increased impact, because readers will have to constantly refer to them to find the clues. Your online areas will get thoroughly examined, too, because users will be busy searching there for answers. Neat, huh?

By the way, I'm particularly proud of this puzzle idea. If you decide to use it or any of the other ideas presented in this book, please tell people where they came from. Remember, sharing ideas *and* credit is a key tenet of cyberspace culture.

Well, the ideas in this chapter should keep your subconscious busy creating direct response tactics. Meanwhile, your conscious mind can move on to educating the market.

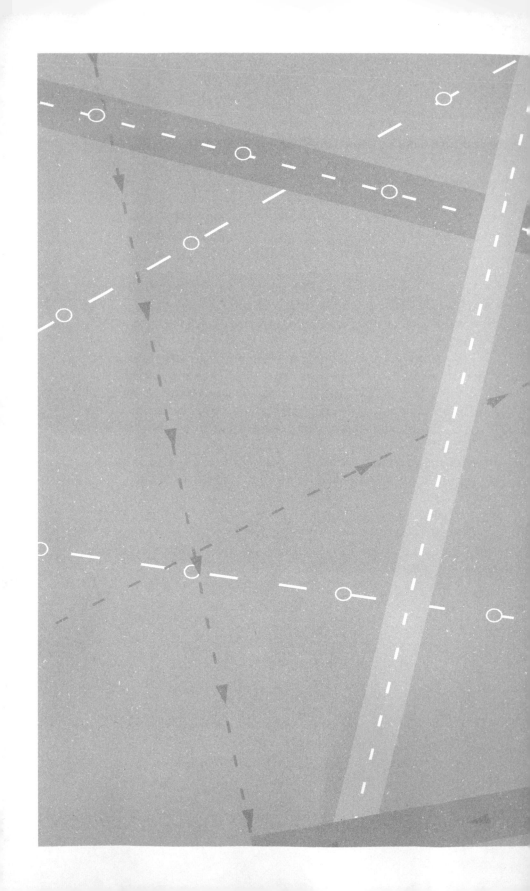

Chapter 10: Market Education: Teach Them Well

Market education is a process where you leave virtually no stone un-turned to give prospects a thorough understanding of your product, company, and industry. The more people know about your business, the better they feel about doing business with you.

Market education is not limited to companies dealing in technology. It also works for selling real estate, photo processing services, and a host of other products and services. Whatever your business, you need to educate the market about the features and facets of your product or service. In some cases, this education goes beyond telling people about the technical aspects of your offering; it also describes your company's operating procedures or explains industry trends. The need for market education is not limited to new or little-known companies. For example, most everyone knows of software giant Microsoft. Nevertheless, this company is spending literally millions of dollars to educate the market about the capabilities and benefits of its new Windows PC operating system, Windows 95.

To determine if market education is a tactic your company should use, ask yourself a few basic questions. Will you close more sales at a faster rate if prospects have an in-depth understanding of your products or services or how they come to the market? Will market education help you to differentiate your products, services, or company from competitors', resulting in better positioning?

Are there opportunities to improve your market position if you take the lead in educating the market about new developments or upcoming trends in your industry?

Say your business is real estate. If you educate your market about a financial trend that people can capitalize on by refinancing their mortgages, and these people benefit by taking your advice, you'll be a hero. People you helped will do more business with you and refer their friends to you as well.

Some companies are reluctant to educate the market in this way because they think it involves baring their souls to the public or going out on a limb. But if you entertain these questions at least long enough to see how the options and opportunities play out, you may discover a cybermarketing avenue that leads to great dividends.

In this chapter, I give you a close look at ways to implement market education tactics in cyberspace.

Some Basic Ways to Educate the Market

You can educate the market for your products or services in several ways: teach them about complex products, about the benefits of using your product or service, about the design or production process, and about your company itself.

Educate the Market about Complex Products

If your product fits into the new- or advanced-technology category or if it has complex features, don't underestimate the value of market education in moving prospects closer to a sale.

Before someone plunks down hard-earned cash for new technology, even if it's just a $19.95 beeper, he or she wants to have a good understanding of what that product does. The purchasers' comfort level with the product has to be high enough that they feel they're making the right choice.

Purchasing agents who must buy lots of products for their organizations will want to know even more than individuals making personal purchases about the products the agents evaluate. No one wants to be the sacrificial goat if what they bought turns out to be the wrong thing.

Complex products are not necessarily just those that are difficult to use. For example, a car is fairly simple to drive: you insert the key, turn it, press the gas pedal, and you're off. But the machinery that lies under the hoods of recent model cars requires almost a rocket scientist to understand it. I'm sure many car salespeople spend hours answering the *whys*, *whats*, and *hows* regarding the complexities of the vehicles they sell.

The "Why-ners"   Market education is valuable even if you sell complex products whose technology is generally understood, such as stereos and TVs. Why? Because there are people in this world, many of them in cyberspace, who never got past that dreaded childhood stage of always asking "why."

The "why-ners" want to know everything about anything they plan to buy, borrow, or just look at. The more complex the product, the more they want to know. These people can "why" you to death before deciding to buy. However, the more you educate them and answer their questions, the faster you can move them to closing the sale.

The FUD Factor   Market education is also good because of another type of prospect. This is the person for whom purchasing is a process governed by fear, uncertainty, and doubt (FUD). The FUD factor can drag out the sales process like a bad soap opera.

The more complex the product and the less people feel they understand it, the greater the FUD factor. You can often move these people a
little closer to closing with education tactics designed to remove the
FUD factor.

Complex Services   Complex services also can be sold faster by market
education. For example, when my company was one of the first to offer
cybermarketing services, it was then difficult to get companies to retain
us. I realized early on that, because cyberspace was so complex, many
people didn't understand it, how to market there, or where my company's services could fit into the picture.

The only way to deal with a prospective client's misconceptions
and misgivings about cybermarketing was to incorporate education into
our marketing efforts, which we are now starting to see pay off.

These efforts include writing articles for several publications, delivering speeches on cybermarketing, conducting press meetings, and writing this book. We include key information from these activities in our
sales presentations and our online areas.

Each effort helps people to better understand cybermarketing, its
benefits, and how our company's approach can enable them to market
online more effectively. Collectively, these activities are shortening our
sales cycles.

Educate Them about Benefits

You may choose to focus your market education campaign on a product's benefits, rather than its features. For example, you can educate people about new benefits they can derive from not-so-new technology.

Many companies are comfortable using PCs for productivity but
they are hesitant to use them in ways that might produce new benefits
such as, say, in cybermarketing. Perhaps if Compaq Computers and
other computer manufacturers can figure out how to make these hesitant companies more comfortable with cybermarketing, they will sell
more computers.

When my company promoted AT&T's PassageWay computer-telephony integration (CTI) system through BBSs, our challenge was to
help people who have used phones and computers for years to understand that linking the two devices offered significant new benefits.

It was apparent to us early on that, without market education, we
would have a difficult time selling PassageWay. Although comfortable
with using phones and computers separately, prospects feared they
would be overwhelmed by the "new" CTI technology.

One of the ways that we met this challenge was by developing a briefing paper for AT&T's PassageWay product that explained CTI benefits in an easy-to-read manner that didn't intimidate people. We also presented examples of how different types of companies could benefit from the technology. Our objective was to raise readers' comfort levels about CTI by describing situations and companies that prospects could relate to.

To make the briefing paper come alive for people, we used the PassageWay Solution Game.

This funky little interactive game with wild, New Age graphics (this isn't your father's AT&T!) puts you in the role of stockbroker at a small brokerage firm. Stockbrokers are a main target market for PassageWay. You work against a giant brokerage firm in a race to raise $100,000.

Each step of the way, you encounter a selection of people to call and approaches to use to get these people to invest in your venture. If you make the right choices fast enough using simulated PassageWay CTI features, you win.

Together, the briefing paper and the interactive game helped people understand CTI and got them excited about buying the PassageWay product.

Educate Them about the Delivery Process

If you sell products or services with few features or benefits that distinguish them from competitors, consider showing people your design or production process that results in a better finished product.

Burger King effectively practiced this type of market education. While a hamburger is not a complex product—nor is one raw burger much different from another—Burger King generated lots of sales with ads that showed how the process of flame broiling a burger, only after a customer had ordered it, made its burgers better than the ones competitors fried and left to fossilize in a warming bin.

Another example: If you have a service that develops crucial documents for trial lawyers, you can win sales by educating lawyers about how your research process is more thorough than your competitors' and why that matters.

And, if you plan to actually do financial transactions online, you can reassure prospects as to the security of this process by educating them in how it works and the precautions you will take.

Educate Them about Your Company

Another strong card to play is educating the market about your company, particularly if it's new. In many industries, prospects feel more comfortable buying from companies after they learn something more about the management team.

Perhaps knowing the financial strength of your company or its investors will encourage people to do business with you. This information can indicate that you have the financial resources to stay in business for the long term.

You can educate prospects about many aspects of your company in order to help close sales: the services provided by the customer support department; your company's commitment to R&D that ensures customers will always have access to the best products; nationwide or worldwide locations of sales and tech support offices; or partnerships with well-known companies.

When you educate the market about your company, be sure to tell them who your key customers are. Hans Gomez of Adobe Systems says, "My perception is that this type of information helps customers feel like they are making the right choice since [they see] other industry leaders are also using the same product."

You can wrap any or all of the tactics I've described in this section into a market education campaign that shows prospects how your company differs from your competitors'. While many people tend to take "us versus our competitors" arguments with a grain of salt, if you present your case effectively, you can position yourself as a desirable alternative to your competitors. Strengthen your case with the right supporting documents, such as customer testimonials.

Taking Market Education to Cyberspace

There are several ways to capitalize on the unique qualities of cyberspace and make your market education campaign a success.

Deliver Information Fast and Cheap

Cyberspace is one of your best communication channels for educating the market about new technologies and complex products. Here is an audience that is predisposed to appreciating new technology and prone to asking, "why, what, and how"—ad nauseam.

Cyberspace is also a medium that can deliver tons of educational information immediately and cheaply. Claris, for example, maintains 4,000 technical articles on its gopher site. Borland keeps nearly 5,000 technical documents on its BBS.

CUC International offers online access to descriptions and ordering information for 250,000 products. Geoworks stores over 5,000 files with product and company information on AOL.

The preceding numbers are just tips of the respective companies' information icebergs. Yet, there's still plenty of room in cyberspace to stand up, present your case, and educate your market.

Bolster Sales Staff and Resellers

Cyberspace gives you an opportunity to use market education to resolve the potentially tricky problem of compensating for any lack of technology expertise among your sales staff or the resellers who handle your products.

Whether it's computers, engineering, medicine, finance, or any field that requires a high level of education or skill to master, technologies and techniques used in such industries advance so quickly that even experts can barely keep up. Unless you have deep financial pockets, enlisting a sufficiently competent sales force is a big and costly challenge.

First, you must recruit the sales force—and technically knowledgeable people are increasingly hard to find. Of course, you have to pay them, and the more they know, the more they cost. When you do bring people on board, you have to train them about your particular business, which is time consuming and expensive in itself. Then once you finally get your salespeople up to speed, they become targets of every headhunter on the planet.

If you use a retail channel to distribute products, recruiting competent resellers stresses your resources and sanity even more than getting your sales staff, since retail businesses are more hard-pressed than you to find, train, and keep people competent enough to sell your product.

With retailers, you have the added geographic problems of training people who are scattered across the map. You also have to deal with the fact that retail operations are responsible for selling many products other than yours, and the salespeople there often don't have time to learn the intricacies of every product they sell.

You can counter these problems with some of the same market education information that you offer your prospects. Use this content to educate your sales staff and retailers faster, less expensively, and more efficiently than you could with conventional training. (Obviously, you have to customize this content differently for salespeople and retailers, with such information as tips to overcome sales objections, but the core information is the same.)

You can even incorporate some of your online content into your sales staff's presentations. Consider the improved effectiveness of a salesperson who spends ten minutes describing your product in general terms— and then takes a customer online to show him or her detailed information on topics of specific interest.

In cyberspace, you get an added bonus from your content because it educates prospects even while your salespeople sleep at night. Russ Jones, director of programs for Digital's Internet Business Group, relates how that company's Net server filled in nicely for its sales team.

"An Italian software developer with no prior experience with mini computers needed to write a proposal to create a mini computer-based system. It was 4:00 A.M., and not having anywhere else to go at that hour, he went on the Internet. Digital was the only vendor with the information he needed. He got his mini computer education and wrote the proposal using Digital specs. He subsequently won the bid, and Digital sold a system."

Distribute Briefing Papers

For companies that market complex products, a common market education tactic is to distribute briefing papers. These documents describe your product's technology or your industry in detail, with few or no references to your company.

If you label documents "Briefing Papers," make sure they are objective, otherwise, people are likely to take offense and feel that you tricked them into reading promotional literature.

You can give prospects detailed technical information about your product and how to use it by putting this information into documents labeled "Tech Notes" or "Product Info Sheets." People can then access these documents when they want more information about your product, such as descriptions of features or how to use different features to solve specific problems.

To get more marketing value from your briefing papers, put a tag line at the end of each paper that directs people to your tech notes, where they can learn what your company is doing in each particular technology area. Good briefing papers will build interest in products that incorporate the technology discussed—*your* products.

Service companies can similarly use briefing papers to educate the market about the industry or discipline that their services address. For example, our company posts briefing papers at our Web site that describe different aspects of cybermarketing. By educating people about this new marketing discipline, we make it easier for them to determine how to understand our services.

Bring Your Content to Life

Cyberspace is a New Age medium, so when you use it to educate your market, look beyond text-based content. Remember, this is an interactive medium. Use it to present interactive and fun educational materials.

For example, the PassageWay Solution game that I described earlier in this chapter is an entertaining way to teach people about something that's fairly complex. But whether your products are complex or simple, try to find ways to put humor and entertainment into your content.

Another thing you can do to liven up your content is to set up "live" seminars in online services' chat rooms or your BBS. These online areas are great, because they enable you to communicate with people in real time. As soon as you type something, seminar attendees see it on their computer screens. Likewise, you can read others' comments as soon as they are typed.

Cybersurfers love these chat sessions, because they can interact immediately with a real person who knows a lot about the product in question and the company that produces it. Attendees also can communicate with each other at these seminars, thereby helping each other to learn. And this opportunity for interaction contributes to the community feeling that you want to develop in your online area.

"Geoworks supplements its online postings of briefing papers with a monthly real-time conference on AOL with a guest speaker from the company," says Geoworks' online manager, Steve Main. "Every night of the week, we offer a chat room hosted by a remote volunteer customer service rep. Customers always have a place to come and learn more about what we're doing."

Educate the People in the Know

Many cybersurfers are on an eternal quest for information, so anticipate that hunger by volunteering information about your product or service that surfers will want to stop and check out. For example, set up a "Did you know?" section in your online areas with information that visitors normally wouldn't find without looking for it.

A variation of "Did You Know" is an "Insider's Connection" section that discusses complex issues regarding your technology or industry. A section with "insider" information should be quite popular since most people like to be recognized in their business or social circles as "the person in the know."

To see how doing this translates into bottom line benefits, think back to those why-ners I mentioned earlier in the chapter.

In electronics stores, for example, there are people who make quick purchase decisions about stereos or VCRs, yet have little understanding of the technical complexities inside these products. But if you look around that store long enough, you may also spot some why-ner asking a poor sales rep enough questions about product features to try the patience of a saint.

It's a good bet that many of the people making a "buy" decision in five minutes at some point asked for advice from a why-ner. Your Insider's Connection section is for this person who does lots of homework before buying, asking the endless questions and reading tons of spec sheets. The person in the know, to whom everyone else goes to for advice, is most likely a why-ner.

By setting up popular education centers for these people, you create a lot of advice givers who eventually send prospects your way, primed to do business with you without asking a lot of questions. They've already received their market education—without taking up your time.

People in the know probably also have influence beyond cyberspace. This can be an added bonus for you when they advise individuals who don't go online and otherwise wouldn't see your online content.

By the way, many why-ners don't actually whine, and they are valuable people to engage in direct conversation. Because they ask a lot of questions in general, they often have a lot of information to share.

Enlist Others to Educate

Educating prospects about the benefits to them of using your products or services is as important as teaching them about features. However, educating people about benefits requires a different tack than hitting someone with reams of technical materials. You need content that people can relate to in some personal way.

You can present convincing arguments about the benefits that your merchandise offers, but cybersurfers tend to be a cynical lot. They also want to hear about the benefits of your product straight from the horse's mouth—your customer's, that is.

For example, have you ever seen the occasional news story that shows someone who's 105 years "young" swearing that his or her longevity stems from a drinking glass of wine every day? Think about it. Wouldn't that make a great online presentation for a wine company?

You can incorporate into your content quotes from customers or third parties (press, industry analysts, and so on) or assemble information that comes directly from these sources. It's ideal if these sources are also online and you can hyperlink your online areas to them. Just make sure that your audience in cyberspace can relate to the third-party sources that you quote.

If you want to present the benefits of your products or services in a way that positions you against your competitors, you will definitely have greater success with third-party material. Never attack your competitors. Doing this would result only in a bad reputation for your company. But articles, product comparisons, research reports, or newsgroup discussions that compare you favorably to competitors are valuable content to post or hyperlink to.

Besides distributing written materials with third-party endorsements, you can also bring others in to help educate by hosting a panel of experts or customers in chat room seminars or newsgroups.

For example, AT&T could recruit several PC and telecommunications industry journalists to participate in a discussion in an appropriate newsgroup about the benefits of CTI. Maxis could host an AOL conference about the benefits of simulation games in schools, and include on the panel parents and teachers who use simulation software.

The upside of hosting a panel is that you can control its direction by selecting topics to discuss and setting a general focus for these topics. The flip side is that, to have credibility with the cyber crowd, you can't orchestrate this session too much, particularly after it starts. If you try to do this, or if you don't let people participate fully in the discussions, you'll lose their interest and support.

Let Your Company Be Your Ace in the Hole

If the greatest strength for marketing your product or service lies in the company that stands behind it, then put your company up front and center. Unlike most marketing channels, cyberspace lets you educate your market about your company through direct and indirect two-way communication.

Bring your company execs online for monthly live chat sessions like Geoworks does. Or do an online press tour (a series of meetings with editors) and have your management team go online in the chat rooms of various online publications. Have your top people distribute columns or newsletters online to customers, similar to what Amway's chief operating officer does on his company's CompuServe forum.

You can also take advantage of the graphic capabilities of Web sites and the online services by presenting pictures and background information on the key people in your company, from the management team to the Employee of the Month. This gives your company presentation greater depth because cybersurfers then have faces and names to go along with your briefing papers and spec sheets.

If you are in manufacturing, post videos online that users (granted, not everyone—yet) can download to see your machinery in operation. Or you can post maps of your branch offices or store locations that users can click on to get more information about each location.

Become a Leader and a Spokesperson

While educating your market with information, you can also establish your company as a market leader or position your executives as industry spokespeople. One way to do this is to set up a section within each of your online areas as a resource center for your industry or profession.

Along with the content that you prepare, stock these sections with materials developed by third parties, such as briefing papers, published articles, and news feeds from wire services that discuss trends or provide general industry background. Hyperlink your resource centers to other related content, appropriate Internet newsgroups or directories, and other online areas that your market will find valuable.

As you design your resource centers, remember that these places are valuable to you because they build traffic and loyalty to your area. People will have one place to go to find the information they need, rather than spending time searching cyberspace for it.

An example of a resource center is the Online Press Center that my company created for Symantec's Web Site, which is marketing new software utilities for Microsoft's Windows 95 operating system. This center contains useful content for journalists, who are constantly on deadline and in dire need of practical information that they can access with minimal hassles.

Symantec's press center includes briefing papers on Windows 95 topics, a list of useful terminology for journalists covering Windows 95 and articles by Symantec and third parties that provide additional Windows 95 background material.

The center will also include commentaries by Symantec executives on late-breaking Windows 95 news, plus a listing of industry analysts, corporate contacts, newsgroups, and other sources of information about software utilities or Windows 95.

Our goal is to create thought-provoking content with hard-hitting news value that positions Symantec as a leading press source for Windows 95 information. As a result, Symantec will receive both direct and indirect coverage in Windows 95 articles written by journalists who access its resource material.

You can create resource centers similar to Symantec's, whether for the press or consumers. For example, if you market sports products, you could create a center containing sports management information for people who manage professional and amateur sports programs.

If you market financial services, you could set up a data analysis center for people who follow financial trends. You could include economic reports from leading universities, a directory of financial planners, your company execs' analyses on stock market news, and hyperlinks to other companies' investor relations information.

If you offer outdoor equipment, assemble a clearinghouse for documents on issues, legislation, and business developments that impact the environment.

If you sell software, you have a sea of options, from educating people about copyright legalities to presenting theories on using business management software to help companies survive changing economic conditions.

Keep in mind, though, that you have to be more than a source of information if you want to establish a true leadership position for your company. Your content must incorporate third-party content, offer analysis, and encourage input from users. These centers should be places where people learn through vigorous and even heated discussion.

Using Various Areas of Cyberspace

For posting market education content, BBSs are a valuable online tool. BBSs guarantee that anyone with just a modem can gain access to your areas, which is not true of any other medium of cyberspace.

BBSs can also hold mega amounts of information, so you have the space to address endless technical issues, complex products, extensive company and product backgrounds, and so forth. And you can set up interactive systems on BBSs so your company executives can interact with customers.

FTP and gopher sites are tops as far as reaching the maximum number of Net surfers. Even companies that have BBSs keep the same data and more on these Internet sites. Practically anyone on the Net can access FTP and gopher sites, and if you primarily want to distribute information with little interaction with people, these sites will work fine alone.

If user interaction is important to you, though, supplement your FTP and gopher sites with either a Web server, a BBS, or the online services; all three have interactive capabilities.

The online services are good to use for market education too, because on them you can set up real-time seminars, conferences, or round table discussions, plus their chat areas let you strike up conversations on the fly or set up impromptu conferences.

Claris's Marc Stobs says, "We run a monthly live conference on AOL because this service is very conference-based. We go for an hour and have up to 110 people at a time participate. Sometimes we have general Q&A sessions, but when we're rolling out a new product, our product managers and developers participate."

AT&T Interactive's and Microsoft Network's hyperlinking features (described in Chapter 4) and ability to present good graphics will be particularly valuable for setting up resource centers. Information created with dozens of hyperlinks can be just as useful to cybersurfers as material posted at your site, because linked sites can be accessed so quickly. Creating links also saves time in content development.

Internet Web servers let you be more graphical with your presentation than other online mediums, so with them you can design more entertaining and effective materials. If you do use visuals, try to limit your graphics to photos and diagrams when possible so that you don't overload the bandwidth of people's Net connections.

The ability of Web sites to link anywhere in the Net, plus the fact that the online services and many BBSs have Net connections, lets you create resource centers that are conduits of information from almost the entire realm of cyberspace.

Listservs and newsgroups are useful for distributing educational materials to people who want to have the materials delivered directly to their e-mail mailboxes or want to pick these materials up without accessing your online areas. Although listservs and newsgroups don't offer the real-time interactivity of BBSs and online services, you can still use them to conduct educational discussions about a specific company, for example, or a particular industry development.

A Market Education Project for You

All of the online areas can play as valuable a role in educating you and your entire company as they do in educating the market. By just accessing the same kinds of online areas that I've recommended for distributing information, you can learn a lot in a short period of time about your industry and competitors.

Here's a good project you can do before implementing market education tactics. First, decide on something that you want to learn about, preferably something related to your business. Then go online to find out about it.

See what's listed on the topic at hand in all the online areas. See how educational information is organized and how it's accessed. Ask other people you encounter for their opinions of the information that you're looking at. You might be surprised at what they have to say.

During this project, you may discover some new competitors or helpful allies. Regardless of what you find, you will be a smarter marketer because of it.

With an understanding of educating your market, you're ready to move on to product demonstration and distribution.

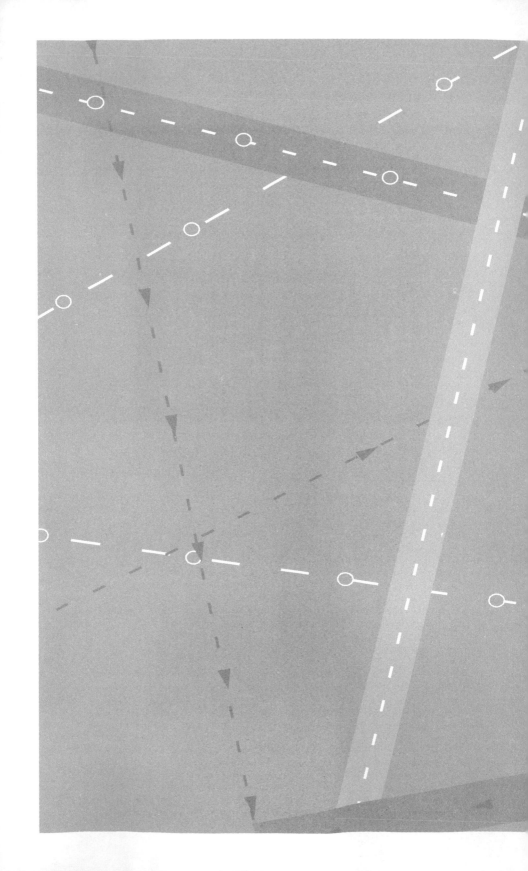

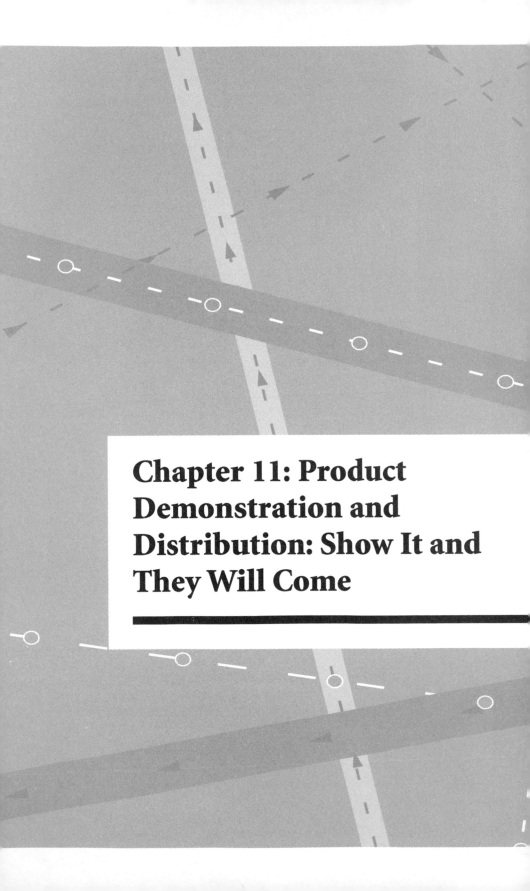

Chapter 11: Product Demonstration and Distribution: Show It and They Will Come

Product demonstration is the category of cybermarketing tactics that can have the most direct impact on generating sales for your company. If you can demonstrate all or most of your key product features online, you will move prospects closer to ordering that product, either online or through conventional channels such as the telephone or local retailer.

If you've watched good salespeople demonstrate products, you know how powerful this tool can be. A person can be transformed from a reluctant, skeptical prospect to a smiling customer as he or she is guided from one feature of the product to another, witnessing how each delivers valuable benefits.

Your goal should be to duplicate this process in cyberspace, with one major difference: Where most conventional product demonstrations are predominantly one-way communication from seller to prospect, in cyberspace the demonstration should be an interactive, two-way process.

This interactive process corresponds with every cybermarketing strategy I've discussed so far: Your online visitors want to try things for themselves, at their own pace, communicating with you at various steps along the way.

If some of you are wondering how a company that sells fine china, clothing, or real estate can demonstrate products online—much less companies that sell intangibles, such as consulting services or financial planning—bear with me; it can be done.

The obvious products to demonstrate online are those that can be digitized, such as software, music CDs, and videos. If you're in the business of selling information, such as consulting services, research data, or database information, you can demonstrate or preview that information for prospects.

To demonstrate tangible products such as automobiles, office equipment, or hotel rooms, you just have to stretch your creativity. Later in this chapter, I show you some innovative approaches to online demonstrations of products like these.

Along with product demonstration, in this chapter I discuss product distribution as well. If you can effectively demonstrate your product online, it makes sense to give people the option to order that product when they are most excited about it. It then follows that, if you can, you should deliver your product through the same medium that customers use to buy it.

Options for online product distribution are restricted by the physical limitations of cyberspace, just as are those for demonstrating products online. But don't discount this possibility for your product until you've examined your options carefully—and with a creative eye.

Some General Guidelines for Product Demonstration

Before moving to specifics for demonstrating and delivering your product online, look at some general guidelines for creating effective demos in cyberspace.

As I've mentioned often, maximize the interactivity of your demonstration so that people can experiment, explore at their leisure, and examine features of your product in whatever order makes sense to them. You can increase the impact of this interactivity by giving people the opportunity to personalize the product for their specific needs.

For example, if you're demonstrating software, let users input their own data into the demo. If they can see your software solving problems at their workplace, users will be more convinced that yours is the product to meet their needs.

Try to make your product demo become indispensable to your prospects' day-to-day lives. For example, companies that market newsletters can offer a two-month free trial and have the newsletter electronically delivered to prospects' e-mail boxes. Once prospects get "hooked" on that information in those newsletters, they're more compelled to order the full subscription.

If possible, don't restrict prospects' use of your product demo. For example, CUC International (the company that sells memberships to its shopping clubs), allows prospects to sign up for three months of unlimited use of its services. After this trial period, people are billed if they want to continue their memberships.

Finally, don't make it difficult for customers to order the product you've demonstrated; always provide an easy transition from the demonstration to ordering options. Remember, you want to give people every opportunity to order while they're most favorably disposed to purchasing your product. Give customers several options for ordering (e-mail, telephone, regular mail) and paying: Accept credit cards, checks, money orders, or whatever is practical and legal.

Three Ways to Make Your Products Come Alive Online

There are three types of demonstrations you can put online; which you choose depends on the products or services that you market.

1. *Direct experience.* In this type of demonstration, you let people hold and use your product, usually for some limited time. Computer software, visual products such as videos and digitized artwork, information services, and consulting services are some of the products with which prospects can have a direct experience. This experience can be either online or on prospects' PCs after they've downloaded the demos or information.

2. *Indirect experience.* This type of demonstration lets prospects use a product's features but not take possession of it. For example, a service company that provides information from a medical database may let prospects access data, but the access will be very limited and data can be viewed only on-screen, not downloaded.

3. *Simulated experience.* Companies with products that cannot be accessed physically from cyberspace can use this option to strut their stuff online. A cruise line, for example, can use a combination of still shots, an interactive database, and video and audio clips to let prospects see and hear what life will be like for them on one of the line's deluxe vacation cruises.

Next I look at the three demonstration types in detail, showing specific ways to make each effective. I also discuss how to weave product distribution options into your product demonstrations.

Direct Experience

Whenever you can, try to give people a taste of the real thing. Here are three types of companies that can do just that.

Software   Software is an ideal product to demonstrate and deliver online. One reason is that people can download full-working versions of it as easily as they can download any other file. They can use it immediately, and if they like it and your online area is appropriately equipped, they can then order and download the finished product.

This entire process conceivably can happen in your online area, but the more likely scenario is that people will download the demo, play with it off-line, and then later log back on to order the software. It pays to have a screen of information built into the demo that directs people in ordering the product either online or through an 800 number.

Ideally, the demo can access users' PC modems, dial their BBS, and automatically walk users through an online ordering process. (I suggest a BBS here because many people who have modems do not have online service or Internet access.)

If you're creating a software demo, make sure it's more than a collection of screen shots that users can only look at and not manipulate. A lot of people will throw demos like these away if you give it to them in person: If they spend time downloading this type of inert brain-dead demo, they'll be none too pleased when they discover what they've got— and your chances for a sale will be slim.

What you should develop in a demo is a fully functional piece of software with limits on the amount of data that it will store or the number of days that a user can try it out before it stops working. Some companies give away older versions of software that is fully functional but lacks the newest features. This is an effective strategy, unless the older product is so outdated that people won't use it.

Take into consideration the size of your software files. If they are collectively more than 1MB, your demo is probably too large to download for users with 14.4 bps or slower modems. Unless users can convert the demo into a fully operational product (usually by buying a special code to activate the software), they may be reluctant to spend an hour or more downloading it. The ability to turn the demo into a "real" product with just a phone call gives them the perception that the demo is more valuable.

File size is a nonissue, however, for companies with ISDN or T1 telephone lines, which allow downloading of these files in minutes. If these companies are the target market for your software, you don't have to worry about the size of your files—within reason, of course.

Make sure that your software demo includes an optional large file of sample data. People not only want to load some of their own data into the software and see how it operates; they also want to see how the software processes large volumes of information.

Information Services   I define information services as companies that market either packaged information (research reports, newsletters, financial analyses, and the like), access to data sources (such as legal or medical data bases), or the means to track data (such as news reports and stock prices).

It's fairly easy to get prospects to take information services on a "test drive," if you will.

One option is to give prospects a free trial for a limited time. This is particularly effective if you market an information-tracking service, where typically the information being tracked changes rapidly. You can give away enough to get people addicted to your service—but there's always new information that you can convince them to buy.

Farcast and Individual, Inc., are two companies that use this give-away method to demonstrate their news-tracking services. The companies allow users to select topics for news stories that they want to follow. During the trial period, users receive e-mailed stories on their chosen topics from various wire services and publications. After a month of receiving up-to-the-minute news, many people find it difficult not to continue the service.

If you market access to databases, you could give prospects the full-working service, but with old data . For example, Ziff-Davis could do this with Computer Select, the company's CD-ROM-based database of computer technology articles from numerous publications. Its service demo could be the fully working database, but with five-year old data.

Prospects who receive a demo like this would get a true feel for how efficiently the CD-ROM searches for and retrieves data, as well as an idea of the depth of information that the service provides. The demo would generate sales for the company because customers who are interested in this type of information need to have the most current information there is.

For companies that sell information through subscriptions, such as medical or insurance industry newsletters, two possible tactics are to give away samples of older materials or to use a limited trial offer. Ideally, the information service delivers this material electronically to prospects' e-mail boxes, saving on production and mailing costs.

If you use any of these tactical options for demonstrating information services, be sure that your demos have built-in mechanisms for prompting orders. My company saw the effectiveness of this tactic when we tested Individual's news tracking service; we received daily reminders to order the full service during the last ten days of our free trial.

Consulting Services   Delivering a demo of a consulting service may seem farfetched. but you can do it quite effectively with some careful forethought and planning. The biggest challenge is in providing enough service to make the demo valuable for the recipient, without giving away the store.

An easy tactic for doing this is online posting of briefing papers or summaries of research reports that educate prospects about various aspects of the field of expertise. You could also post articles written by senior members of your firm that have been published in well-known journals or publications. These documents should demonstrate your firm's competency and breadth of knowledge.

JP Morgan, the Fortune 500 investment banking firm, uses an interesting tactic to demonstrate its consulting services. In contrast to many firms in its industry that calculate the potential risks of various investments, but only members of the firms actually manipulate the data, JP Morgan set up its analysis system called RISK Metrics on the firm's Web site so people can do their own calculations. Besides giving people more control over the data they access (a big plus for building loyalty to the firm's site), RISK Metrics also shows people how JP Morgan processes data and arrives at the advice they give clients.

Because the firm makes it easy for people to understand complex financial calculations, these prospects are inclined to choose JP Morgan when they're shopping for an investment banker.

Presenting case studies of how your firm solved problems of various previous clients is another way to show what you can do.

To illustrate, a friend of mine works for Arthur Anderson's Business Systems Consulting (BSC) group, which helps clients select, install and manage computer systems to help these companies operate more efficiently. My friend has interesting stories about how BSC tackles difficult problems. These tales of life in the trenches could translate into popular online documents giving readers a sense of how their companies could benefit from BSC's services.

BSC could make these case studies even more engaging for cybersurfers by first presenting a problem and then asking readers how they would solve it. After taking a crack at the solution, readers could be directed to another area to find out how BSC resolved the issue. (Remember that including some sort of incentive helps to make surfers' efforts worth their time.)

A tried-and-true way to demonstrate your consulting expertise is to bring your senior staff online to interact with people either "live" or through e-mail. To make this tactic work, though, these individuals must contribute valuable information, and their comments mustn't be blatantly self-serving. Doing the online "lecture circuit" is time consuming for these staff members, but it's a sound investment in future business for your company. (For tips on how to demonstrate consulting strengths by participating in forums and discussion groups, see the April 1995 issue of *CompuServe Magazine*.)

Having learned about the categories of products that are suited to the direct demonstration experience, read on to learn about those that require indirect demonstration in cyberspace.

Indirect Experience: The Alpha Project

For an example that really defines the indirect experience in product demonstrations, look to Digital Equipment Corp's Alpha project.

Digital had developed a new line of high-powered computers with significant speed and performance advantages over those of its competitors. The problem was convincing potential customers that this was true, when every computer company claimed to have bigger, better, and faster machines. How do you prove that your machine is superior without putting one in every prospect's office? And doing that, of course, would be a financial and logistical impossibility Unless you're Digital Equipment Corp.

In a beer-based brainstorming session with two engineers at a Silicon Valley micro brewery pub, Gale Grant, currently of Open Market, suggested using the Net to deliver Digital's new computer (the Alpha) to the desk of anyone who wanted it. Simply stated, Digital would set up an Alpha at its office and give users Net access to load software from the users' computers to the Alpha—and let users put the Alpha through its paces.

Grant became the spearhead of this incredibly creative project. All she needed to make the plan work was software to register the users who accessed the Alpha, and two people (her brainstorming team, as it turned out) to keep the Alpha up and running. Once the details were settled, the Alpha project was on its way. The promotion worked out much better than anyone had expected.

Thousands of people accessed the Alpha, including people from smaller companies that wouldn't have been able to get a loaner computer to test (and who may not have become customers). Digital attributed a sizable number of sales to this promotion.

Digital also received several indirect benefits from the program, according to Ira Machefsky, who now guides the Alpha marketing effort: "Knowing that many people were using the system simultaneously, users were more impressed with the Alpha's speed than they would have been using the computer alone at their offices. Others were so impressed that we took such a big risk letting the world pound on our computer that they accepted our claims without testing the Alpha. We also found that our sales cycles shortened dramatically."

Whether or not you can use this particular approach depends on what you sell; it is primarily suited to heavy or expensive equipment that manipulates electronic data. This can include medical diagnostic equipment, computers, test equipment, and possibly home entertainment equipment.

All the World's a Stage   Included in the indirect experience category of product demonstration are companies in the entertainment industry— film, stage, concert producers, and so on—whose promoters want you to experience full-working features of their "products," but they certainly don't want you to experience entire products before you buy them.

The video and audio playback capabilities of the Web enable companies to preview excerpts from any live performance. Together with liberally intermingled still shots, companies can effectively demonstrate the Bam! Pow! Biff! excitement of Batman; the intensity of Hamlet; or the sensuality of the singer formerly known as Prince.

When it comes to using cyberspace to demonstrate products, Hollywood is already the leader in the entertainment world. In fact, of all the companies that have taken their business online, movie studios seem to be doing the most to push the technology envelope to its outer limits. The music industry is also becoming aggressive in using cyberspace as a product demo vehicle. You can pick up some valuable tips by spending time reviewing sites for new movies and record producers.

Cyberspace is also a good venue for budding entertainers to demonstrate their talents. Small town dance troupes, waiters or waitresses waiting for their big acting breaks, or junior Spielbergs in training. Like any small business, these future stars can go online and leverage cyberspace as effectively as the big guys to tell—or sing—their story to the world.

Simulated Experience

Most companies doing business online will probably need to simulate the experience of using their products. If your company falls into this group, don't consider this a poor cousin to the first two demonstration options. You can develop engaging simulated demos, especially if you use the new technology that lets you create 3-D Web sites and sites with increasingly sophisticated interactive capability.

Reaching for New Hyatts with Demos

Many products are inert, nontechnical, relatively unexciting, and about as far removed from electronic show-and-tell as you can possibly get. Or are they? The people at Hyatt Hotel would definitely tell you "no way."

Hyatt's VP of resort marketing, Steve Yastrow, one day went on the Internet and saw there the future of hotel marketing. Yastrow says: "When we evaluated the Net with a long-term perspective, we saw this as being the way the world is going. By getting online early, we're learning something new every step of the way. We'll have much more experience than other businesses that come online later."

As Web site development tools mature, Yastrow says that he envisions making the Hyatt Hotel properties come alive for people online. How? He will soon be able to create 3-D room displays so that travelers can "walk" through hotel lobbies and into restaurants and then click to get pictures of different menu items.

Visitors will be able to "ride" the elevators, see the rooms and suites and even check out the view. A Hyatt site in Hawaii currently has a camera mounted on the roof that sends pictures from the beach to the Web site. Potential vacationers can check anytime to find out when "surf's up!"

At the click of a mouse meeting planners will be able to compare different meeting room layouts to determine which setup best meets their needs. Jerry Michalski, an industry analyst with Release 1.0, suggests maximizing this idea by developing software that tabulates the costs of the various setups (including items such as projectors, screens, tables, and so on.) As planners modify the setups, they automatically see how the changes impact the costs.

Simulation demos that use interactive photos are particularly effective for restaurants, museums, amusement parks, or any business whose "product" consists of land and buildings. You don't have to wait for the new 3-D tools, either. You can do a lot with existing technology if you're creative about how you link your graphics and direct people through your online areas.

Simulations also solve a dilemma for companies that need to keep enough product readily available to meet the diverse needs of a large number of people who want to demo it.

Martin and His Amazing Technicolor Web Site   When his first cars came off the assembly line, Henry Ford would tell people, "You can buy our Model Ts in any color you want—as long as it's black."

Well, times have changed. Many products, including cars, come off the assembly line in every color imaginable to suit the buying public's diverse tastes. But while it's one thing to deliver a product custom-tailored to meet your customer's needs, it's quite another to show every prospect a custom-designed product before he or she buys it.

Take cars, for example. There are so many options, accessories, and colors for every car that you'd need a showroom the size of Detroit to show prospects all the possible variations for one car model. You would, that is, without a site in cyberspace.

Martin Rood, owner of Rood Nissan/Volvo in Seattle, Washington, has found that he can show prospects many more options at his DealerNet virtual showroom on the Web than he can in his Seattle showroom. Visitors to his site scan through thousands of pictures and video clips of autos, RVs, boats and parts.

Yet, as much as DealerNet has expanded Rood's ability to show a wider range of cars to prospects, he knows that the ultimate demos are still to be made. In cyberspace you can potentially create a system that lets users take the image of a standard car, electronically manipulate different features and colors until they have created their dream car, and then order the car while they're still online.

Clothing companies could use similar technology to create online areas where users entered their physical features (height, weight, skin tone, and so on), picked clothing from a catalog, and then changed colors, patterns, accessories, and so forth until they'd created the outfits they liked. Customers can then be directed to a screen for ordering their fashion creations.

In fact, any business which markets products which come in a variety of colors, shapes, styles, and sizes can use the power of cyberspace to let people demo the options before buying.

Granted, some people are genetically disposed to accepting nothing short of the in-store shopping experience; for them, simulation is out of the question. But if your prospects are comfortable with catalog shopping, cyberspace and simulation demos should pay off for you, providing you can get prospects to access your demos.

Product Demonstrations in the Marketing Mix

Once you have an idea of what type of product demonstration you'll provide, consider how that demonstration can be used in combination with other cybermarketing tactics, such as direct response activities, press relations, and research. Draw attention to your online demos by publicizing them in all of your conventional marketing materials and ads.

If possible, offer people immediate rewards for accessing and using your demo. For example, make arrangements with online services to offer cybersurfers free connect time if they download your demo. If you eliminate the charges for the time required in downloading an item, people will certainly be more willing to do so.

Use contests or special giveaways (those tried-and-true mugs and T-shirts) to encourage people to access your demonstrations. Design a contest so that people have to use your demo to get answers to the clues.

At various places throughout your demonstration, put subtle reminders for placing an order. (Practically every screen on the Hyatt Hotel's site has a hyperlink to the hotel's online reservation center along with a list of general information links.) At the end of the product demo itself, include a specific direct response call to action.

In every press campaign, either online or off, alert journalists to your product demonstration. Although these people understand that such demos are promotional in nature, they still may view a well-produced one to get a better understanding of what your product does.

You may want to develop a product demonstration that helps gather feedback on new product designs or solicits ideas on marketing the product. If so, set off an area where you can password-restrict entry, (unless you don't care if your competitors know what you're up to.) Then invite your valued customers to view the demo and then either e-mail feedback to you, or enter a chat room for a real-time discussion.

Generate participation in your marketing research by giving users free products or access to your service in return for their time. Build interest in your research by asking for user feedback as you design your demo, and then let the people who responded see the demo before you release it to the world.

As you read through the following chapters and think back on previous ones, more ideas for integrating product demonstrations with other marketing tactics should come to you. Now let's move on to press relations and see how to better communicate with the Fourth Estate (the press) in cyberspace.

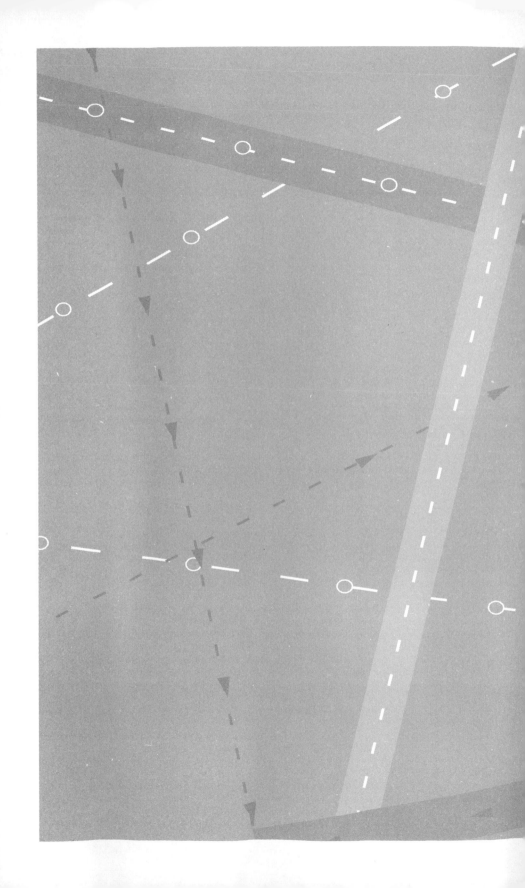

Chapter 12: Public Relations: A Whole New Ball Game

This chapter focuses primarily on working with the press, so it is especially relevant to those in your company who are responsible for PR. I talk about how journalists use cyberspace, and how you should use it to communicate with journalists. I also discuss how to get coverage in the newspapers and magazines that are publishing online.

I then address how your public image online can impact your press coverage. If you have a community of loyal supporters in your online areas, it will have a positive influence on journalists who also visit your sites. (In conjunction with reading this, you may want to review my earlier comments about community development in Chapter 8.)

The Journalist as Cybersurfer

My company recently conducted a qualitative research survey for the purpose of gaining insight into how journalists are using online services and the Internet to do their jobs. We also wanted to solicit advice from journalists on how PR professionals can work more effectively with them in cyberspace.

We took the qualitative rather than quantitative route because we were more concerned with collecting feedback and advice than with creating charts, graphs, deviant curves, and all that voodoo that researchers do so well. To get the most candid responses, we guaranteed anonymity to respondents.

Our 64 survey respondents were primarily from computer publications (most of the business magazine and daily newspaper journalists did not reply to the survey). However, I believe that the comments and advice given by this group apply to journalists across a broad spectrum of publications.

The feedback was highly interesting. While you might find that some of the journalists' suggestions on the techniques that PR people need to improve upon are rather blunt, try to remember that many journalists sincerely believe that PR people—and their companies—can benefit a great deal from these comments.

Survey Says…!

We found the characteristics of the journalists who completed our survey to be in keeping with those of typical cybersurfers I've described in the early chapters of this book.

For example, journalists roam cyberspace primarily looking for information or those who can provide it for them. As one editor stated, "I gather information, and there is a hell of a lot of information out there to be gathered." Cybersurfing journalists are intelligent people who tend to form communities through a few newsgroups rather than at a specific site.

How Journalists See Cyberspace

Most journalists surveyed believe that cyberspace will become very important to them—if it hasn't already—because it will enable them to tackle certain aspects of their jobs faster and more efficiently than they can using the phone or fax.

However, most journalists apparently see cyberspace as a supplement to other means of communication, not a replacement. Said one: "I prefer the face-to-face meeting or the phone. The Net is a great way to ask questions and get specific information, but I don't think it's an environment for briefings, demos, or other conversations."

Another respondent commented, "The Internet can help me do my job better in a world in which phone tag is a part of daily life. Simple questions can be answered quickly and painlessly. Also, I can turn to cyberspace for research." Journalists know that they can instantly reach an abundance of people and information online.

Journalists also value the convenience of using cyberspace. As one stated, "It's open 24 hours a day." An executive editor adds, "I can get nearly all of the information I need right at my desk by tapping into the right sources. If I need to, I can schedule an interview or even conduct one over the Internet. I also receive stories from freelancers and columnists over the Net. It's a significant time-saver and a genuine convenience."

Journalists who are into pain avoidance view cyberspace as a great communication tool. For one editor, cyberspace plays well into his daily routine because "I hate answering the phone and going to the library." For another, "It's easier to get information [online] than calling up a PR person who may not have a clue as to what you're looking for."

Others find that cyberspace takes the pain out of taking the pulse of the marketplace. Without too much effort, said one, "I can query or observe people who are spending their hard-earned money on these products."

Of course, not every journalist agrees wholeheartedly that cyberspace will make his or her professional life better. Some expressed skepticism about this because a significant number of companies and consumers have yet to go online; also, the quality of content posted by many companies that are online is poor, and it's difficult to find information online quickly.

Remarked one editor, "I think it's still more hype than anything else." Others share this feeling, although they still find some redeeming value to the medium. For example: "It's too time-consuming at present to get information, but it is a big help," commented one journalist. "Generally there's more junk and advertising than useful information. But there's no question the potential is there."

In the same vein, an editor stated that "At this point, I rely probably more on faxes than on e-mail for my job. That's because many companies aren't on the Internet yet." But one respondent warned companies not yet in cyberspace that, "as more people and information become available, those without Internet access are going to be sorely disadvantaged."

Journalists Don't Lurk

Some PR people think of journalists as illusive individuals who lurk in some mystical corner of cyberspace comparing notes, surveying the terrain for news, and recovering from a hard day at the office. If that place could only be found, PR pros could lay siege on journalists with press releases and company backgrounders that would guarantee their clients or companies "good ink."

Well, lay the misconception to rest. Most journalists who responded to our survey said that they don't have the time or inclination to *hang out* in cyberspace. But one journalist responded with an electronic grin, "if there was [a place where journalists hang out], I probably wouldn't tell you guys."

Journalists did tell us that when they are online to do more than send or read e-mail, they go to vendor sites or other specific places to pick up information relevant to a particular story.

Journalists Rely on E-Mail and Visits to Vendor Sites   Half of the journalists surveyed use e-mail to communicate with companies and each other. Nearly two-thirds also visit companies' online sites and participate in Internet newsgroups to pick up news information.

Many journalists look at e-mail as a convenience because "I don't have time to answer all the calls I get, but I usually have time to answer e-mail since I can do it at odd hours." One top editor: "E-mail is still the most effective tool [in cyberspace]. I think most Web sites could do better by the press."

Another editor concurred, saying, "I think that electronic communication is efficient and beneficial all around," though she worries that e-mail boxes may soon become as cluttered as some people's desks.

Others use e-mail to circumvent the PR "palace guard": "I use it as a way to communicate with engineers so I can get the real story instead of getting slimed by marketing speak of internal company PR," comments an editor.

One editor-in-chief uses e-mail to "send technical questions to corporate technical types instead of having to wait for PR people who never know the answer." This same editor stated that every PR person should have a personal e-mail address. Hope springs eternal, I guess.

They Make Selective Visits   Besides depending on e-mail, the journalists we surveyed visit companies' Web sites and forums and participate in newsgroups and listservs as well. Journalists surveyed also access online databases to get company background and product information. For example, Ziff-Davis's Computer Select, located on CompuServe's ZiffNet, is particularly popular with the computer press. Other databases are accessed for information about companies in different industries.

Journalists sometimes visit vendor sites to observe what customers are saying about companies' products, services, and so on. They spend time in companies' customer conferences and online forums, "which is where the rubber meets the road, and we can break down the marketing hype," said one journalist. Another adds, "I look for both praise and complaint about products. I am interested in how well companies respond to user inquiries, and I look for extra tidbits of information made available to users from vendors."

Several journalists commented that an advantage to communicating in cyberspace is that it's good for managing the 101 nitpicky details of gathering information without wasting time with telephone tag. "It can take some of the small obstacles out of the way, such as having a place online to get historical material or to post detailed technical questions and get answers," said a product reviews editor.

Once these details are taken care of, journalists will use e-mail to schedule face-to-face or telephone meetings. States one journalist about cyberspace: "There is only one thing that is CERTAIN—there will be some questions that cannot be answered without a dialogue with a representative from a vendor."

If You Build It—And Journalists Need It—They Will Come

We designed our survey already assuming that many journalists access companies' online areas to gather information. What we really wanted to learn was what *kind* of information is valuable to journalists.

Using a tactic that lawyers might call "leading the witness," we asked journalists if they were on deadline, would they visit a site online "if you were certain" of finding useful information. All but five people—not surprisingly—said "yes." But what my company found particularly useful, was that some of the people answering "yes" had a few interesting comments about "useful information."

Stated one journalist: "[this question] unfortunately implies the presence of truly useful information by vendors. It's hard to find useful stuff when companies are the providers of the information." Added another: "In general, it's slower than picking up the phone when I'm on a deadline. Technical difficulties, poorly written resources, and unanswered questions come up on the Internet."

Not everyone criticized the quality of information online, but more than a few indicated that finding valuable content is often a hit-and-miss proposition.

We wanted to find out straight from the horse's mouth what content was considered valuable information, so we asked journalists what would draw them to a company's online area.

We found that while journalists do appreciate the usual press releases and company backgrounders, they won't journey into cyberspace to get them because they tend to get them via snail mail and e-mail.

What *will* they go after? Many journalists indicated an interest in white papers, company business info, financial or marketing strategy outlines, and a detailed competitive analysis. FAQ sheets (Frequently Asked Questions) are also of interest. An afterthought from one respondent: "Oh, if the information were up to date, that would be a nice thing."

A significant number of journalists want industry and customer contacts—these crucial information sources seem to be harder to find the closer editors get to their deadlines. Some editors said that they'd like to get suggestions for newsgroups that they could join in order to get additional information and feedback about a company's industry or marketplace.

Companies can also help journalists by directing them to sources of independent assessments of companies' products, such as published articles or research reports from industry research firms not hired by the companies; you can help journalists by directing them to these services. You can also direct journalists to online databases, such as Computer Select, which list additional information about companies or industries (just be sure that your company is listed in these sources before directing journalists to them).

One editor felt "Policy statements on potentially controversial issues would be nice, but I doubt they'd be there." He's probably right.

Whatever you decide to put online for the press, consider this advice about content from an editor who's been online a few years: "It must be more than an electronic version of a press kit. It must prompt actual discussion and an exchange of information between two groups that are quite pressed for time: the people who make the technology and the people who evaluate and report on the technology."

Back to Basics

Posting the right information online is just half the battle in wooing the press—the passive half. The other half involves active communication with journalists, primarily through e-mail.

The journalists we surveyed addressed this issue with greater intensity and in greater detail than any other part of our survey. One editor-in-chief commented, "If a person has poor [press] communication skills in real space, then cyberspace won't help them."

As PR professionals begin to use cyberspace to interact with the press, journalists are finding that PR people still commit with incredible regularity the four cardinal sins of conventional press relations:

- They don't target their press contacts.

- They don't send the right information.

- They don't know enough about the product they promote.

- They e-mail journalists to ask "Did you get that release I sent?"

When we asked journalists to offer "tips for how PR people can use cyberspace to help rather than annoy" members of the fourth estate, much of their advice was directed toward the committing of these four "sins." An editor-in-chief warned that if PR professionals drag these faults into cyberspace, "bozo filters will become extremely popular." (A *bozo filter* is software that automatically deletes without reading e-mail that comes from someone the user doesn't care to communicate with.)

Target Contacts   As one journalist summed it up, "The rules are the same online as with conventional media relations: PR specialists need to understand both the needs of their clients and the specific characteristics of the publications they approach. Shotgunning e-mailed press releases (especially with long lists of cc:s to other publications), pitching inappropriate companies or stories, and generally using electronic media to throw out more information in the hope that it sticks will only hurt perceptions of clients, not help."

Another journalist commented, "Don't use it to send even more blanket releases than you do now. If I recognize an annoying sender's ID, it's awfully easy to hit that delete button."

"I prefer (but others do not) press releases by e-mail. However, it is easy to abuse this too," warned one journalist. "PR people who don't know who to mail things to will drive editors as crazy electronically as they now do on paper. We still get mass shotgun mailings, and mailings to obsolete people at obsolete addresses."

Commented another, "Vendor people usually send stuff to the wrong press people (the same fatal mistake PR people make with faxes, letters, and calls). For example, I'm editor-in-chief, but I DO NOT handle new product info or 95 percent of the other things a vendor wants to communicate to our publication. Because I have other priorities and duties, sending product info to me usually delays it by days and even a month, by the time I sort through and forward it to the appropriate person. So be sure you know *who* you should be contacting, rather than sending it off to the highest-ranking title you can come up with and hoping that person will do the rest of your job."

To reinforce the point, "I hate to get a release that shows up automatically on our 15 or so addresses. It's similar to the thoughtlessly released story that comes in four copies to every editor in the building, and we all throw them away. I don't like getting releases that have been compacted. I got one story in three files, all compacted into some file format that I had never heard of."

Some editors apparently feel that PR people not only need to target individual press contacts better but also do a better job at targeting publications. An editor at *Byte* magazine explained: "Try to understand my needs. For example, *Byte* is not really a product/news magazine. It's about technology, so I'm not that interested in new product announcements unless it's some new technology or new application of technology."

Once you've targeted the right contacts at appropriate publications, take heed of this editor's side note: "Make e-mail addresses known, in case I need to reach you quickly." Wouldn't it be a shame to reach the right people, but not give them a way to get back to you?

Send the Right Information   Much of the survey feedback that fell into this area stemmed from problems discussed in the preceding section. PR people who don't spend the time to carefully target their mailing lists are almost guaranteed to send the wrong information to at least a few journalists.

Said one editor: "Don't flood an editor's mailbox with a too-frequent stream of insignificant announcements." So think about it; a writer who covers new product announcements may have no use for your releases about financial achievements or newly hired executives.

Some of the suggestions we received did identify information that journalists prefer to receive by e-mail. For example, "If vendors set up Web sites, I would just as soon they let me know where they are, passively. When I want information, I'll ask for it."

This kind of advice usually prompts PR people to ask what they're supposed to do when they have important news that an editor may not know about. After all, a story could grow old waiting for an editor or writer to happen by and see it.

One journalist advised that, when you have something new or time-sensitive, "Make your e-mail information concise and accurate. Tell me what's out there, give me a precise location, and a sample of the content. There's too much going on to rely on blind luck." Another journalist wrote, "I don't want my e-mail box to be flooded with press releases I find worthless. I'd rather just get a quick note asking if I *want* more information and let me choose."

"Keep in mind who the target readers of the various pubs are and try as hard as possible to personalize the pitch for that pub. This saves time and ensures a better hit rate."

"Provide clear positioning statements about product strengths and core technologies. Pay attention to what we're writing and make comments on what, in your opinion, we're missing."

Know Your Product   Knowing your company's product means much more than just understanding how it works. To effectively present products to editors, PR folk also need to understand their product's role in the marketplace.

One editor commented at length about how market awareness will help PR people do a better job for the companies they represent.

"Generally, PR tends to make one big mistake, and that is thinking about their clients from the clients' perspective, instead of from the perspective of the recipient of the information. While this may keep the clients happy initially, the failure to explain your clients within the larger perspective or context that the public will perceive them can only lead to ineffective communication."

"Some thinking on the part of PR about why I should care about their message means that they have to think about where their clients' products or companies fit into the real world being described in my magazine. It ain't so much the fact itself that is interesting, but where the fact belongs with all the other facts."

Don't Ask: "Did You Get It?"   A number of respondents weighed in on our survey with straightforward advice about the habit PR people have of checking back to see if their materials were received. The overwhelming consensus: Don't do it!

One editor stated: "Send me e-mail and leave me alone. E-mail is a terrific method of communicating; why ruin it by annoying me with 'did you get my release?' questions?"

Another: "Send me e-mail. Trust that I got it. Don't call to follow up."

And finally, "Send info, then don't bug me about it." Everyone else who commented on the "question from hell" said pretty much the same thing.

There were a few other tips offered by journalists for PR people. For example, be sure to include your phone number with any e-mail that you send. Accompany any requests for copies of stories with a postal mailing address. And, "Each PR person should reply *promptly* and with alacrity to any e-mailed question from the press."

These points may seem like excerpts from PR 101, but don't take them lightly. I've been involved in PR for over ten years, and I still hear editors complaining about these same shortcomings in PR professionals. It seems you just can't teach some old dogs—or even some young ones—new tricks.

If you're interested in getting the entire survey report, titled "A Quest for Insight: PR in Cyberspace," it's free at our Web site:

http://webhead.com/success/report.html

Stop the (Online) Presses!

Magazines and newspapers of every size and interest have been tripping over each other in a headlong rush to get online. This can be good news (literally) for you in terms of gaining additional press coverage.

The publications currently online fall into two categories: those that reprint most of what you see in their newsstand copies, and those that transform their online editions into new publications, capitalizing on the unique formatting and reporting opportunities that cyberspace offers.

You'll find your best opportunities with the publications in the latter category, where you have the opportunity to help shape content and get coverage for your company as well. To get coverage in publications in the first category, your PR efforts must be successful at getting your company into the hard-copy editions.

Working the Circuit

The first order of business when dealing with the online pubs is determining which of your target magazines and newspapers have electronic editions and in which online areas they're located. The online services make it easy to cross-reference your press list by listing all the online pubs that they carry. On the Net, however, you'll have to search several Net directories to find out which pubs are online and where.

Of course, you can get this information by calling all the major pubs that you work with and asking them if they have online editions. But I often find this a rather painful process, especially with publications that have been online for only a few weeks. Few people you'll get on the phone at the workplaces of these latter-day cyber converts seem to know that the publication is even online, much less whom to contact with story ideas.

Once you've put your target list of online pubs together, the creative challenge begins. You need to visit these pubs online to determine how you can create special news events—panel discussions, user/company chat sessions, and so on—that fit into the electronic formats that the respective publications are developing. The key here is to create events that will draw large audiences of the publications' existing or potential readers.

For example, you might try working with a few of the pubs to create "virtual trade shows," with your company's information, photos, and graphics posted in online "booths." Or, industry-specific or special interest magazines might work with you to sponsor online conferences to discuss topics of interest to their particular readers.

Don't leave out adapting conventional PR tactics to the galaxies of the cyber realm; often these online pubs are receptive to ideas, for example, conducting online interviews with your executives, working with press releases to develop stories, or writing about creative ways in which customers are using your products.

In reality, practically any idea for online press coverage can be a winner. Just be creative, understand the publications' missions and audiences, and present your case well. It also pays to spend some time chatting with the online editors of these pubs to get a good feel for what can or can't work. And it definitely pays to integrate your online press efforts with your conventional press campaign.

When you get coverage in print publications like *The New York Times* and *Business Week*, increase the impact of these stories with real-time interviews and special events in the online areas of the same publications. Remember, step one: introduce your story in conventional media; step two: present it fully in cyberspace.

After developing your strategy for pursuing coverage in your target online pubs, spend a few minutes using the Net directories to scan for e-zines that might offer you press coverage potential. E-zines are electronic magazines designed exclusively as online publications. Many are written by individuals who see the Net as a low, low cost publishing vehicle.

Although many e-zines are written by people who are amateurs to the publishing business, quite a few are developing loyal online followings. If there are e-zines whose readers fall into your products' target markets, don't neglect to get coverage there, too. You can present the e-zines with the same story and event ideas that you created for the "traditional" online pubs.

Shaping Your Public Image—Online and Off

As I mentioned earlier in this chapter, everything you do to build a strong community around your online areas helps to create a positive public image for your company both online and off. When people leave cyberspace, they tell their real-world friends about the good, the bad, and the ugly that they see online. They also pass information to journalists they meet online, who use it to write stories for their print publications.

Two recent events demonstrate the far-reaching effect that cyberspace can have on a company's public image.

A Tale of Two Cyber Cities

Intel, the maker of Pentium and other PC chips, and Hewlett-Packard (HP), which makes computers, printers, and other computing products, each have an extensive Internet presence. In 1994, each company also had a relatively minor problem occur with one of its leading products. But the two companies dealt with their respective problems very differently—and this difference was evident in the results.

Intel's problem became a major national PR headache for that company, which generated volumes of negative press and cost a tremendous amount of money to rectify. HP's problem was deftly handled and became a PR feather in HP's cap.

Intel   In 1994, Intel's Pentium chip was the biggest and the coolest (according to the Intel PR machine) PC microprocessor to come down the pike. However, it turned out that the chip had a little problem doing a particular type of complex mathematical calculation. But the problem was so obscure that very few people would ever run into it.

Well, Murphy's Law kicked in, and one day while doing some calculations a researcher discovered the Pentium's problem. This person mentioned the problem to the people in a newsgroup to which he belonged, asking if anyone else had uncovered it. After a few days, during which several people commented to each other and to Intel about the problem, a minor buzz developed in cyberspace. Intel initially ignored the buzz, apparently seeing it as a trivial issue that would soon go away.

But as a few days passed, the buzz became a little more intense. Intel then issued a statement that downplayed the problem by telling people that they had nothing to worry about. Oops! Never trivialize people's problems in cyberspace, particularly when you're a well-known company with a prominent place in the public eye. What might appear to be a logical response to a minor problem elsewhere takes on the appearance of gross arrogance in this arena. And what's perceived as arrogance quickly breeds disgruntlement.

The cyber community's buzz of disgruntlement toward Intel became a steadily increasing roar of displeasure. This roar was picked up by a few members of the press, who started reporting Intel's problem in minor stories here and there. Then Intel's CEO, Andy Grove, issued a statement explaining the Pentium's problem in detail, telling customers that they had little to worry about, and indicating that Intel had no plan to replace the problem chip. Oops again—wrong response.

The steady roar then became a mighty cacophony of outrage. Flame throwers were everywhere in cyberspace. Unflattering Pentium jokes proliferated in e-mail boxes like rabbits. Then the press became fixated with the Pentium story, as it blossomed from filler material to front page headlines in computer *and* mainstream publications. Do you suppose these were the kinds of stories that gave Intel stockholders a warm and fuzzy feeling? I don't think so.

There was something particularly interesting and new about the press coverage of Intel's problem: rather than quoting Intel's people in many of their stories, journalists were quoting online users, Intel had assembled a sizable PR crisis management team to put an Intel spin on the news, but the press darted right around it to get unfiltered commentary from customers online.

Before the dust of the fiasco finally settled, Intel had to replace many more Pentium chips than it likely would have had the company taken the problem seriously and resolved it immediately (these chips cost a few hundred dollars each, so replacing them in mass must have been quite costly). What's more, the volume of negative press really injured Intel's image in the short term. While the company is now doing better than ever, I'm sure it would have preferred avoiding this embarrassing incident altogether.

HP   Around the same time that Intel was having its problem, Hewlett-Packard was dealing with its own potential customer crisis.

HP's problem centered around misfeeds occurring in one of the company's printer lines. In an effort to increase the type of media that users could print on (regular paper, transparencies, labels, and so on), HP had changed the rubber compound on the rollers that grip the paper and send it through the printer. The new compound caused the rollers to grip too much paper lint and consequently created misfeeds that jammed the printers.

When complaints from customers started to trickle in HP quickly investigated the situation and developed a solution for the problem. HP then began searching for owners of the problem printers in order to let them know about the solution—a difficult job since customers didn't have to register the products or be listed in an HP database. To meet that challenge, HP turned to its Web site, which became a key communication vehicle for getting the word out.

Because of the company's swift response and willingness to take public ownership of the problem, HP received significant praise from both customers and the press. E-mail such as this note started streaming in: "I was delighted to find that, not only did HP recognize the problem, but that a solution was being offered free of charge. Your Web site was instrumental in passing this information along. Much appreciated."

Granted, the press stories were fairly low key; CNN didn't interrupt its OJ trial coverage to break the news about HP's product fix. But minimal *good* news coverage is far better than major negative news. What's more, HP's online community became stronger and more supportive of the company than ever.

Steps for Keeping Your Company Image Clean

I can't overemphasize how important it is to study and understand the characteristics of the cyberspace environment. Though much is changing in the online world, some key principles still remain stable.

For example, you must constantly provide a high level of service and support online for your customers and for prospective customers as well. Because your business is online, cybersurfers expect it to meet certain high standards of proficiency and quality; if it doesn't, they will ignore its existence. When you do provide good service on a regular basis and customers come to expect it, don't repeat Intel's initial crisis strategy. If you do, your customers will publicly crucify you—and *then* they'll ignore your existence.

Maintain a high level of responsiveness to your online community, even when people aren't asking for service or support. Here's a story to illustrate my point: One weekend I was surfing through Compaq's site doing research for this book. I really liked its home page because of some fancy graphic elements that it had. On the following Monday, when I revisited the site to capture the home page on disk, the basic image was the same—but the fancy graphics were gone.

At 7:00 p.m., I sent an e-mail to the WebMaster asking about the graphics (I didn't mention that I needed them for a book). By 9:00 a.m. the next day, I had my answer. I was particularly impressed at this, not only because the response came faster than I expected, but also because I couldn't imagine that my question could have really been that important to someone who must receive dozens of e-mail messages a day.

On the same Monday night that I sent my e-mail message to Compaq's WebMaster, I also sent a question to Dun & Bradstreet's WebMaster asking about one of its subsidiaries and indicating that I wanted to do business with the subsidiary. To this day, I have not received a response from D&B to my question. Not a positive sign of responsiveness from a company that is a leading provider of information services, is it?

Another stable principle for doing business in cyberspace is that a single voice will always carry weight far beyond its measure. Ignore this phenomenon at your peril.

Of all the departments in your company that impact your presence in cyberspace, remember that your PR department or agency must play a primary role in shaping your public image. PR should be responsible for keeping your primary messages online consistent with what is being communicated through conventional channels, particularly during major press campaigns.

See that your PR team constantly monitors your online areas to spot any problems with customers, prospects, or the random visitors who wander into your areas from time to time. If any problems do occur, this team should nip them in the bud. More importantly, make your

PR team responsible for taking *proactive* measures to address anticipated problems, in much the same way that HP did with its printer problem.

Finally, see that your PR department has a plan for damage control, should you need it. The larger and more well-known your company, the more crucial it is to have such a plan before a crisis strikes. In cyberspace, *news* travels quickly; *bad news* travels almost instantly. (It's much harder to create a good fire-fighting plan when the hounds of hell are yapping at the gate.)

Enough said on that for now. Let's move on to research in cyberspace.

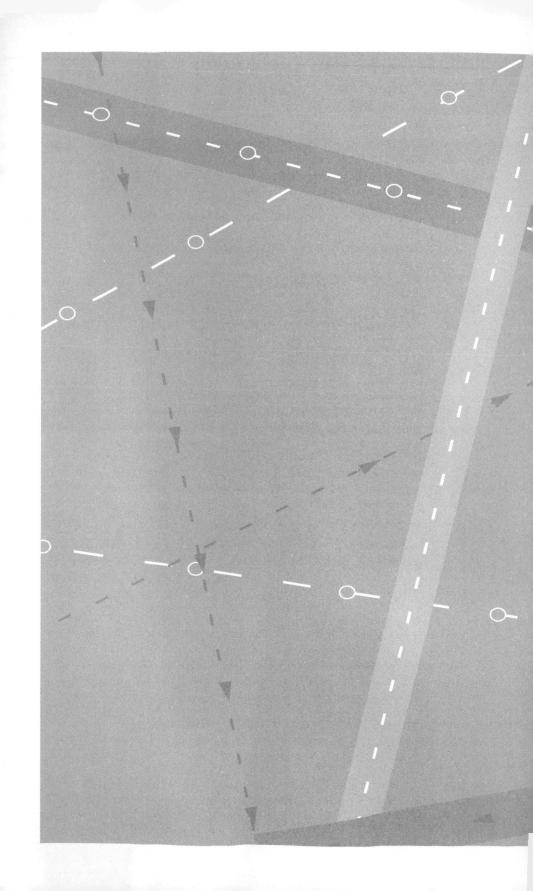

Chapter 13: Research in Cyberspace: Seek and Ye Shall Find

If there is ever a situation where you might die from too much of a good thing, doing research in cyberspace is it. The incredible wealth of data online can meet a variety of your business needs. But at the same time, the sheer volume of this information can overwhelm the people it's supposed to help.

And if the current amount of online information isn't enough to stagger the imagination, new information is being added to cyberspace with such intensity that you will practically need a small army to keep up with it.

This chapter offers tips and techniques for collecting information from this vast stockpile of data so that your marketing, service, product development, and other departments can use it to improve your business operations.

Ready-Made or Custom Designed

In cyberspace, research information comes in two forms: that which has already been collected and is available for you to pick up, and that which you collect directly from cybersurfers.

Of the information that is ready for access (called *secondary* information), some of this is categorized and packaged neatly for easy access, such as in research databases as well as information on the online services. Other info is cataloged so you can determine how to package it yourself to meet your particular needs (for example, from Farcast, the information service provider that I mentioned in Chapter 11).

However, for the time being, the bulk of information in cyberspace lies in poorly chartered waters. When you do find the source for the information, it's often a major undertaking to sort through all the information to find the specific data that you need.

For some research projects, such as competitive analysis, information that you need is not only hard to access, it's also "disguised." For example, if you market games, an area that is an entertainment site to most surfers (such as a newsgroup whose members talk about interactive games) can be a major source of information about your competitors' new products. Smart cybermarketing includes learning to recognize such disguises.

The form of research information that you collect directly from the people in cyberspace (called *primary* information) can be gathered through surveys that you conduct at your online areas or at other areas in cyberspace. You can also pick up this type of basic research by talking to people in chat rooms or through newsgroups and listservs.

In the next section, I focus on making your case for conducting online research. Then I discuss in detail some methods for doing both forms of research.

Despite the benefits of market research, in some organizations it is still difficult to sell top management on the concept of doing any kind of formal research, particularly since the costs of doing conventional research are so high. However, I believe that justifying the cost of online research is easy—because online research can be easier and less expensive than conventional research.

It Makes Sense to Get It Online

Why do research online? Well, to paraphrase an editor's comment from the preceding chapter, research is gathering information, and in cyberspace, there's a hell of a lot of information to be gathered.

So Much Information, So Little Time

You can best take advantage of the huge amount of information available online by understanding and effectively using the sources for finding it: information databases, Internet directories, BBSs, and popular online "hangouts."

Information Databases   One of the ways that you can obtain information for research is by scanning information databases such as Lexis/Nexus, the premier source for legal information. The online service Delphi offers access to over 400 databases; CompuServe offers access to a sizable number of databases, too. The number of databases you can access on the Internet is unknown, but you can bet it's a whole heck of a lot.

The particular value of online databases is that the information at each usually addresses a certain topic (such as law, medicine, or oceanography), which narrows down your search quite a bit. You can focus on your area of interest without wading through unrelated materials.

Managers of these databases file and categorize their information, and provide software search features that enable you to fine-tune your search to find just the information you need.

Many database providers charge you to search through their information, but this cost is often justified since it might take days of constant searching to otherwise find the same information. However, the cost of using databases such as Lexis/Nexus is expected to drop dramatically in the future because many databases on the Net are now offering searches free or dirt cheap.

Internet Directories   Another area of cyberspace that offers seemingly endless sources of research data are Internet directories. There are the top-tier directories, such as Yahoo, EINetwork, and Lycos, which have catalogued tens of thousands of sources of information on Web, gopher, and ftp servers. These directories even list some newsgroups.

If you access these top-tier directories and then do a keyword search on your topics of interest, you can find an amazing number of sources. But there's more.

Hundreds of smaller directories also list sources of information on the Net, and many of these directories focus on a specific topic, type of person, company, or such. For example, in one of my own searches, I discovered—and used—a directory that listed information of interest to people who manage computer systems at large corporations. The possibilities and direction of these searches really are nearly endless.

Here's a tip for you: When you start a research project, go to the top-tier directories and do a keyword search on the word *directory*, as well as on whatever other words fit the topic of your search. Yahoo, Lycos, et al. will then give you a comprehensive list of directories that you can scan to find specific directories to facilitate your research.

BBSs   In addition to using databases and Net directories, there are the gezillion BBSs throughout cyberspace. The upside of doing this is that many of these BBSs contain files of information that may be useful for a research project. Also, there may be people who frequent these BBSs who are great sources of additional information.

For example, a BBS for genetic researchers may include various document files on a particular subject that you can download. But while you're fishing around the BBS, you may also "bump into" a world-renowned geneticist who can offer additional insight into your project.

The downside of BBSs is that maps or directories to find them are few and far between. The only way to find out about many of them is through word of mouth or through the few magazines that may have partial directories of BBSs. *Computer Shopper* and *Open Access* are two pubs that regularly list BBSs and their phone numbers. Some BBSs advertise their existence, but not many of those that do are valuable research sources.

It's also getting easier every day to access information available online. Wading through this sea of information to find only the information you need is facilitated with Internet directories that are continually becoming more comprehensive, sophisticated, and easy to use. More and more BBSs are developing electronic gateways to the Net, which means that soon they should start to appear on Net directories—and thereby be easier to find.

Hangouts   And finally, in our hit parade of endless sources of research information are popular "hangouts" where millions of cybersurfers spend their online time: the myriad of forums, chat rooms, Web sites and every other nook and cranny in cyberspace. These people are your best sources for primary research data. They are available, opinionated, and generally quite agreeable to talk if you approach them in an appropriate way.

Newsgroups and listservs number in the thousands, with new ones popping up by the hour. They are great places for doing preliminary primary research among cybersurfers. There you can interact with a limited number of people and get their feedback on different topics, as well as scan through previous message threads to pick up additional comments.

The feedback that you obtain from these popular areas can be useful for designing surveys, online focus groups, and the like. When you want to conduct surveys of larger numbers of people, turn to the other online areas where people hang out—starting with your own forum or Web site.

Getting It Online Is Easy

If you've ever done conventional research, you know that the process of data collection is a righteous pain in the neck. You have to hire and manage data collectors, make hundreds of phone calls, mail thousands of questionnaires, and tabulate the data. These are the trials and tribulations that cause many companies to avoid research like the plague. But cyberspace eliminates a great deal of these hassles.

How? To begin with, if you have an in-house BBS, forums on the online services, or a Web site, you already have your data collectors in place. All you have to do now is design, post, and promote your surveys. Potential respondents will show up and complete them, and software programs will collect and tabulate the data automatically.

You can set up some of your surveys to collect data on an ongoing basis, so you can track changes in attitudes, buying habits, and so on over a long period of time. You can also change a survey by the month or by the day if you need to get feedback on different issues, promotions, product prices, and such. These kinds of changes are logistical nightmares in conventional research.

Data collection is also becoming easier with the continual refinement of the technology for *search agents* which are software programs that automatically find data based on search criteria that you input. Improvements in this technology will result not only in better information search capabilities, but also in the ability to have information delivered directly to your e-mail box.

Using a search agent, you could input the criteria that would, for example, let you find information on new real estate investment opportunities located in the state of Nevada and posted online since June 5th. The agent would take your criteria, do an automatic search of a particular area of cyberspace, find anything that matches the criteria, and bring it—or a description of its location—back to your computer. (Is this a great technology, or what?)

Some of the online services, such as CompuServe, Microsoft Network, and AT&T Interchange, have agent technology that search some or all of their respective services' information. Several companies are developing similar technology for the Net, and several of the information services companies on the Net have their own agent technology.

If you have good software developers who work for your company, or if you can afford to hire an outside software consultant, you can create your own search agents to meet your specific needs.

Besides being comparatively easy, conducting research online can also be inexpensive.

Much of the information on the Net is free. Your only cost is in the time you spend finding it and the connect-time charges of your Net provider or online service. Also, because so much info on the Net is free, many of the information providers who charge for database searches and other services are being forced to lower their prices.

Since surveys can be completed online in your online area and then automatically tabulated, the administrative costs of this particular type of research is limited to the time that you spend developing or revising your surveys. Even if you distribute surveys by e-mail or conduct online focus groups, the associated costs are still much lower than those incurred with similar conventional research tactics.

The Bottom-Line Benefit: Better Decision Making

You don't do everything that comes along just because it's free or easy, right? If you're going to do online research, you need to know that it will meet specific company objectives. Most companies find that their research objectives fall into one or more of these business areas: marketing, customer service, and product development.

Marketing To get the maximum benefit from online research for your company's marketing objectives, your marketing department should, first and foremost, use online research to measure the effectiveness of your online areas. If you do not regularly gather feedback from the people who visit your areas, it is likely that your site will stagnate and people will stop visiting. This feedback is what helps you make changes and enhancements that keep people interested in your area.

Your marketing staff can also evaluate actual or potential marketing campaigns, specific promotions, ads, and so forth by posting surveys or hosting online discussions. You can keep these activities either secret or open, depending on how much information you reveal during the research and whether or not you want your competitors to see what you're up to.

Your marketing department should set up procedures (which I discuss shortly) for gathering secondary information. These staff members should join appropriate newsgroups to keep their fingers on the pulse of changing market trends, industry developments, or competitors' activities. They should also use live chat and e-mail to talk to cybersurfers and get opinions that will help you analyze your secondary data.

Service To get the most from online research for your company's service area, your customer service department should use a combination of online surveys and discussions to measure customers' satisfaction with your products and services. Some of the feedback that you get from these tactics (along with your company's responses) can be posted directly to your online areas for other customers to read and learn from. This feedback will also serve as an early warning system to alert you to problems that can potentially become major traumas.

You can build questions into these surveys that will provide feedback on how to enhance the customer service and support that you currently provide, as well as how to develop new services for your customers.

Product Development Your product development team can collaborate with marketing and customer service to not only track market trends, but also to determine what new product features you should develop to address emerging trends. Collaboration doesn't have to be an internal function only. In the early days of the Net, for example, it was used heavily by researchers at different organizations who were working on the same project in noncompetitive ways.

Cyberspace is a good place to test new product ideas, as demonstrated by companies such as IBM and Computer Associates. These two large computer products companies have used private forums on CompuServe to manage what's called *beta testing* of their products. In beta tests, you distribute new products, which you are nearly finished building, to select customers who give feedback that helps you fine-tune the final development of the product—or realize that you need to go back to the drawing board.

If you can demonstrate your products online, as described in Chapter 11, beta testing online may be a valuable way for you to test drive new products before they are released to the entire market. It's better to find out ahead of time that your product has problems, or that you need to redesign its features, before that product is out there for the whole world to see. It's also cheaper to fix any problems before going into mass production of the product.

Making the Most of Secondary Research Information

To really make the most of information you'll find already collected online, you need to first know what you're looking for and then how to manage it.

Know What You Want and for Whom You Want It

Before you wade into the waters of cyberspace's endless secondary research info, understand that *planning* is key. You and the managers of various departments within your company (marketing, customer service, business operations, R&D) should sit down and determine what kind of information will be valuable to each respective department.

Marketing people, for example, typically need information that's different from that used by customer service or human resources. Another difference is that marketing often needs information delivered much faster than other departments do, because marketing opportunities can come and go within days. R&D, on the other hand, may require research data only near the beginning and the end of its projects.

While you're discussing who needs what, determine in which format the information is needed. Some may prefer tabulations of responses from survey reports with charts and diagrams, while others may want to see only specific comments and no numerical data at all. A few people may want just written summaries of data that are offered by particular sources and the locations of those sources.

Once you and your department managers have decided what kind of information they need, designate a person to be a research coordinator. This person will conduct online searches to find out if the data that everyone wants and needs is available.

This person should also create and distribute directories of all of the online information sources that he or she feels are appropriate at Web sites, newsgroups, databases, and so forth. Included with the directories' addresses for these sources should be directions for getting to each location, as well as directions for accessing the information once people get to it. Make sure that all departments know what info is available.

This research coordinator should keep abreast of online search tools and new online areas that may be of value to the company. More people can be assigned to work with the research coordinator as the need arises.

This is a good time to discuss an issue that seems to make a lot of executives skittish: whether to give Internet access to all or most of the employees in your organization. Some execs hesitate to give many of their employees online access because they worry that workers will fritter away the hours searching out X-rated Web sites and playing games. (Many of these same execs just ten years ago discouraged putting PCs on every desk for similar reasons.)

My advice? Give your people total access to the Net. Companies are discovering that employees who have free reign to roam cyberspace find valuable software, contacts, and information that help them or others do their jobs better.

Since there is more information online than an army of workers can track, the more pairs of eyes there are scoping the terrain for you, the better. The work time that may be lost by a few goof-offs will be offset by the increased productivity of those with a wider array of information at their fingertips.

While I do feel that it's advantageous to give everyone in your company access to cyberspace, I also think that you need some sort of centralized management of the information-gathering process. This will reduce duplication of efforts and ensure that data that is useful for several groups doesn't stay on just one person's desk.

Consider creating a data collection structure similar to that used by the investment banking firm JP Morgan. This company gives its employees total access to the Net. But the firm also has a research team that tracks online information about new developments in economic modeling, academic papers, newsgroup discussion, and anything else that can help their colleagues provide better financial advice to customers. The team posts the locations and brief descriptions of everything of merit in a central place so that employees can reference this listing before starting individual information searches.

Automate, Automate, Automate

Once you begin to actually uncover information sources, consider automating every part of the data collection process that you can. There is so much information online—and it changes at such incredible speed—that the only way to ensure that your organization doesn't get swamped with information overload is through automation.

Software search agents, whether custom designed or "off the shelf" from software vendors, should be the backbone of your automation efforts. Establish a schedule of how often you and others need particular information, and then schedule your agents accordingly to pick up this data.

Ideally, your agents should deliver the information to a list of appropriate people. However, you may find that you need a second software package, such as Lotus Notes, to take information from the software agent to individuals' computers via e-mail. If this is impractical for your company, then have the agents deliver information to a commonly accessible location.

When you subscribe to information providers (again, Farcast is a good example), try to work with those that have search agents that filter out information according to your needs and then deliver it automatically to your e-mail doorstep. Microsoft Network, CompuServe, and AT&T Interchange all have search agents that are flexible enough to meet a variety of needs.

As new technology for managing life in cyberspace comes to market, it should become easier to automate the data-retrieval process.

A Finger on the Pulse: Conducting Primary Research

The central avenue for collecting primary research information will be your own forums, newsgroups, BBSs, and other online areas. Here, you have complete control over the process of designing and administrating data collection tools such as surveys and focus groups.

Another advantage of using your own sites for data collection is that you can determine when and for how long to conduct research, and you can change your procedures whenever necessary. For example, CUC International, which has multiple product promotions running simultaneously, may create new surveys every week in different sections of their online areas.

It's possible to use sites managed by other organizations to post and distribute surveys, too, or to use listservs and newsgroups that seem to reach the audience that you want to poll. However, I think the lack of control from using these avenues would create problems that would outweigh any benefits that you might receive.

Survey Design Guidelines

Because Gale Grant, of the Net service provider Open Market, has considerable experience developing systems for gathering cybersurfers' feedback, I asked her what some design issues are that people should be aware of.

Grant answered: "People will not answer surveys that they don't find interesting or beneficial to them. Questions that ask 'How much money are you planning to spend?' or 'When do you plan to purchase?' are not very popular. However, people do respond to questions that ask for their opinions about existing products or services, or ask them to input suggestions. It also helps to tempt them with prizes."

She continues, "You have to be up front with people and tell them how their information will be used, or if you will release a report of the survey results. If you tell people after the survey how the company responded to their input, even if you disagree with their suggestions, those whose ideas you don't use will not get upset and feel they were ignored."

When we develop surveys for clients at Successful Marketing Strategies, the surveys usually include questions such as "How many people are at your company?" and "Are you the primary decision maker?" We carefully work these questions into questionnaires that ask people to contribute information that will help our respective clients to create future content.

For example, the question "Are you the primary decision maker?" would be couched in a question that asks "To help us develop content that addresses your specific needs, what is your role within your organization?" We would provide multiple-choice answers, with one of the answers being "primary decision maker." Coming up with the appropriate phraseology for such questions does require a little extra work, but the right questions will generate more useful responses.

Another guideline is that, unless you have a fabulous prize to offer for completing a survey, don't make the survey too long. Six to ten questions should be the limit. You can, of course, break up a long survey and distribute sections throughout your online area.

Some companies turn surveys into games, such as a scavenger hunt, which are much more enticing than a regular questionnaire. Games allow you to scatter questions throughout your areas, taking the tedium out of answering one question after another. Scavenger hunts are also good because they get people to look at more of your content while they hunt for hidden items and clues.

Other companies, such as Hewlett-Packard, use surveys as a "key" that allows people to access certain sections of a site's content. If you use this approach, though, be certain that the information that people access justifies the time required to complete the survey. For example, HP uses a questionnaire in one of its sections that has valuable tech notes that engineers who use HP products are very interested in receiving.

If your newsgroups and listservs have a large following, you can use them to distribute surveys. You can also send surveys to your database of e-mail addresses—*if* you warn people about potential surveys before they give you their e-mail addresses. Unsolicited surveys, like unsolicited e-mail in general, tend to irritate people a lot.

To summarize: Ask the right questions, keep the surveys short and entertaining, and offer a bribe of some sort when practical and affordable.

Data Tabulation

As with collecting secondary research, you want to automate collection of primary data as much as possible. If you post surveys in your online areas, this is often easy. On Web sites and BBSs, you can develop a system that does a running tabulation of data as people complete your surveys. At any time, you will then have a tally of results as of that moment.

You can also transfer these tabulations into a database program to do complex analysis of the survey results. This option makes sense if it's important for your company to have detailed statistical data. But if all you want is a general idea of what people think about your products, or you just want to collect people's comments, you can forego the detailed analysis.

For administering and tabulating surveys from your sites on the online services, you must make arrangements with each respective service to develop the software that sits on their computers and collects responses. This information is then given to you so that you can transfer it into a software program that does your tabulation and analysis.

If you distribute surveys via newsgroups, listservs, or regular e-mail, this data collection can be the most difficult to tabulate. The biggest hurdle is finding a way to automatically transfer survey responses to data tabulation and analysis software—a challenge that I leave to the software geniuses of the world. I prefer to administer these beasts from an online area whenever possible.

You're now familiar with the basics of online research. To stay abreast of how new technology will help research in cyberspace become a more sane process, check in regularly at this book's Web site. Next take a look at providing service and support online.

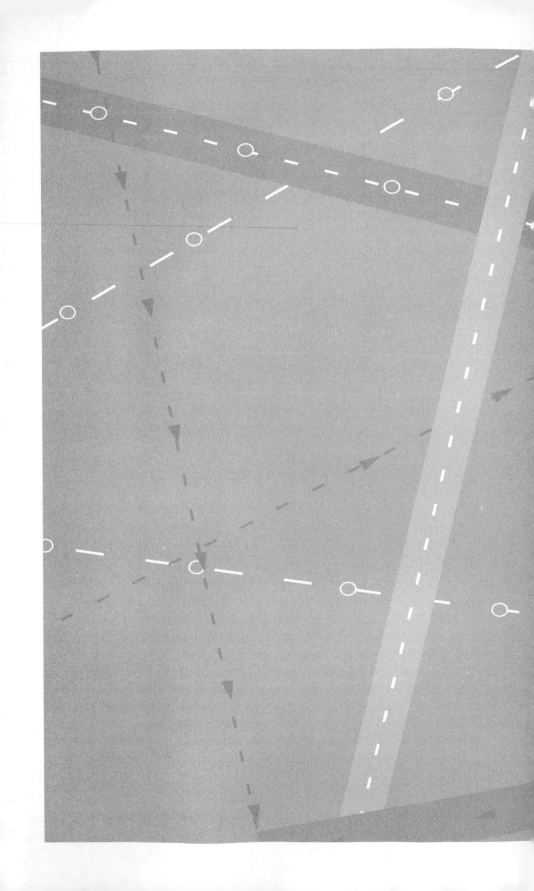

Chapter 14: Service and Support: You Can Never Give Too Much

Customer service and support will be the cornerstone of business success through the rest of the 1990s and beyond. The more personalized the service and support, the more successful a company will be.

As I mentioned in Chapter 8 when talking about brand loyalty, consumers want to be dealt with as individuals and not as members of a faceless herd. They feel particularly strongly about this when it comes to receiving service. If you make customers feel special during the sales process—when you're trying to get their money—you had better make them feel special when they have a problem, big or small.

Cyberspace gives you many opportunities to provide service that, if not always personalized, is at least quick, efficient, and relatively hassle-free. Even though most customers prefer to speak on the phone or in person with a living, breathing soul, going online is often better for them than being placed on terminal hold and listening to bad elevator music.

Cyberspace gives you the added advantage of allowing you to use the same medium to support your resellers, suppliers, and others with whom you do business, as well as your internal staff. In many cases, you can use the same content (with minor modifications) to support all of these groups and customers.

One of the challenges that you may face with providing online service and support is getting the people with whom you do business to go online. You may find that customers, suppliers, and so on have neither the technical equipment, the expertise, or the inclination to access your online areas. Resolving any one of these issues may require a lot of time or money on your part. How will you justify the effort and cost?

First, determine how much money each customer will spend over the course of two or three years. If you have customers such as midsize to large organizations that net you $50,000 or more a year in sales, doesn't it make sense to give these customers a PC, a modem, and a direct link to your online area?

Second, determine how much time and money you can save by supporting people online. You could do this by using the Lotus model, which says that ten people can be supported online in the time it takes to support one by phone—but I like to be conservative. So calculate how much time you spend on phone support currently and then reduce that by number by 50 percent. Do these savings justify the effort of moving these people online?

The bottom line here is that each customer and business relationship should be viewed as an investment that pays bigger dividends the more you nurture that relationship. Using cyberspace for service and support is one way to both nurture these relationships and run your support operations more cost effectively.

In this chapter, I give you specific ideas for providing top-level support online.

With the cost savings that you will realize, I do not suggest that you cut personnel. The goals instead should be to reallocate your resources so that you are able to provide more personalized services when the need arises, and to service more people as the company grows without adding support personnel.

Keeping Customers Satisfied

To keep your customers satisfied with your online service and support, you first have to get them online and then you have to make it worthwhile for them to stay. You also must deal with the ticklish issue of whether to charge customers for online service and support.

First, Get Them There

The first group of customers that you want to entice into using your online areas are those who are already online. They have the technology in place to get to you, and they should be comfortable using it. They just need to know you're online.

Put information about your online support *everywhere*. All of your ads, promotional materials, and product instruction manuals should have your forum or Internet address prominently displayed. Wherever you have the space, explain all the benefits of getting service online: no waiting, 24-hour availability, the sense of community spirit.

Turn your customer service staff, salespeople, and telephone operators into vigorous champions of your online service. Have them tell customers and prospects alike at every opportunity about the advantages of online support. Amway, for example, has its telephone operators tell every distributor who calls in for service about the company's online forum and give instructions on how to get there.

You might also consider offering customers special service packages that are favorably priced for those who get support online. For example, if you offer a two-year warranty on your products, offer a third year for free but limit it to online service. Another option is to run promotions, such as special drawings, for people who access your online support.

With a few good ideas, you should be able to bring those of your customers who are already online to your areas. But what about those who aren't yet online? This is where you have to weigh the costs versus the benefits to determine what makes sense.

You may want to create a separate promotional piece for people who aren't online that sells them on the benefits of getting service online. This piece should also describe the additional benefits of being a cybersurfer.

Because going online is an added expense, try to work out special promotions with the online services so that your customers get free online time or other bonuses if they sign up. You can add to the bonuses by offering "frequent user" points for accessing online support, and then these points could be exchanged for free time online.

Some companies, including Dell Computers and Marty Rood's dealerNet, give their customers free Internet Web browsers on software disks with the respective companies' names on the labels. You could do something similar, with the browser configured so that the first place that people would go would be to your Web site's customer support area.

However, be warned that a hefty price tag goes along with this Web browser promotion. Even though the developers of browsers generally let users download them for free, they do charge companies to private-label them. I've heard six-digit figures tossed out as companies' costs for private labeling.

It might be cheaper to work out a promotion with a Net provider to bring your customers online for a special rate. If you're targeting customers who aren't online, this definitely makes more sense than the free browsers because there's no value in giving away Web browsers to people who don't have Net access.

Another option for getting organizations online that will buy a lot of products from you is to include the PC, modem, et al. 226226as part of a service contract. And if you don't want to hassle with providing customers with access to online services or the Net, you can set up an internal BBS that customers can access instead.

So You Got 'Em Online. Now What?

After you've gone to all this trouble to get your customers to your support areas, don't disappoint them. Give them tons of information.

FAQs   Start with the Frequently Asked Questions (FAQs). All of the questions that people ask your support people on the phone, as well as any that you can anticipate, should be in a FAQ section in your online area. It's okay if you have dozens or even hundreds of FAQs, as long as they're laid out in a logical format and are easy to navigate.

If you're worried about cluttering up your main online areas with FAQs, keep only the newest FAQs in your support areas and archive the older ones on a seldom-used area such as an ftp server or BBS. A handy index in the support area can direct customers to these archived files.

E-mail Bulletin Board   You should also provide an e-mail bulletin board where people can post questions and answers. This will take more of the support load off of you, because customers can use it to communicate with and help each other. In fact, many people now expect this feature as a standard part of any online area that provides customer support, particularly the sites of computer products companies.

If you're worried about having problems exposed on this bulletin board that you'd rather keep under wraps, limit postings to general service questions such as "when will the new XYZ widget be in the stores?" You can require that people with serious problems send their questions in private e-mail. However, this kind of restriction may turn people off, as well as limit some of the value of being online.

Be sure you have the staff and structure necessary to respond to messages within 24–48 hours. People might tolerate longer waits for answers to general questions—for a little while, at least—but not for service or support problems.

Complement your message boards with an interactive, problem-solving database that lets customers solve their own problems. These databases are similar to, but much more inviting than, many companies' automatic telephone support systems whose electronic voices prompt you to "Press 1 if you have this problem; press 2 if you have that problem."

Though they take some effort to develop, these databases are great because they empower customers by allowing them to take control of the support process and not have to wait for e-mail responses.

Spec Sheets and Tech Notes   Post all of your product spec sheets and tech notes. *Tech notes* are documents that focus on particular aspects of a product or its use that are not covered in the instruction manual; for example, if you manufacture farm equipment, you might have a two-page tech note that describes ways to use the optional wheat cutter.

Posting spec sheets and tech notes makes sense particularly with mechanical, technical, and other complex products, because manuals for these products can include only limited information due to size constraints. Tech notes can fill in the gaps that manuals leave, as well as elaborate on certain product features. Some companies post literally thousands of tech notes.

Tech notes are also beneficial because people tend not to read manuals. However, they are inclined to read information about particular product features that either pique their interest or address an immediate need.

If you sell furniture, clothing, or other durable goods, the equivalent to tech notes for your product might be tips on how to repair rips, prevent undue wear and tear, restore older products to look like new, or other advice that enhances the use of your product. Companies with other types of products and services need to determine whether or not tech notes are useful in their circumstances.

Stories and Background Information   You might also post stories on your support areas that tell how customers are solving particular problems or enhancing your products in order to get more value from them. Doing this will build interest from customers, because people love to talk about themselves. It will also contribute to the feeling of community that you want to have in your area.

If you create extensive product background materials as part of your market education effort (see Chapter 10), either include this information in your support section or have links from the support section to this content. Also include reprints or links to any articles that favorably critique your products.

Turn Online Support into a Revenue Stream

The question of whether to try to turn your online support into a revenue stream is complex.

On the one hand, it's nice to charge for providing service and support, because these are business operations that cost you money. Even if you look at these operational expenses as a necessary cost of doing business, you can still use any income generated from them for investment into expanding services, giving raises to your support staff, or spending on R&D or some other area.

On the other hand, charging for support runs counter to the current culture of cyberspace. It could also defeat the purpose of online support by causing some people to call your 800 number rather than pay a fee to get support online. What's more, developing systems to monitor and charge people on some of the online services and the Net would likely be a time-consuming effort.

If you do decide that you want try to generate revenue from your online support areas, there are a few options for doing this. For example, the online services offer companies a revenue-sharing plan. Here's how it works: You collect a percentage of the hourly usage fee that the online service charges each person who visits your area. Percentages range from 10 percent to 15 percent. You negotiate actual amounts with the respective services.

You can factor these fees into your customer support revenue. While the payments may seem small in many cases, it's still more than you earn from telephone support.

MSN and some of the other services will help you set up a special section within your forum for customer support and let you charge premium rates for it. You can let anyone enter this area and have the premium charged to that person's bill by the online services, or you can restrict access to customers who pay you a fee in advance for a special password.

Another option is to have a general service and support contract between you and your customers that includes special pricing for online support provided through your BBS or Internet sites. In this case, your company can keep all of the revenues that it collects.

You can even have different levels of pricing for online support, such as general support for free, and "platinum" support for your key customers for which they would pay a monthly or annual fee. However, doing this creates administrative complications such as additional book-keeping, distributing and tracking passwords, renewals, and so on.

If you do charge customers for online support, you must face the biggest bugaboo of all—determining how much to charge. There is no pricing model to reference, and no wrong or right price; you will just have to experiment. Or perhaps you can be content with the cost savings of online support over telephone support and spare yourself the hassles of charging customers for support at all.

Helping the Hands That Help You

If you want to reap the full benefits of cyberspace as a service and support vehicle, you must broaden your focus beyond just customers to include resellers, suppliers, and others with whom you do business.

Provide increased support to dealers and distributors, and you will be rewarded with increased sales. The tighter relationship that can develop in cyberspace between your company and its suppliers will result in better service from suppliers—which, in turn improves your business operations.

If your business relies on third-party organizations to provide customers with add-on items or services such as training for your products, supporting these organizations online can help them be more effective. This increases customer loyalty to your company, since successful third-party products and services increase the use of your products.

Greasing the Third Wheel

On the dating scene, a third person's presence—the infamous *third wheel*—can intrude on the development of a relationship. In business relationships between companies and customers, the opposite is often true. You can use online service and support to make those third wheels valuable assets.

Dealers and Distributors   For your dealers and distributors, set up an online area that offers product training materials, profiles of your typical customers, and tips on how to effectively sell to them. Cyberspace is also an ideal place for distributing information that changes rapidly, such as pricing, product availability, special promotions, and so on.

Tandem Computers, after trying to keep its thousands of resellers up to date first with printed material and later with info on CD-ROMs, found that a Web site was the only way to keep resellers current with diverse, complex, and constantly changing product information. If you do this with a Web site—or a BBS or another area of cyberspace, for that matter—be sure to keep this area restricted to resellers only.

You can also give resellers your technical support materials and FAQs, which can help them to resolve problems with customers who return for service to the place where they physically bought the product. Rather than have customers get irritated by dealers who push them off on you, give dealers the capability to resolve problems as soon as customers call or bring them in.

When designing support for resellers, keep in mind that these people have limited time to spend at your site because they are selling products from many vendors. Resellers also tend to have high turnover among salespeople. So make your support materials easy to understand and use: The more interactive your content, the better. That way, dealers' personnel can then work on it on their own time, at their own pace, and without structured supervision.

Suppliers   For each supplier that provides your company with products and services, the online content required may be different. For suppliers of products that you order on a frequent basis, such as parts for equipment that you manufacture, an online tracking and ordering system can remove some of the stress from your internal staff.

With a system like this, suppliers will be alerted when you need something and can then deliver it without waiting for a paper-bound bureaucracy to go through its ritual. You may have to create a software solution to manage this particular task.

If your suppliers provide services to your company, your online support for them may be as simple as e-mail links that let your staff and theirs communicate more effectively. Some service providers may need to have access to financial, customer, marketing, or other information from your various departments. Be sure to keep all such content on private sections of your online areas.

JP Morgan requires its software suppliers to get Internet access so the company can have services and software upgrades delivered to it much faster and more efficiently. In a similar vein, if you constantly find yourself waiting for faxes and FedEx from suppliers, seriously consider building online connections between your staff and theirs.

Third-Party Vendors   The content that you develop for organizations that provide third-party products and services to your customers will be similar to that for resellers. Take a look at an example from the bicycle industry.

Rock Shox is a company that makes shock absorbers for mountain bikes. If your company makes mountain bikes, Rock Shox is an important third-party vendor for you because its products make your bikes easier to ride. Your company would in turn be important to Rock Shox, because the more bikes you sell, the more shock absorbers Rock Shox would potentially sell, too.

Your online support area for Rock Shox could include company background info, specs sheets and tech notes, tips on how to sell their products to your customers, price lists, advance notices on special promotions, and so forth. You could post any information that would help a third party to better understand your products and make them more eager to work with you.

Probably the most important online support that you could provide for Rock Shox, from its perspective, would be having information in your general online areas to tell everyone about Rock Shox products. (Computer companies, by the way, are one group in cyberspace that tend to have extensive third-party product information in their online areas.)

You can apply the content ideas in the Rock Shox example to supporting just about any third-party vendors, whether they market products or services.

After expanding the view of service and support to include resellers, suppliers, and third-party vendors, consider one more important group that fits into this picture—your company personnel.

Support within These Castle Walls

With your content in place to support those that you do business with in the outside world, its time to take a look within your company. The content you've developed may prove very helpful internally to your company, too.

Sales

Your sales team can use the same general product information, spec sheets, and tech notes that you develop for customers and others as part of your team's product training section. The selling tips, customer profiles, and other content developed for resellers can be useful to your salespeople as well. Of course, you may want to supplement this with traditional sales training materials to help sales people brush up on their basic sales skills.

Develop and post sales presentation materials that salespeople can download before visiting prospects. These can include charts, graphs, customer testimonials, and such.

Also consider posting portions of a sales presentation, along with company background info, on a BBS that your people can access via laptop computer and modem, from a prospect's site. Although this material could be shown from a person's laptop alone, doing a live link to the home office will impress upon prospects that you're an innovative and leading-edge company.

Marketing, Advertising, and PR

The same training and support materials that you post for salespeople are valuable for anyone who markets your product, including ad or PR agencies that you may retain. You can supplement this information with market positioning papers for each product, marketing strategy guides, and any other documents that will help this staff achieve its marketing goals.

Besides training and background materials, the most valuable support data that you can give marketing people is the resource and general market information that you can retrieve from the Net and online services. With the preceding chapter as a guide, you can create systems that will funnel appropriate news and other information directly from cyberspace to staff members' desks.

Field Staff

If you have staff working from remote sites or branch offices, or road warriors such as traveling sales or tech support people, you can use cyberspace as an ideal way to support them with content pertaining to their specific jobs as well as general company info.

Cyberspace is often a more convenient, cost effective, and efficient means of communication than mailing, faxing, or even phoning information, particularly to people in foreign countries and different time zones. You can also give these people online training rather than sending trainers out to them in the field, or disrupting field operations by bringing these staff people to the home office.

Human Resources

You can use your online areas to support the efforts of your human resources department to communicate with people both outside and within your company.

For example, HR can post job descriptions and general company recruiting information that can potentially reach more qualified job candidates than classified ads in local or national publications. If your company is really aggressive, you can try to arrange links to your HR's content from the Net sites of the colleges that produce the kind of graduates that your company seeks.

JP Morgan and Schlumberger Ltd., a $6.7 billion maker of oil drilling equipment and electronics, are two companies whose online sites' aggressive online employee recruiting efforts merit close evaluation by your HR managers.

Your online areas can also be effective distribution points for the slew of materials that HR must provide for your employees. New employee orientation materials, company policies and guidelines, career advancement opportunities, and the plethora of government regulations companies must make available to employees.

Building the Ties That Bind

There are a number of ways to use your online areas to foster better internal communication and build closer ties and camaraderie among the troops.

For example, you can create a company events message board that will serve a dual purpose of building ties and eliminating the kinds of personal e-mail that can bog down your computer network (announcements about softball games, bridal showers, garage sales, and so forth). Better still, create a company news center to announce promotions, sales performance, events, and other news that make people feel good about the place where they work.

It may be valuable to have an internal "newsgroup" for discussing issues and company developments. Of course, you don't want this to become an electronic gripe session; the purpose would be to provide a place where employees could contribute ideas and observations to improve company operations. Since this would be an open area for everyone within the company to read, employees should feel comfortable that others won't steal credit for the ideas that they post there.

The more you use your online areas to foster vigorous conversations and exchanges of ideas among employees within and between departments, the more cohesive your company should become. And if you create a similar online dialog between management and employees, your company should have a clearer focus as it pursues its goals in the marketplace.

Having covered in detail the seven areas of cybermarketing tactics, let's see how these tactics can be worked together with your cybermarketing strategy to form one comprehensive plan.

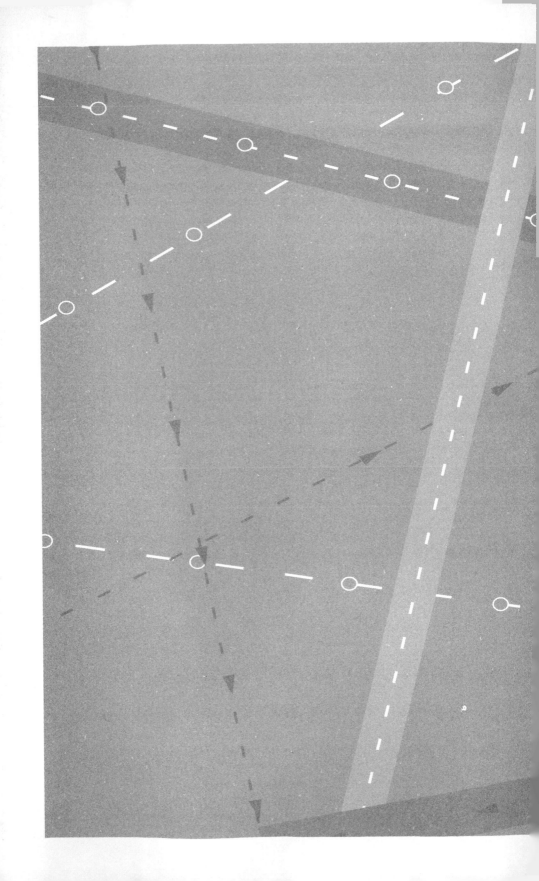

Chapter 15: The Written Word: Your Cybermarketing Plan

Now that you've learned about adapting to the people and the environment of cyberspace, developing a four-dimensional cybermarketing strategy, and working with a seven-point framework for creating tactics, it's time to create a written cybermarketing plan.

Your written cybermarketing plan will be more structured than the list of ideas generated from your brainstorming session, which I talked about in Chapter 7. This plan will pull together all the pieces of your campaign: strategy, tactics, resource issues, timelines, and so on. Its a document that will serve as your blueprint for a campaign that produces the results you want.

Lack of a plan in any marketing area often results in floundering and resource squandering. People are often too busy either trying to get a product out the door or putting out fires of one sort or another to devote enough time to planning. Planning is especially tricky in cyberspace, where things are changing so rapidly that it's hard to put a plan into place before your main marketing vehicle changes again.

This chapter shows you how to quickly develop an initial cybermarketing plan. This plan will not cover everything from soup to nuts, but it will be useful until you can write a more comprehensive plan. Just keep in mind that this has to be flexible so you can modify it as developments in cyberspace—and your company—change.

Get a New Plan, Stan

When you begin to devise your cybermarketing plan, you'll focus on three areas: your objectives, the best places in cyberspace for reaching those objectives, and the appropriate tactics to use.

Objectives

Begin by defining your strategic objectives; that is, determine what you want to do online.

For example, do you want to market to existing customers, prospects, or both? Do you want to convince people to order your product or access service and support online, or do you intend to distribute information that directs people to order through conventional means, such as the telephone or the mail?

Refer to the four-dimensional strategy discussion in Chapter 5 to answer these and other questions, and then make any necessary revisions to the cybermarketing mission statement discussed in Chapter 7.

Place this statement in the first section of your cybermarketing plan, titled "Objectives."

Besides your primary mission statement, you may have secondary objectives to put in this section. These can include such aims as using your presence in cyberspace to manage investor relations, creating the backbone of a communication network between national and international branch offices, or recruiting new employees.

Your objectives will dictate which places in cyberspace you'll use for cybermarketing and which specific tactics you'll employ.

Target Areas in Cyberspace

Once you've decided what you want cybermarketing to achieve for your company, you're ready to determine which areas of cyberspace will enable you to reach those objectives. Title the next section of your plan "Target Areas in Cyberspace," and fill it out with answers to questions like the following ones.

Are you going to use a bulletin board system (BBS) to store and distribute content or to send information to other BBSs? Does it make sense to use the commercial online services such as America Online or CompuServe?

If you're going to use the Internet, will you focus only on the Web, or will you store content on gopher and ftp sites as well? Will you use newsgroups and listservs to proactively distribute information?

The answers to these questions will be dictated in part by demographics (which places in cyberspace your customers or prospects are most likely to visit) and by how many staff people you can muster to manage and maintain your online areas. Where you set up shop in cyberspace will also be affected by fast and furious changes in the online services.

Tactics

Now bring out the list of ideas generated from your brainstorming session (discussed in Chapter 7) and possibly conduct another session or two. Then weed out the weak ideas and put those that seem to be most practical in the third section of your plan: "Tactics." (Keep the other ideas in a binder or computer file that you can put your hands on quickly should you need it. You can never have too many ideas for backup as you start your cybermarketing campaign.)

Subdivide your "Tactics" section into seven points: the Big 7 of cybermarketing, which I covered in Chapters 8 through 14. This makes for a neat and logical presentation that's easy for everyone on your team to follow.

Building Brand Awareness and Loyalty   The first section under "Tactics" is for the tactics that will help you build a community of customers who are loyal to your product (or *brand*). Besides addressing your customers, these tactics will inform as many other cybersurfers as possible about what your product and company have to offer. Some of these people may not be customers today, but who knows about tomorrow.

Your brand marketing tactics may consist entirely of promotions and creative sponsorships, but they can also include aggressive hyperlinking of your Internet information with other sites and seeding BBSs with product information.

Direct Response Marketing   Next in your plan comes direct response marketing. Unlike the long-term impact of helping to build brand awareness or loyalty, direct response tactics serve to induce people to take a specific action—and, preferably, right now (buy a product, pick up literature, and so on).

If yours is a new company with immediate cash-flow needs, you may be more inclined toward "buy one, get one free" offers or giveaways that induce swift action. As the number of companies online increases, even established firms with loyal customers may have a greater need for direct response promotions to help them rise above the increasing marketing noise.

Market Education   Tactics in your market education section go beyond making people aware of your brand; they include giving customers and prospects an in-depth understanding of your product or service, your company, or your industry. Many people are more likely to buy a product when they fully understand how it (or the company behind it) works.

Some of the tactics that you include in this section—and much of the content developed to support them—may also be useful in areas such as public relations or service and support. Keep in mind the principle that a speaker at a panel discussion on electronic commerce told the audience: Content, once developed, can easily be sliced, diced, and repackaged for different venues and additional purposes beyond that for which it was originally designed. Makes sense to me.

Product Demonstration and Distribution   While market education is an effective way to build people's comfort levels so they'll be more inclined to buy your products or services, one of the best ways to educate prospects about products or services is to demonstrate them. You will derive even greater benefits from this tactic if your prospects are able to demonstrate your products or services themselves.

Because the nature of some companies' products or services will make online demonstrations difficult—for example, those of oil rig manufacturers or morticians—this portion of your cybermarketing plan may go through the most changes. Be prepared for a good bit of trial and error as you pursue these tactics.

In this section of your plan, note how your company will keep current with new technologies in cyberspace. As these technologies evolve, especially in the areas of audio and visual presentations, your options for demonstrating products will increase. For example, for real estate professionals, the ability to create 3-D Web sites can significantly enhance the capabilities for "demonstrating" properties.

Public Relations   Public relations are the activities you engage in with the press in order to produce coverage that shapes how the public views your company and products. PR also includes activities that you engage in directly with the public to get press coverage that shapes your public image. When filling out this section of your plan, keep in mind that cyberspace adds new dimensions to the age-old business practice of public relations.

It is difficult to make online PR tactics effective unless they are integrated with traditional press relationship-building tools such as press tours, press releases, and wire services. For that reason, coordinate this section of your plan with whatever plan your PR department or agency has already developed.

If you do work with an agency, this part of your plan should detail how the agency personnel will work together with whoever manages your online areas in order to keep content and online projects in sync with the agency's day-to-day activities. It would be counterproductive to communicate two different messages to the press or the public.

Research   When considering tactics to include in the research section of your plan, don't be tempted to sell this area short; one of the most overlooked benefits of cyberspace is its research potential. Feedback can make the biggest difference in your company's profitability. This feedback can come from customers, the market in general, others in the industry, and even your competitors. Cyberspace can deliver more feedback than you know what to do with.

Regardless of the tactics that you decide to pursue in this area, explore how software tools can help you make research tasks more manageable and less expensive. Having these tools (or the people who can develop them) at your disposal may dictate how aggressively you can pursue particular research activities.

Since things change rapidly in cyberspace—including demographics, as more people come online—your research activities should lean towards ongoing data collection. Allow for exceptions, such as testing the effectiveness of new marketing ideas or gauging the market response to particular events in the news.

Service and Support   If you've determined that providing customer service and support online is an important strategic objective, you need to develop tactics to make this happen. Consider a range of activities that address everything from shifting customers from telephone to online support to offering incentives to customers who regularly volunteer to help others online.

To make your online service and support areas pay really big dividends, determine how to expand support to resellers, suppliers, business partners, and your employees. You may need to solicit feedback from people in different departments of your company in order to check this portion of your plan and make sure that your tasks are practical.

Logistics: The Devil Is in the Details

For any plan to be successful, its details must be carefully handled. Give plenty of attention to the logistical details of your cybermarketing campaign—gathering content, allocating resources, and establishing a timeline—and you will see the payoff in the results.

Content

After laying out your tactics, title the next section of your plan "Content." Here, list whatever documents, graphics, visuals, and so forth you will need to make your tactics successful.

Resolve such questions as whether or not you will use the same content in all of your online areas. What will the content include: product literature, technical briefing papers, stock information? If you don't use the same content everywhere, determine which will go in to the various areas.

Also decide what information you will provide to visitors that will be more valuable than typical ads and brochures. What information can you give them about your product or company that they can't get in traditional marketing channels? The technical design and limitations of some parts of cyberspace will determine what content you can place there and how your content will look, so be sure that you become familiar with each of the areas that you will use.

After listing the content that you will need, outline in the plan general document management procedures that everyone involved with creating and managing your content should follow.

Will you use Hyper Text Markup Language (HTML), Adobe Acrobat, or some other software to design and format content for your Net sites? How will you train people to use these programs? If you use interactive databases, will they be custom designed or will you buy ready-to-use software?

Under your content listing, map out the flow of documents from their originators, through a timely approval process and on to whoever actually posts the content online. Determine whether you will use document management software to automate this flow. How will you monitor documents to make sure that outdated content is removed in a timely manner? Where will old content be archived in case it has to be retrieved by either customers, your staff, or others?

While considering document flow to the outside world, also determine how you'll manage incoming items such as e-mail from your online areas and materials retrieved by software agents. Make a note of this in the plan. Some online managers I spoke with recommended Lotus Notes to manage incoming documents that arrive as e-mail messages.

After answering these questions to your satisfaction, move on to describe resources that you will need to carry out this plan.

Resources

Title the next section of your written plan "Resources." This is where, after deciding what content and promotions you want, you determine who will be responsible for creating them. Will it be marketing, sales, or an ad agency? Will customer service or human resources also develop content? Can the people in these departments deliver new content areas frequently enough to your online areas to build repeat traffic? If they can't, who will?

Looking for a Few Good Online Managers

After various individuals in the company have committed to contributing to content development, you must next address the direct care and feeding of your online areas. Building and maintaining online areas requires resources dedicated specifically to this task.

If you're going to outsource the maintenance of your Internet presence to an Internet service provider and have a presence only on the online services or a BBS, then you can probably get away with not having a dedicated online manager. Different staff members can work part-time to develop content. Send it to the service provider or BBS, and post it to your other online areas.

However, if you're planning to make a more extensive and serious cybermarketing effort, you will need at least one person dedicated to managing your online areas. A serious effort usually also involves having in-house Net servers and BBSs. Many companies that are going full tilt in every area of cyberspace have four to six people dedicated to this cause.

With a full-fledged effort, someone will have to learn to use the different online services' software development tools as well as the development tools for Internet and BBS sites—none of which is particularly easy. Then there are the tasks such as physically posting content, keeping all the systems up and running, and managing document and communication flow between your company and cyberspace.

Ultimately, your particular circumstances and needs will determine how many staff members you'll need to dedicate to your cybermarketing effort, or at least how many to appropriate part-time from various departments.

Getting Everyone on the Bandwagon

Since people in many departments of your company may be resources for your content, it's important to get buy-in for your cybermarketing plan throughout the company.

If you're the president or an executive VP, you may have the power of righteous mandate. Still, cybermarketing can bring together departments that typically don't work with each other, and pulling these people together can be a tough balancing act. You'll probably be more successful at this if you use tactful salesmanship with a hint of authoritarianism, rather than figuratively whacking people on the head. Remember that it doesn't take much discontent in the ranks to spoil the best laid cyberplans of mice—or executives.

If you're middle management, or just someone in the company who believes in the saving power of cyberspace, you have two options. The first is to create an area online in your spare time, generate sizable traffic, and then go to the marketing department and say, "Look at all these people we have coming to our online area. We'd really have killer traffic if we did a little more work on the site." You'll either get the resources you need or get banished to the mail room (most likely, the former).

As members of your company become more accepting of life in cyberspace, sell them on creating a formal plan and doing cybermarketing the right way. The more success you have with the site in the initial days, the more resources you should be able to pry loose.

Your second option is to take the idea of cybermarketing door-to-door, starting with marketing and finance because these can be particularly hard nuts to crack. Traditional marketing people may hold out because cyberspace isn't a traditional marketing medium. And finance will hold out because bean counters can't see an immediate sales advantage to cybermarketing.

If the people in these departments give you too much flak, get the rest of the company department heads on your side. Then go back with your allies in tow and really put the heat on. If, on the other hand, these people buy into your idea right away, you can consider the battle pretty much won. The rest of the company decision makers should go along with no problem, especially if you assure them that they will each play a role in the cybermarketing effort.

Whatever you do, save the company lawyers for last—after all company-wide consensus is pretty much a fait accompli. Cyberspace is a place so lax in rules and "wrought with peril" that it gives many lawyers hives just thinking about it. They can come up with 100 reasons to not go online in the time it takes to say "Perry Mason."

Timeline

The final section of your written plan will be called "Timeline"—which no good plan goes without. It's up to you how detailed your timeline should be.

I recommend that you plot specific calendar dates as milestones for instituting or completing key elements of your cybermarketing campaign. For example, dates for content completion, promotion launches, online seminars, and so on. Be as detailed with dates and events as you feel is necessary.

Time to Hit the Cyberroad, Jack

This book has given you a foundation for cybermarketing. When you access its online component, you'll get the next layer of information in the form of real-world examples of lessons learned in these pages.

I will regularly update this online component with new information and examples of how companies are coping with the latest developments in electronic commerce. I will also try to provide you with additional support with the book's online message board.

From this point, use *Cybermarketing Essentials for Success* as just a reference guide. What you design for your online areas, the problems you encounter there, and the solutions you devise will all be learning experiences. Even if you've been online for years, practically every day of cybermarketing will bring you a new lesson.

Good luck as you begin this most excellent adventure.

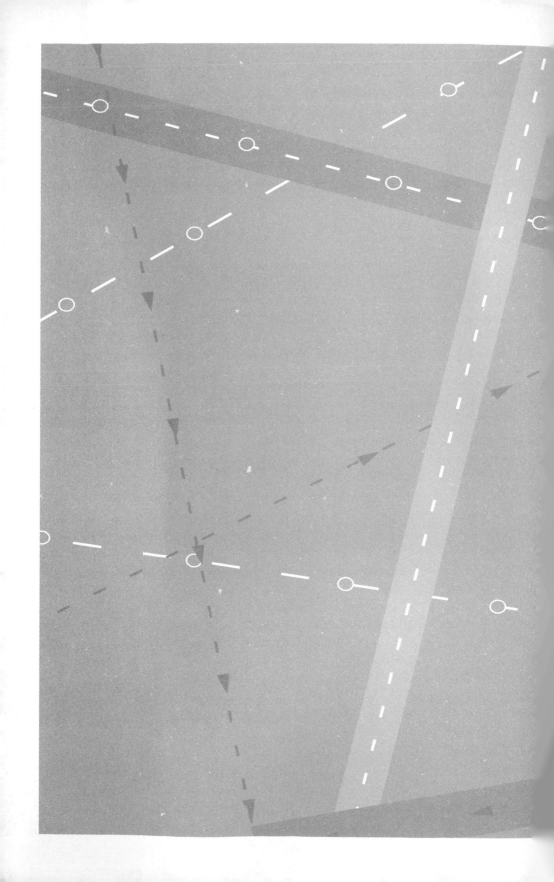

Appendix: Cybermarketing Essentials for Success: The Online Supplement

You can find an online supplement to *Cybermarketing Essentials for Success* on the Internet's World Wide Web and on Microsoft Network (details on how to access these online areas are given later in this appendix). The supplement will help you get the full value of reading this book, with "live" examples of the lessons presented in it and extra information to help you in your cybermarketing adventures.

Timely and Lively

There are two reasons for this online supplement: timeliness and liveliness.

The world of cyberspace is changing so rapidly that it's almost impossible to produce a conventional book fast enough to keep up with the pace. For example, since I wrote Chapter 4 of this book—about commercial online services—the world of online services has undergone some dramatic changes with the introduction of Microsoft Network.

Look to the online supplement for timely updates to information presented in the printed version of this book. When you visit the book's online area, you will find a What's New section that points you to this updated information. Both the Web site and Microsoft Network will have links to online publications where you can keep pace with daily news that affects cybermarketing.

You will also find regularly changing case studies, as I document new ways in which companies are pushing the cyberspace technology envelope to its outer limit. I will enhance lessons taught in the book with new tips picked up on an ongoing basis from my cybermarketing consulting experiences and from readers such as yourself.

While the printed book provides the fundamentals of cybermarketing, the digitized supplement keeps your finger on its pulse. The online version also makes the lessons and examples taught in the printed pages come to life.

When you use the links to many of the online areas described in this book, you will see cybermarketing in action. You'll be able to visit sites, review and download documents, participate in promotions, and strike up e-mail conversations with cyber surfers. At the Microsoft Network site, you can go into the chat room for real-time conversations with other readers of this book to exchange observations and ideas.

Accessing the Supplement

There are three ways to get on the Internet and access the online supplement: through an Internet service provider (ISP), a commercial online service, or Windows 95.

To access the Net through an ISP, you need at least 8MB of RAM on your computer and a modem faster than 9,600 bps. You should be able to find a provider in the yellow pages or a local computer publication, or by calling around to a few computer stores.

Once you get a Net account, you need to get on the World Wide Web. You can do this by going to a computer store and buying one of the commercially available Web browsers. Or, to get a free Netscape browser, you can go onto the Internet through FTP access (which most Net providers offer) and send a message to

ftp.netscape.com

When you get to Netscape's site, download the appropriate file for your computer's operating system.

The free browser will be sufficient to get you to the book's Web site. The commercially available browsers have extra bells and whistles that you might want if you plan to spend a lot of time online.

An alternative to getting an Internet account through an ISP is to subscribe to one of the online services such as America Online, CompuServe, Delphi, or AT&T Interchange, each of which offer Web access directly from their respective services. This option lets you enjoy all of the benefits of the online service as well as getting to the Web.

The third alternative for accessing the supplement is buying Microsoft Windows 95. If you do this, you can check out the online book either on Microsoft Network itself or on the book's Web site, which MSN lets you access.

To get the specific Web address, the Microsoft Network location, and any final instructions about how to access the online supplement, send e-mail to **book@successful.com**.

INDEX